"Back in the days before Vaticaɪ
ing to understand manuals such ﹍
Gredt, OSB, while their contemporaries at secular schools were excited by existentialism or phenomenology or analytic philosophy, they would turn to the works of
Étienne Gilson. In my recollection, Gilson's luminous historical works helped them
both to understand Aquinas and to situate his thought in relation to such modern
philosophers as Descartes, Hume, and Kant intelligently and without distorting cari-
cature. Turning to these *Medieval Essays* with a certain sentiment of nostalgia, then,
I marveled to encounter the subtle scholarship, the wide-ranging erudition, and the
detailed knowledge of the authors and texts in relation to issues that still burn today.
Gilson's even-handed defense of the study of medieval philosophy is imbued with an
understanding of the justice of the Renaissance and Enlightenment complaints against
scholastic thought; but it takes the readers by the hand and leads them into an utterly
refreshing appreciation of those old authors and texts that is rarely, if ever, matched
in the depth of its gratitude to his masters and in its profound courtesy towards those
with whom he disagrees. These essays take the readers back to school and offer the
opportunity to experience the thrill of discovery even with regard to texts and issues
with which they may have had a great familiarity."

—FREDERICK LAWRENCE, Boston College

"This is too small a collection of Gilson's essays. Why? In reading his article on St.
Anselm, who died in 1109, I learned more about fourteenth-century philosophy and
theology than from most works on that era itself. From Gilson's inaugural lecture at
the Sorbonne, we all could discover what it is to be gracious toward those who taught
us. In essence, these essays lead to a richer understanding of the nature of history,
philosophy, and theology, and also of the life of a scholar."

—STEPHEN F. BROWN, Boston College

"We are in debt to James G. Colbert for his fine selection and translation of these essays
by the renowned Étienne Gilson. These essays illustrate well the vital importance for
recovering in our contemporary culture medieval quests for wisdom."

—MATTHEW L. LAMB, Ave Maria University

"I've been struck by the timeliness of these essays. Gilson's prediction about the future
of scholasticism has come true: historical research is indeed placing philosophy into its
theological context (but this has led to the dismissal of thomists focusing on Thomas's
philosophy). His remarks on the ontological argument fit into the debate on recent re-
formulations. Anslem's proof involves not causality but entailment: 'necessarily, if God
is thought, He is thought as necessary,' a reading not unlike many proposed today."

—WALTER REDMOND, The College of St. Thomas More

MEDIEVAL ESSAYS

MEDIEVAL ESSAYS

Étienne Gilson   *translated by James G. Colbert*

CASCADE *Books* • Eugene, Oregon

MEDIEVAL ESSAYS

Published under license from Librairie Philosophique J. Vrin.
Étienne Gilson, *Études médiévales*
<< Vrin-Reprise >>
© Librairie Philosophique J. Vrin, Paris, 1986.
http://www.vrin.fr

Cascade Books
An Imprint of Wipf and Stock Publishers
199 W. 8th Ave., Suite 3
Eugene, OR 97401

www.wipfandstock.com

ISBN 13: 978-1-60899-387-1

Cataloging-in-Publication data:

Gilson, Étienne, 1884–1978.

[Etudes médiévales]
Medieval studies / Étienne Gilson ; foreword by Jean-François Courtine; translated by James G. Colbert.

x + 222 p. ; 23 cm. — Includes bibliographical references.

ISBN 13: 978-1-60899-387-1

1. Philosophy, Medieval. I. Courtine, Jean-François. II. Colbert, James G. III. Title.

B2430.G473 E88 2011

Manufactured in the U.S.A.

To
Ana

CONTENTS

FOREWORD TO THE FRENCH EDITION

O F NECESSITY THERE IS something arbitrary in assembling nine essays from the prolific opus of Étienne Gilson, for which we still[1] do not have a complete bibliographical listing. C. J. Edie's bibliography published in *Mélanges offerts à Étienne Gilson*[2] stops at 1958.

The contributions gathered here range over thirty-five years and represent "classical" studies of doctrinal history or models for essays in the history of ideas. In any case, the scholarly research which involves so many explorations into the "doctrinal jungle" that is the Middle Ages, sketches the powerful perspectives of our philosopher-historian and contributes to the articulation of *fundamental* questions about the respective status of philosophy and theology. Guided by the watchword, "back to theology," which Gilson launched at Rome in 1950, the historical critical research partially assembled here can not help but nurture philosophical reflection for a long time to come, if it is true, as Auguste Comte maintained, that "in the famous commitment that scholasticism constitutes," it is "theology [that] makes itself dependent on metaphysics."[3]

Jean-François Courtine

1. [Translator's note: see, however, McGrath, *Etienne Gilson: A Bibliography*.]
2. [Translator's note: see Edie, "Writings of Étienne Gilson," 15–59.]
3. Text quoted by Gouhier, "La pensé médiévale," 310.

ix

1

CRITICAL HISTORICAL RESEARCH AND THE FUTURE OF SCHOLASTICISM[1]

W̶HAT CHANGE OF PERSPECTIVE does critical historical research suggest for our approach to scholasticism? What indications does it provide about its future? The question posed is broad, so we may be excused if we simply touch upon its main point within the brief space of a paper.

A century ago in 1850, Barthélemy Hauréau published *De la philosophie scolastique*, followed by his *Histoire de la philosophie scolastique* in 1872 and 1880. Since then, works on medieval philosophy are countless: in 1900 Maurice de Wulf, *Histoire de la philosophie médiévale*; in 1905 François Picavet, *Esquisse d'une histoire générale et comparée des philosophies médiévales*; in 1921 Martin Grabmann, *Die Philosophie des Mittelalters*; in 1928 Bernard Geyer, *Die patristiche und scholastiche Philosophie*. We could mention others without even considering innumerable works devoted to the philosophies of Thomas Aquinas, Bonaventure, Duns Scotus, and Ockham. But for every ten histories of medieval philosophy, how many histories of medieval theology do we find? For twenty volumes on the philosophy of Thomas Aquinas, how

1. This is the complete text of Étienne Gilson's remarks in the last session of the International Scholastic Congress, Rome, September 6–10, 1950.

many historical expositions of his theology are there? For a century historians of medieval thought generally seem to have tended to represent the medieval ages as inhabited by philosophers rather than theologians.

There are several reasons for this, the first a dogmatic one. Since philosophy was overtly established as a science separated from theology in the seventeenth century, there has been a desire to contrast scholasticism, *qua* pure philosophy, with other pure philosophies that attacked it. This trend started in the sixteenth century but accelerated towards the end of the seventeenth. In 1667, under the pseudonym Ambrosius Victor, the Oratorian André Martin, devoted his five-volume *Philosophia Christiana* to turning St. Augustine into a philosopher. In 1679 Antoine Goudin's *Philosophia juxta Thomae Dogmata* came out, and innumerable *Cursus Philosophiae Thomisticae* were to follow up to our time. In 1746 Josephus Antonius Ferrari would defend Aristotle's philosophy *rationibus Joannis Duns Scoti subtilium principis*. What a distance had been traversed since the time of Duns Scotus! In the fourteenth century, he used Aristotle to defend the faith! In the eighteenth century it is he who is conscripted to defend Aristotle. In 1782 Carolus Josephus a Sancto Floriano published his *Joannis Duns Scoti Philosophia*, which was not to be the last. Then as now, it was a question of comparing philosophy to philosophy, which is why medieval theologians who never wrote any philosophy in life, composed so much after death. But strictly historical factors complement the previous consideration. In the measure that history of philosophy was established as a distinct area of study, it became more and more difficult for it to neglect the Middle Ages. Might it not be that there was a great deal of philosophizing in the faculty of arts? Above all, one could not help noticing the striking difference that distinguishes modern philosophy at its inception from Greek philosophy at its end. Metaphysics emerged from the Middle Ages different from the state in which it entered them. Thus something had happened in philosophy, even within the theology faculties. That is why so many studies wavering between theology and philosophy had to be published, treating theologians as philosophers; in short, doing what could be done without troubling oneself excessively about theoretical distinctions. It was certainly necessary to search out medieval philosophy where it was.

Yet, did this involve adopting a medieval perspective on the Middle Ages? It was clearly perceived that it did not. The general stance of the great thirteenth-century doctors seems faithfully defined by the text of his *In Hexaemeron* (II, 7) where the Seraphic Doctor distinguishes

four types of writings, each of which occupies a different level and deserves the respect that corresponds to its rank: 1) Holy Scripture, which
contains what man needs to know to achieve his salvation; 2) writings
of the Fathers in order to interpret Scripture; 3) Commentaries on the
Sentences to interpret the Fathers; 4) books of philosophers to interpret
the Commentaries on the *Sentences* or the *Summas* of theology. To be
sure, one may have reservations about St. Bonaventure's testimony, for
he expressed his bad humor against philosophy and philosophers quite
bitterly, above all in 1273. As has been noted, it is true that philosophy
does not occupy the first rank in his thought, but when did it ever occupy first rank in the thought of any theologian worthy of the name? It
certainly did not in that of St. Thomas Aquinas. With whatever personal
nuances we please and which history demands, no medieval master of
theology seems to have disputed the hierarchical order described by St.
Bonaventure: Scripture first, the Fathers as interpreters of Scripture, the
theologians as interpreters of the Fathers, philosophers to understand
theologians. It is natural and healthy that for forty years historians with
theological training have recalled this evidence to those whose formation was chiefly philosophical. Their warning can be summed up in the
criticism directed by one of them against a book on St. Bonaventure's
"philosophy": What you call philosophy is only mutilated theology. He
was right, but that is equally true of every book about the "philosophy"
of Thomas Aquinas, Duns Scotus, or Ockham. Our first conclusion
will be that historical research, which originally focused on medieval
philosophies, will tend more and more to reintegrate these philosophies
into the theologies that contain them.

The second development is all the more remarkable, because, while
linked to the first, it initially seems to contradict it. A century ago, one
referred comfortably to *the* scholastic philosophy. Barthélemy Hauréau
even tended to reduce it to one problem, as if everything came down to
variations on the theme of universals. Nearer to us, some went so far as
to maintain that St. Thomas' doctrine on this point was the common
doctrine of his time, that it could be expounded without citing him and
appealing only to texts of his contemporaries. In fact, historical progress
has led to differentiate doctrinal positions, and without denying what is
common in their Aristotelian technique, to individualize, so to speak,
the use theologians made of it. The special originality of each great doctrinal synthesis becomes increasingly apparent to us, and we perceive
those syntheses to be more distinct than they once seemed. The unity

of the schools themselves seems less rigid than we used to imagine. Albert the Great no longer appears to be simply a Thomist before his time, and today we would hesitate to affirm that Giles of Rome belongs to the school of St. Thomas Aquinas, something formerly regarded as indubitable. Now, in the eyes of a historian, this growing differentiation of scholastic theologies appears to be linked to that of the philosophical instruments they use. We re-encounter the lesson of the scholastic gibe: *Qualis in philosophia, talis in theologia.* Thus, our very effort to return to theology has situated us in the presence of as many distinct philosophies as we find distinct theologies. The fact is so important that it is worth considering it attentively.

In one sense that effort justifies so many historians devoting their preponderant attention to medieval philosophies. The very nature of theology validates them, because theology is *intellectus fidei*, and naturally, different ways of achieving that understanding within the unity of faith will engender different theologies. A theologian's "philosophy," even when integrated into his theology, will thus continue to occupy an important place in future history of medieval thought, but it will not be exactly the same as before. History has reached a point of no return. Experience teaches that the more a historian separates philosophy from theology in medieval doctrines, the more the former tends to be reduced to a common technique, increasingly stripped of originality, which at the extreme melds into Aristotle's philosophy as revised by Avicenna or Averroes. In this regard it is notable that the historians who most diligently extract a philosophy free of any theology from medieval texts, ordinarily are the same people who insist on the existence of a kind of common philosophy or at the very least of a scholastic "synthesis," which might be called that of the whole thirteenth century. From their point of view these historians are right. They are even absolutely right: act and potency, form and matter, the four causes, metaphysics as science of being, truth as taken from being just as it is, so many guiding theses—one could easily mention others—defined a philosophical interpretation of the world common to all our theologians. That is true, but if it were the whole truth, it would be necessary to conclude that the Christian Middle Ages remained philosophically sterile and that, as some still think, it only repeated a more or less deformed Aristotle *ad nauseam*.

It is here that the second conclusion to be drawn from so much historical research insistently demands our attention. Experience makes us see that the more medieval philosophies are reintegrated into their theological syntheses, the more original they appear to be. The same fact can be expressed in several ways. We can say, for example that philosophical thought became creative in its theological function at that time, or that the greater theologian a master is, the greater philosopher he is. Only the fact matters, and it is that the decisive progress of western philosophy in the Middle Ages occurred at the points where *intellectus fidei* in some way called for originality. At the same time as it justifies the medieval *qualis in philosophia talis in theologia*, historical research invites us to complete the saying by *qualis in theologia, talis in philosophia*, which is no less true and no less important. Indeed, these are two formulations of the same truth and well known to theologians themselves; because, if theology is intellection of faith, the intellection can neither be isolated from the faith whose understanding it gives, nor the faith from the intellection it seeks. In brief, medieval philosophy owed its fecundity precisely to being a theological instrument.

This historical lesson in turn poses doctrinal problems that the historian as such is not competent to resolve, but whose solution would not be without importance for the future of scholasticism.

If we recognize the thirteenth century as the golden age of scholasticism, that is doubtless because we judge it has succeeded in its endeavor, and if it is true that *res eodem modo conservantur quo creantur*, it seems that we could not hope to succeed as well in the future without proceeding in the same manner. But history here comes to the rescue to tell us how the thirteenth century proceeded. Despite excuses that may be found, the greatest objection to separating scholastic philosophy from its theology is that this inevitably creates the illusion that theologians worked by introducing a completely finished philosophy, just as they found it in the philosophers of their time, into a completely finished doctrine of the faith. Hence, the conclusion is often articulated that to redo the task of the thirteenth century would first involve our taking as point of departure the philosophy and science of our time in order to reconstruct a new scholasticism that would be in agreement with modern mentality and acceptable to our contemporaries. That seems to read a misinterpretation into history. Thirteenth-century theologians did not part from the philosophical sciences of their time to adapt theology to them. They parted from the faith to take up the philosophical sciences of their time, metamorphosing them in the light of faith. Centered on the *intellectus fidei*, they took in unchanged a great deal of philosophical or scientific knowledge of their time without necessary relation to Christian faith, and this is precisely the obsolete part of their work that we have no reason to conserve. But if nothing is more transitory than positive science, nothing is less transitory than Christian faith, and in order for thirteenth-century scholasticism to be taken up again where it left off, faith, not science, would have to have changed since then.

Though I want to be brief, I beg leave to insist on the capital point just stated, because not all errors of perspective are on the same side. To those who call for a new scholasticism founded on modern philosophy, some will respond that there is only one true philosophy, which is that of Aristotle, and that scholastic theology is true because it is founded on it. But neither Duns Scotus nor Thomas Aquinas founded their theology on any philosophy, not even Aristotle's. As theologians, they used philosophy in the light of faith, and thereby philosophy emerged transformed. What metaphysics there is in Thomas Aquinas or in Duns Scotus is their own metaphysics. Each Aristotelian formula that they take over receives from the notion of *esse* or of *ens infinitum* a sense Aristotle never thought of, which he would hardly have been able to comprehend, and which their very disciples, when they come to confuse their master with Aristotle, no longer always understand in all its depth. It will never be said enough: to make over scholasticism starting from Kant or Hegel would be to wish to redo what has never been done.

Let us try to imagine what would have happened if our scholastics had started from Aristotle in constructing their theologies. Aristotle's god did not create the world *ex nihilo*. He exercises no contingent action on the sublunar world. He never intervenes in the guise of particular providence but abandons the world to a necessity that only chance interrupts. In Aristotle, man, instead of being an immortal person called to his own destiny, is merely a completely perishable individual, with no other function than to repeat the species in a transitory way. Is that the philosophy on which our theologies rest? Yet it is Aristotle's philosophy! Let us note here with Duns Scotus, whose judgement imposes itself on Thomists as well as Scotists, that there is a profound reason why Aristotle's philosophy was this way. It is precisely that Aristotle's metaphysics was a direct development of his physics. Precisely because they refused to speak as theologians, the medievals who started from Aristotelian science naturally ended like Averroes, in the same metaphysics. If it were true that our theologians had built their theologies on a metaphysics itself linked to now-obsolete science, it would be right to say that to redo their project would have to consist in theologizing starting from philosophies that are so many developments of today's science. But, at once, one would come to the result that the work would immediately have to begin again. This has never been clearer than in our time, where one generation has seen three different physics succeed each other, that of gravitation, general relativity, and wave mechanics. Yesterday science was determinist, it is indeterminist today, it will become determinist again tomorrow. Are we going to change theology each time that, by changing physics, we must change metaphysics? But the absurdity of the proposition makes it quite clear that our theologians themselves have never done any such thing. Philosophizing, not in the light of physics, but in that of faith, the medieval theologians left us metaphysics and even philosophies of nature, which there is no need to remake continually, because these doctrines participate in the stability enjoyed by the light in which they were born. To philosophize as a scholastic cannot be to adapt Catholic theology to the science of our time nor to philosophies that are inspired by that science, but rather to adapt this science and these philosophies to the metaphysics created by our theologians in their effort to attain a certain intellection of faith We intend to do no more here than record certain lessons of history objectively. Perhaps the chief initiative of the medieval masters, because they were theologians, was never to have done their thinking *starting from* science or philosophy. Thus it is to misread history to say: Scholasticism tied faith to Aristotle's old philosophy; let us do the same thing with the philosophy of our time. Scholastic theology created (in the human sense of the term) a new metaphysics, whose truth, independently of the state of science at any moment of history, remains as permanent as the light of faith in which it was born.

Thus the future of scholasticism does not consist in adapting medieval metaphysics of being and causes to the movement of science and philosophy, but to make it constantly take up the achievements of knowledge in order to rectify them and purify them. To do otherwise, would be to suppress scholasticism by putting it in a state that did violence to its nature, and to lose along with it one of the most precious benefits that we owe it. It is by associating metaphysics with itself that medieval theology liberated metaphysics from physics, without thereby enslaving metaphysics to itself. For the first time, it broke the bonds that even in Aristotle still held first philosophy captive on the terrain of positive science, by encouraging it toward the heaven of faith. It is impossible for philosophy to lose itself there, because it cannot attain this heaven, but by tending toward it, it liberates itself and finds its true equilibrium. Its future fecundity lies in fidelity to its essence; to remain intimately associated with the intellection of faith.

The seventeenth-century adventure ought to serve us as a lesson. Whatever anyone says, the bad thing then was not ignorance of new science, but the illusion that it was necessary to defend the obsolete science of Aristotle against the new science; for what was necessary was to put the latter in its true place, in the light of metaphysical principles whose sense had been lost. We have to get hold of their authentic, profound sense again today, and one can say that buried under more than five centuries of rubble, ignorance of itself is the worst illness that scholasticism suffers. To return it to itself, let us hear the counsel of history: *Return to theology!* Please trust us that the distinction between faith and reason is not at issue. Nor should we forget the formal distinction of objects of philosophy and theology, so dear to dialecticians. Neither the one nor the other is at risk, but formal distinction of objects is not real separation in exercise. To exercise the intellect in the transcendent light of the virtue of faith is different from attempting to deduce philosophically demonstrated conclusions from an article of faith. Here yesterday's truth merges with tomorrow's. It is by restoring scholastic philosophies to their natural place that history will increasingly understand them better and better as they were: *non erubesco evangelium* is a phrase that we should be able to proclaim in every order, even that of scholarship. It is by returning to its place that scholastic philosophy can have the hope, or rather the certitude, of flowering and bearing fruit again. Only a prophet could say what will be its future, but a historian can announce by whom it will be done. The true *scholastic philosophers* will always be theologians.

THE MIDDLE AGES AND ANCIENT NATURALISM[1]

TODAY A CHAIR OF history of philosophy in the Middle Ages replaces the chair of Celtic languages and literatures that two scholars, D'Arbois de Jubainville and Loth, have graced. So, a new subject area has been created. However, no one would believe me if I pretended to create it from nothing. Rather, I certainly see the desire on the part of the Collège de France to promote, by participating in it, a historical movement to which masters like Denifle, Baeumker, and Martin Grabmann have contributed or still contribute in Germany, Maurice de Wulf and the whole Louvain group in Belgium, Father Ephrem Longpré and the Quaracchi workshop in Italy. In France itself, how could we forget forerunners like Victor Cousin or Barthélmy Hauréau? Among so many other scholars who ought to be cited, above all, how could we pass over Father Mandonnet, the author of *Siger de Brabant*, which was and remains an ever-new point of departure, and his Saulchoir school, the glory of French scholarship?

If I had to tell all, I would have to acknowledge many other debts, but there are two that I would never forgive myself for failing to mention, because, although they are not owed to medievalists, the very

1. Opening lecture in the course of History of Philosophy in the Middle Ages, at the Collège de France, April 5, 1932

spirit of this new subject area will always bear their imprint. To Lucien
Lévy-Bruhl I owe having been turned early toward the study of medieval
philosophy. I would like to have learned better from him how to clarify
from within thinkers being interpreted and to restore each one of them
in his own individual difference. For me, to do for Abelard, St. Thomas,
and Duns Scotus what Lévy-Bruhl did for Descartes, Hume, Berkeley,
and Compte is a goal whose difficulty I think I can measure exactly.

My second debt was contracted in this very place during Bergson's
admirable lectures, which were the most intense and deepest intellectual
delights for his students. From that teaching, so rich in so many ways,
the historian comes away with the desire to recover the simple movement beyond the formulas in which a philosopher's thought is expressed,
which engenders them, runs through them, and confers an indivisible
unity upon them. He will also retain the sense that our historical concepts need to become ever more supple and be recast, as it were, to at-
tach themselves more precisely to the reality they express. Thus, instead
of sketching a superficial outline of the philosophical Middle Ages, I
intend to remain faithful to the spirit of his teaching by attempting from
this day forward to seek a vantage point that aims at its very essence: the
relation of medieval thought with ancient naturalism.

I don't know whether the question is at all surprising. Interpretation
of the Middle Ages is inseparable *de facto* and *de jure* from interpretations of the Renaissance, the Reformation, and Humanism. Now
naturalism and the taste for Antiquity are regarded as the monopoly of
Humanism and the Renaissance. But if this is their peculiar contribution to the movement at its height toward the beginning of the sixteenth
century, by that very fact, is it not also the affirmation of what the whole
Middle Ages denied, is it not a resolute protest against the thirteenth-
century religious supernaturalism, the long awaited revenge of Greek
thought against Christian dogma?[2] The notions are widely held. To

2. "The Renaissance in France is, I believe, the transformation of conduct, ideas,
and sentiments that takes place during the sixteenth century under the influence of
ancient literature, partly through the mediation of Italian Civilization and the culture
of the Northern peoples. Thanks to the critical method and spirit, thanks to the sense
of beauty, this transformation culminated in a more or less complete elimination of
the medieval ideal. It finally accomplished an ideal of free, rational culture, similar to
that of antiquity, by rendering the general conceptions of life, nature, art, and the world
independent of Christianity. Thenceforth, the Christian element ceases to occupy a
preponderant place in civilization, when it is not directly opposed or systematically
omitted. Free examination conquers everything theology loses. Humanity notices that

challenge them, it does not suffice to recall that the Middle Ages were not insensible to the beauty of forms and did not always scorn literary elegance. Bernard of Chartres, John of Salisbury, Hildebert of Lavardin, twenty other writers, the painstaking effort to conserve the writings of the ancients for us and improve their texts, all array themselves against these oversimplifications for which nobody today would take responsibility. However, the problem is to discover whether the Middle Ages ever understood this Greek naturalism that it could not ignore or rather, as the more usual opinion has it, mistook its true sense that the Renaissance had the merit and honor of discovering.[3] Whatever the reasons I may use in support of the first thesis, I am afraid of being regarded as defending a paradox and of special pleading if I undertake the demonstration myself. That is why, by letting Erasmus and Luther speak, two witnesses whose right to be heard in the name of Humanism and the Reformation will be challenged by no one, I am going to ask where they opposed medieval philosophy and exactly what part of it they denied.

it can go it alone. To sum up, the Renaissance is a movement of emancipation, which supposes the diminution of the Christian ideal. That is the great change that explains the whole development of literature since the sixteenth century." Lefranc, "Diverses définitions," 494. Cf. Plattard, in Bédier and Hazard, *Histoire*, I:130.

3. "What did the Renaissance contribute? Is it precisely ancient texts? Not at all! We know only too well that the Middle Ages possessed Latin literature almost in its entirety. 'Latin letters,' Victor Le Clerc was able to say, 'were definitely not resurrected because they were definitely not dead'" (*Histoire Littéraire de France*, XXIV:326). If Victor Le Clerc meant that the Middle Ages possessed the text, the letter of Latin literature, he said what is completely true. He is mistaken if he means that the Middle Ages possessed the spirit, the feeling of Latin Antiquity. For two things escaped the Middle Ages: its philosophical thought and its beauty of form. With the liveliest respect, even as the medievals devoted an excessive, childish cult to antiquity, which only allowed them to admit moral or even theological doctrines as true under the more or less artificial authority of sacrosanct antiquity, though satiated with reading and quoting the ancients, the Middle Ages understood antiquity badly. An excellent consequence came from this: the Middle Ages remained a functionally original period. But on the day when this vein was exhausted, everything became prosaic, everything was empty or flat." Julleville, "Esprit de la littérature," 357. Cf. 393–95: "One can go on forever finding medieval survivals in the Renaissance, pointed arches, mysticism, mysteries, scholasticism. We must not lose sight of what is essential because of what is accessory, forgetting that the Renaissance represents individual liberation from dogma in the order of spirit." Cohen, *Ronsard*, 286–87. See 9 n. 9: "In this sense, our teacher Abel Lefranc could define the Renaissance as "intellectual laicizing of the humanities," (*Revue des cours et conférences*, II:724–25. Further on: ". . . the separation of the Church and Poetry . . . ," 10).

Along with Erasmus's *Enchiridion*, one of his most important theoretical writings is the *Paraclesis* or "exhortation to the very holy and very
salutary study of Christian philosophy."[4] Perhaps his style has not been
studied sufficiently. Always elegant and polished, Erasmus himself tells
us, however, that he did not wish to take ancient rhetoric as his model;
only the truth, the more powerful in proportion as it is simpler, seemed
capable of opening to his teaching the hearts he desired to touch. When
a Christian writer confronts the urgent problems of theology, Cicero
himself is no longer a master we should follow. Indeed we have learned
the secret of a less flowery but more powerful eloquence than his.[5] To be

4. Erasmus, *Paraclesis Studium*, 137–44: . . . *dum mortales omnes ad sanctissimum
ac saluberrimum Christianae philosophiae studium adhortor . . . Paraclesis* first appeared
in *Novum Instrumentum* in 1516, but it was often reprinted thereafter. It was very fa-
vorably received. See for example in Allen and Allen, *Opus Epistolarum*, V:2, number
1253. Other instructive texts concerning Erasmus's attitude toward medieval theology
are found in his *Epistola Apologetica*, columns 7–9, notably, 8 C: *quaeso quid com-
mercii Christo et Aristoteli? Quid sophisticis captiunculis cum aeternae sapientiae mys-
teriiis?* "Responsio ad Albertum Pium, art Scholastica Theologia," columns 1167–69;
Hyeraspistae Diatribes, book I, columns 1294 C–D.

5. . . . *si minus picturatam quam fuit illius, certe multo magis efficacem. Paraclesis*,
column 137 E. Cf. *Quanquam illud potius optandum, ut Christus ipse, cujus negotium
agitur, ita citharae nostrae chordas temperet, ut haec cantilena penitus afficiat ac moveat
animos omnium. Ad quod quidem efficiendum, nihil apud nos Rhetorum epicherematis,
aut epiphonematis. Hoc quod aptamus, non alia res certius praestet, quam ista veritas,
cujus quo simplicior, hoc efficacior est oratio. Paraclesis*, column 137 A.

It would be interesting to return to the problem of Erasmus's literary conceptions,
because he explained himself completely clearly on the subject. The alleged mystery of
Erasmus perhaps simply points out that we do not succeed in finding anything in his
writings to justify the preconceived idea we have formed about him. For him, writing
well in philosophy is writing like Jesus Christ and his disciples. If St. Thomas and Duns
Scotus write badly, it is because they use technical and therefore barbarous language
(*Ratio sive Methodus*, column 82 C–83 A.) As for profane literature, Erasmus does not
disapprove if the future theologian, "cautim ac moderate degustatis elegantioribus dis-
ciplinis per aetatem instituatur ac praeparetur . . ." (*Ratio sive Methodus*, column 79
CD) When he says "per aetatem," he understands that their study is suitable to a young
man much more than to a mature man. For the former they will be an apprentice-
ship, a prelude to the study of Scripture: "velut tyrocinio quodam praeludere in litteris
Poetarum et Philosophorum gentilium . . ." (*Enchiridion*, column 7 D) Accordingly, it
is necessary to use them with moderation —*modice*—in passing—*quasi in transcursu*—
without lingering in them—*non autem immoretur*; in a word, one must not tarry near
the Sirens' rock. The danger that threatens the student of ancient literature is the risk
of adopting pagan mores: *Verum, nolito te cum Gentilium litteris, gentilium et mores
haurire* (column 7 E). If Humanism really consists in turning away from Christianity to
return to ancient naturalism, Erasmus's humanism is rather tepid. Besides, what does
he mean when he invites us to use ancient literature "*cautim ac moderate*"? That the

sure, we have forgotten its source and it is precisely toward the source that Erasmus wants to lead us.

When he looks around, our humanist is pained by a spectacle that ought to have gladdened his heart, were he as he is described. One might think that he would suffer seeing himself surrounded by so many Christians and so few Greeks. But what he deplores is seeing so few Christians and to be surrounded by so many Greeks. In an epoch when the most curious and difficult studies are cultivated arduously, the philosophy of Christ, so profound and so simple, is mocked by some, neglected by most. It is studied only by a small number—*a paucis*—and even then coldly—*frigide*—as occurs with a doctrine without interest for the conduct of life. Whereas Platonists, Pythagoreans, Academics, Stoics, Cynics, Peripatetics, Epicureans, in a word, all of the Hellenizers, completely master the dogmas of the sect to which they adhere, draw the sword to defend it, and would die rather than desert their masters, those who profess Christianity are far from putting their hearts into the service of Christ in the same way. Any disciple of Aristotle would be ashamed to be unaware of his opinions on the cause of lightning, of prime matter, or the infinite, questions where science can neither guarantee our happiness nor ignorance our unhappiness. Initiated in Christ, in so many ways bound to him by so many sacraments, we do not feel how shameful,

---

true method of explication of classical texts is what the Middle Ages applied to the Bible and what it was severely reproached for applying to Virgil. Therefore, it is necessary to explain allegorically and morally not only fables (like Tantalus and Phaethon, *Ratio seu Methodus*, vol. V, column 82), but also even Homer: *Sed uti divina Scriptura non multum habet fructus, si in littera persistas haeresque, ita non parum utilis est Homerica Virgilianaque poesis, si memineris eam totam esse allegoricam* (*Enchiridion*, vol. V, column 7 E). When he calls for avoiding obscene poets, this self-proclaimed pagan or paganizer, betrays scruples that many medieval readers of Ovid did not feel. Erasmus is so serious about this that he intends to emend texts in name of religious scruples: when an ancient text contradicts the Gospel, either it is badly understood, or it hides a trope within itself, or the text is defective (*Ratio sive Methodus*, vol. V, column AB: *aut codicem esse depravatum*). What prudence in this return to Antiquity! His position cannot be summed up better than he did himself: "Breviter, omnem ethnicam litteraturam deliberare profuerit, si quidem id fiat, ut dixi, et annis idoneis, et modice, tum cautim et cum delectu; deinde cursim, et preregrinantis non habitantis more; postremo, quod est praecipuum, si omni ad Christum referantur" (*Enchiridion*, ch. II, column 8 A). Every word of this wisely constructed phrase matters. Those who seek a definition of humanism will find them worth meditating on. Furthermore, it is useful to compare everything Erasmus wrote on these matters with St. Augustine's *De Doctrina Christiana*, with which Erasmus is deeply impregnated.

how frightful it is to be ignorant of his dogmas that bestow completely guaranteed happiness on everyone.[6]

So, Erasmus is far from demonstrating excessive enthusiasm for Greek thought. To compare Aristotle to Christ is the action of "impious madness."[7] We might think we were listening to a medieval Augustinian protest against the abuses of philosophy, when Erasmus returns to the classical theme *Christus unus magister.*[8] The methods he advocates to study this unique master's lessons are neither Socratic dialectic nor Platonic analysis, but humility, faith, docility.[9] Some will tell him that this pure and simple acceptance of the Gospel is the philosophy of the illiterate. So be it, says Erasmus, but however crude it is, it is the philosophy of Christ, his Apostles, and of the martyrs.[10] Nothing is more surprising than the ease with which this refined spirit accepts *haec crassula et idiotica*, connecting across three centuries with *et eramos idiotae* of the Poverello of Assisi. At least let us not imagine that he is insincere, because the quite precise goal he pursues is to reject Greek philosophy outside of Christianity, into which the Middle Ages introduced Greek philosophy with the risk of corrupting this Christian Wisdom, which St. Paul already said had convicted the wisdom of this world of folly.[11] Indeed, has it ever been seen that the Apostles taught Averroes or Aristotle? So if we are Christians, let us act like them, and let nothing be more venerable for us than the Gospel.[12]

Cur est nobis quidquam hujus litteris antiquius? Thus spoke Erasmus. It is he indeed who reproaches thirteenth-century theologians for introducing the whole of profane literature into the Gospel without discernment—*quidquam usquam est profanarum litterarum huc*

6. Here we follow *Paraclesis*, vol. V, column 139 BC

7. . . . *cum hoc ipsum impiae cujusdam dementiae sit Christum cum Zenone aut Aristotele, et hujus doctrinam cum illorum, ut modestissime dicam, praeceptiunculis conferre velle. Paraclesis*, vol. V, column 139 D.

8. For example St. Bonaventure, "Christus Unus Omnium Magister," 567–74.

9. Erasmus, *Paraclesis*, vol. V, columns 139 F–140 F.

10. *Quod si quis obstrepet, haec esse crassula et idiotica, nihil aliud huic responderim, nisi quod haec crassa Christus praecipue docuit, haec inculcant Apostoli, haec quantumvis idiotica, tot germane Christianos, tot insignium Martyrum examina nobis prodiderunt.* Erasmus, *Paraclesis*, vol. V, column 141 A. Cf. Letter to Henry VIII, number 1390, in Allen and Allen, V:321.

11. Erasmus, *Paraclesis*, vol. V, column 139 F.

12. Ibid., vol. V, column 141 D.

provehentes.[13] Consequently, the situation is more complicated than the schematizations of literary history let us suppose. On the one hand, Erasmus carried on a struggle that was already heated in fifteenth-century Italy, as a member of the party that wanted to further the study of "good literature" to prepare minds for the reading of the Gospels. His adversaries are the theologians, especially monks, whose shortsighted zeal seeks to suffocate the movement instead of directing it. For them humanism is always and by principle what it was only occasionally and *de facto*: dissembled paganism that affects Christian sentiments in order to continue its campaign untroubled. This very real situation is what justifies the usual point of view about the Renaissance in the measure in which it is justifiable. It is thus true to say that there was violent antagonism at the time between representatives of medieval theologism and those of humanism. They not only fought, they hated each other. What strangely complicates the situation and is not taken sufficiently into account, is that the humanist reproaches the scholastic for what the scholastic reproaches him. The humanist Erasmus can certainly invoke

---

13. It would be interesting to compare Erasmus's text with certain interpretations of Humanism that have been put forth. By way of experiment, we can take Randall, *Making of the Modern Mind*. For example, 114–15: "The new spirit consisted at bottom in an increasing interest in human life, as it can be lived on earth . . . and without necessary reference to any other destiny in the beyond or the hereafter." Now Erasmus writes: "Neque vero minus inaequale praemium, quam dissimilis auctor. Quid enim inaequalius, quam mors aeterna et vita immortalis? Quam sine fine summo frui bono in contubernio coelestium civium, et sine fine extremis excruciari malis in infelicissimo consortio damnatorum? Atque hac de re qui dubitat, ne homo quidem est, necdum Christianus." *Enchiridion*, ch. VIII, canon 20, vol. V, column 56 B. Randall adds (122): "Most of all, the humanist scholars brought from their Cicero and their Greeks the happy, natural, and wholesome enjoyment of the goods of natural life . . ." But Erasmus told us: "Verum nolito te cum Gentilium litteris, Gentilium et mores haurire" (See note 5 above). Randall writes further (133–4) that against the folly of his time, Erasmus had two remedies: "the wisdom of the schools of antiquity, above all his rationalized Christian ethics." Yet we read in Erasmus's text this protestation against the rationalization of the Gospel: "et dum omnibus modis fugimos [regulam], quidquid usquam est profanarum litterarum huc provehentes, id quod est in Christiana philosophia praecipuum, non dicam, corrumpimus, sed quod negari non potest, ad paucos contrahimus rem, qua Christus nihil voluit esse communis." *Paraclesis*, vol. V, column 141 E. Thus it is rather difficult to reconcile the popular Erasmus that we are offered with what we find in his writings. If the Renaissance essentially implies the "diminution of the Christian ideal," Erasmus does not belong to the Renaissance. If he belongs to it, it implies nothing of the sort. Whatever is to be the final verdict of history, there is room to reopen the proceedings.

"St. Socrates,"[14] while as a Christian he indefatigably denounces the collusion of Hellenism and the Gospel in medieval thought. Socrates and Cicero are doubtless his saints, but only because they anticipated Christianity, hardly because they pretended to add anything to it. Their morality was *already* Christian. Christianity is to be no longer *still* Greek. That is why we see Erasmus ceaselessly accuse of paganism those medievals who tried to construct a Wisdom whose technique was Greek and spirit Christian: Ockham and behind Ockham, Duns Scotus; behind Scotus, St. Thomas Aquinas; behind Thomas Aquinas, Albertus Magnus.[15] The greatness of St. Augustine makes Erasmus hesitate, but the only figure he truly cherished without reservation is St. Jerome, because he was the least philosopher of all.

Faced with this situation, how can we avoid asking whether, rather than being the discovery of ancient naturalism, the Renaissance was the collision of two different sides of this naturalism, where the only thing missing was their recognizing each other as complementary in order to be in harmony. Erasmus wants the Gospel pure and simple, cleansed from what centuries of theology had made it.[16] But then we must expel

14. This well known text is found in the *Convivium Religiosum*: "Profecto mirandus animus in eo qui Christum ac sacras litteras non noverat. Proinde quum hujusmodi quaedam lego de talibus viris, vix mihi tempero, quin dicam, Sancte Socrates, ora pro nobis.—At ipse mihi saepenumero non tempero, quin bene ominer sanctae animae Maronis et Flacci." Assuredly we are very far from St. Augustine here, further yet from Luther but very close to Justin, who turns Socrates into a Christian and martyr. On Erasmus's preference for Platonism, see *Enchiridion*, ch. II, vol. V, column 7 F. On the divine inspiration of Cicero, see Allen ed., *Letter to Johann Vlatten*, number 1390, V:339.

15. "Quid Alberto Magno, quid Alexandro, quid Thomae, quid Ricardo, quid Occam, alli velint tribuere, per me sane cuique liberum est . . ." etc. Erasmus, *Paraclesis*, vol. V, column 143 AB. "*Quid*, quaeso, simile in Scoto? Nolim id contumeliae causas dictum videri; quid simile in Thoma?" *Paraclesis*, column 143 B. "*Cur* major vitae portio datur Averroii quam evangelio?" *Paraclesis*, vol. V, columns 143–44.

16. This in no way denies his cult of the Ancients. What the *Convivium Religiosum* says is that Socrates was a saint because he was *already* like a Christian, in fact better than many so-called Christians. But precisely if Erasmus takes everything good that there was in antiquity in a Christian sense, he absolutely rejects the reduction of Christianity to paganism. The humanist can make his choice in antiquity on the condition that the Gospel is his rule of discernment. As for the average Christians, he only needs the Gospel, because there he finds everything that Antiquity has of goodness and more, things that Christ taught but that the wisdom of the Philosophers did not know (". . . quae Philosophorum sapientia non poterat . . .") *Paraclesis*, vol. V, column 141 D. There is nothing classical in what he says on the subject: "Affingant illi [those who maintain Christian Hellenism] suae sectae principibus, quantum possunt, aut quantum libet; certe solus hic e coelo profectus est doctor, solus certa docere potuit, cum sit

Aristotle in his entirety, that is to say Greek ethics, Greek nature on which this ethics rests, and finally Greek dialectic that interprets nature. We must go further and drive away the divine Plato, whose doctrine of the Ideas is henceforth incorporated into the theology of the Word, and Socrates himself, whose ethic is only grounded by grounding dialectic. For a friend of the Ancients what ravages! It is easily understandable that Erasmus himself had doubts. He perceived that his criticism left a gaping hole between the reading of Cicero and that of the Gospel or of St. Paul. The naked evangelism of his *Enchiridion* seemed a bit impoverished even to him and he appealed longingly for a true theology that the Dominican Javelli's *Philosophia Christiana* will soon attempt to establish.[17] But Javelli's very attempt shows clearly how precarious the position of theologians hostile to humanism was. By what right would the sixteenth-century scholastics forbid that good literature regain the place in education that Chartres had assigned it in the twelfth century? If it is because good literature carries pagan perspectives, it is necessary to begin by not setting up Aristotle at the heart of theology. What is more Greek than the *Nicomachean Ethics?* It is decidedly too late. When the definition of virtue and justice have been borrowed from the pagans and accepted, the study of the Ancients need not be held destructive of Christian ethics. The theologians had the right to watch over humanism, to redirect its deviations as necessary, but they did not have the right to deny its basic inspiration, because from it they had their existence. Two conflicting humanisms are found, neither of which is comprehensive enough to assimilate the other. Both sides have treated an ally without whom they cannot logically survive as an adversary.

---

aeterna sapientia; solus salutaria docuit unicus humanae salutis auctor; solus absolute praesitit quidquam unquam docuit; solus exhibere potest, quidquid unquam docuit." *Parclesis*, V, column 139 D. And since some dare maintain that Erasmus's Christ "seems to be reducible to a mere aggregate of moral concepts" (Pineau, *Érasme*, 115), let us further add this testimony: "Is qui Deus erat, factus est homo; qui immortalis, factus est mortalis; qui in corde patris erat, sese dimisit in terras." *Paraclesis*, vol. V, column 139 E. Finally, since the same historians maintains that Erasmus lost sight of the person of Christ to only retain his moral teaching, we remit the reader to *De Contemptu Mundi*, ch. X: "Quid quod et Dominum ipsum Jesum, quasi turbarum fastidio secessus . . ." It would be easy to cite many other examples.

17. See Chenu, "Javelli," columns 535–36 and "Note pour l'histoire," 231–35.

A doubt remains. The theologians' opposition to humanism was only too sincere. Are we sure of Erasmus's sincerity when he protests against the paganization of the Gospel? For my part, I know no text that permits us to deny it, but it becomes an absolute certainty when we remember that Erasmus is always linked to Luther here. Though Erasmus seldom committed himself and was separated from Luther by profound disagreements, he was always with the reformer against medieval Hellenism. Luther, though he had to exert great effort to keep from publicly "vomiting" their opposition, delayed the explosion until the eruption of the controversy on free will, only because he was linked to Erasmus in this essential point about philosophical Hellenism. Luther's scorn for scholastic theology is well enough known.[18] Now, what Luther reproaches in scholastic theology is exactly this very collusion of Greek philosophy and the Gospel: "A theologian who is not a logician," it was frequently remarked about Luther, "he is a monstrous heretic." To which Luther replied: "The very expression is heretical and monstrous." "Without Aristotle," it was also said, "one does not become a theologian." "Wrong!" replied Luther, and stressed: "On the contrary, one only becomes a theologian without Aristotle." "The whole of Aristotle," he adds further on, "is to theology what shadows are to light." And he clarified the significance of his remark: "Against Scholasticism."[19] What does he want, and why does he want it?

It would be easy to evade the question by classifying it as a theological debate without interest for the history of philosophy. That theological

18. See Scheel, *Dokumente*, "Fabulator Aristoteles cum suis frivolis defensoribus," text 111, p. 57. "Sed multo miror nostratium [errorem] qui Aristotelem non dissonare catholicae veritati impudentissime garriunt," text 114, p. 57. "Ve tibi maledicta blasphemia, ut incocta est haec fex philosophiae," text 119, p. 58. "O stulti, o Sawtheologen!" text 263, p. 117. "Nonne ergo fallax Aristoteles metaphysica et philosophia secundum traditionem humanam decepit nostros theologos?" text 277, p. 123. See especially the extremely violent letter to Johann Lang, February 8, 1517, *Briefwechsel*, I:88–89: "Mitto has litteras . . . plenas quaestionum adversus logicam et philosophiam et theologiam, id est, blasphemiarum et maledictionum contra Aristotelem, Porphyrium, Sententiarios, perdita scilicet studia nostri saeculi . . . nihil ita ardet animus, quam histrionem illum qui tam vere graeca larva ecclesiam lusit, mutis revelare ignominiamque ejus cunctis ostendere, si otium esset, habeo in manibus commentariolos in primum Physicorum, quibus fabulam Aristaei denuo agere statui, in meum istum Prothea, illusorem vaferrimum ingeniorum, ita ut nisi caro fuisset Aristoteles, vere diabolum eum fuisse non puderet asserere." (Of this project only the *Disputatio* quoted in the next note survives.) The letter of November 11, 1517 to Johann Lang is written in the same tone, I:121–22.

19. Luther, *Disputatio*, 221–28. The theses quoted are numbers 43, 45, 50 (226).

debate itself could be simplified to facilitate its liquidation. This is often done. As Luther discovered St. Paul and with St. Paul the necessity of grace, why not admit that everything is reduced to grace? Here again the problem is more complex, and I believe, to the contrary, that it is extremely important for the history of the Middle Ages and Renaissance to clarify its solution. For, every doctrine of grace supposes a doctrine of nature, and if the problem of grace relates to theology, the problem of nature involves philosophy at its deepest. Accordingly, to seek what the Lutheran reform condemns in medieval theology of grace is to search out which notion of nature medieval philosophy lived.

For Luther to help us in this endeavor, we must go back to the source of his great rejection. It is not where it is often facilely situated. No one will seriously believe that the Middle Ages left it to Luther to discover that fallen man cannot be saved without grace. Moreover, how could we simultaneously hold that the Renaissance discovered the sufficiency of nature and that the Middle Ages was unaware of the necessity of grace? But the facts speak well enough by themselves. In the *Summa Theologiae*,[20] St. Thomas asks whether eternal life can be merited without grace. The answer is no. Can man merit the first grace by himself? The answer is no. Could he at least, by his own effort, merit healing after the fall? The answer is no. Let us finally suppose that this first grace that he could not merit has been gratuitously received, can he deserve by himself to persevere in it? No, always no. And let us not be mistaken. Behind St. Thomas is St. Augustine, that is, the radical denial of any possible merit, of any real good, of any true virtue, in a fallen nature that grace has not yet cured. Both Thomas and Augustine know Cicero's very Greek definition of virtue: "a habit of the soul in conformity to nature, to measure, and to reason."[21] But what St. Augustine rejects in Cicero is lack of awareness that our nature is wounded and that there can be no virtue worthy of the name for nature while it has not been healed from its wounds.[22] Assuredly the Ancients could do good, but they did it badly, because among them the man who acted was not good. That is

20. Aquinas, *Summa Theologiae*, I^a II^{ae}, q. 114, articles 2, 5, 6, 9, and 10.

21. Quoted by Augustine, *Contra Julianum*, IV, 3, 19, col. 747. Also by Aquinas, *Summa Theologiae*, I^a II^{ae}, 56, 5 respondeo, and 6, first objection. Cicero's text is found in *De Inventione Rhetorica*, book II, ch. 53: "Nam virtus est animi habitus, naturae, modo, rationi consentaneus."

22. Augustine, *Contra Julianum*, IV, 3, 19.

why when he comes to make a judgement on pagan virtues, Augustine does so with a severity that could hardly be exceeded. "Fabricius will be less punished than Catiline, not because he was good, but because the other was still worse."[23] Thus speaks St. Augustine, because he follows St. Paul, and where there was no faith, how would there still be justice? *Justus ex fide vivit* (Rom 1:17).

But it is certainly true that even this is not enough for Luther, because if fallen nature, as St. Augustine and St. Thomas conceive it, cannot be saved without grace, it subsists and can still do something as nature. That is even why, if grace comes to its aid, it becomes capable again of being able to do something to save itself. With enough grace, it can do everything. From the time that God lifts it up, it is certainly nature that merits. Also another question that specifies and limits their sense precedes the ones I have cited from St. Thomas: "Can man merit something from God?" This time the answer is yes. Indeed what the Thomist maintains is that under the action of grace there is a nature that sin has not destroyed and that grace does not have the effect of suppressing but fulfilling by restoring it. "A rational creature determines itself to act in virtue of its free will. That is why its action is meritorious." And again: "Man merits in so far as he does what he ought by his own will."[24] But there is much more; from the moment when grace makes him capable of meriting, he becomes capable of thereby meriting more grace still, so that limits cannot be assigned to his possibilities of recuperation.

In speaking this way, St. Thomas Aquinas finds support in St. Bernard, because St. Bernard agrees with St. Anselm, who in this does no more than follow their common master, St. Augustine. A person who only has a curable illness is not a dead person who could be resurrected.[25] That is why in the text where St. Augustine affirms the necessity of grace most energetically, he always recalls the natural subject to which grace is applied: "Because what we say is that the will of man is aided by God to do the just action. Besides the fact that, indeed, man has been

---

23. Ibid., article 22 column 729, and article 25 column 751.

24. Aquinas, *Summa Theologiae*, I^a II^{ae}, q. 114, article 1, respondeo, and ad 1um.

25. I cannot recommend highly enough Karl Barth's very profound essay in Karl Barth and Heinrich Barth, *Zur lehre vom Heiligen Geist*, "Der Heilige Geist und das christliche Leben." Cf. "So mag eine Wunde geheilt, so kann aber nicht ein Toter auferweckt werden" (62). Let me simply observe that the text from the *Enchiridion*, 32 cited on page 61, means the opposite of what it is made to say, but this accidental lapse does not affect the substance of the question.

created with the free choice of his will, besides the divine teaching that prescribes how he must live, he further receives the Holy Spirit to produce in his soul the delight and love of that sovereign, immutable good, which is God."[26] Here is the summary of his whole doctrine: "Not justified by the law, not justified by our own will, but justified gratuitously by his grace. However, that does not occur without our will, but our will is revealed to be infirm by the Law, so that grace may heal it, and that the will thus cured should fulfill the Law without being submitted to the Law nor needing the Law."[27]

Luther was acquainted with these texts. He looked into them, and he rejected them. When St. Augustine tells us that, although the whole initiative comes from God, the reconciliation of man with God could not be accomplished without the cooperation of man, for Luther, this is a superfluous cooperation. According to his own words, what Luther wants is to magnify, implant, and constitute sin in order to magnify, implant, and constitute grace;[28] to magnify sin by showing it indestructible; to magnify grace, because instead of curing man from sin, it justified the sinner without curing him. Henceforth, justice is applied to him and saves him without becoming his—*non per domesticam, sed per extraneam justitiam.*[29] Grace reputes him to be just while still leaving him a sinner. Completely impure in himself, he becomes holy before God. In short, St. Augustine's God heals a nature, Luther's saves a corruption.

Here we reach the core of the debate, and the Reformation's hostility to medieval philosophy appears in its true light. Since there is no more nature, how could there still be a philosophy of nature? With what right might the theologian recur to the Greeks to inform himself on the conditions of morality and freedom, which have both irremediably ceased to exist after they were abolished by sin? But also, inversely, since

26. Augustine, *De Spiritu et Littera*, III, 5, column 203. Cf. "Non ego autem, sed gratia Dei mecum (I Corinthians XV, 9–10); id est non solus, sed gratia Dei mecum; ac per hoc nec gratia Dei sola, nec ipse solus, sed gratia Dei cum illo." *De Gratia et Libero Arbitrio*, V, 12, column 889. Cf. St. Thomas Aquinas, "Electiones autem ipsae sunt in nobis, supposito tamen divino auxilio," *Summa Theologiae*, I, 83, 2, ad 4.

27. Augustine, *De Spiritu et Littera*, IX, 15, column 209.

28. Scheel, *Dokumente*, 240:98–99.

29. Ibid., 241:99–100. In the same sense, see Luther's letter to Georg Spenlein, April 8, 1516 (the "unvergleichliche Brief"), in *Briefwechsel*, Weimar edition, I:35–36, notably: "Cave ne aliquando ad tantam puritatem aspires, ut peccator tibi videri nolis, imo esse. Christus enim non nisi in peccatoribus habitat." In other words, if grace healed men from sin, since man was healed, there would no longer be a reason for grace.

in their eyes it is after nature's restoration by grace that it truly began to exist again, why did not the Fathers and the medieval philosophers claim for themselves the right to speak of nature and to speak of it in the only manner appropriate, as philosophers? Consequently, under the theological superstructure and Revelation that crowns it, this persistence of ancient metaphysics and ethics through the Middle Ages was regarded as merely the childish illusion of Christians playing at being Greeks for centuries without understanding the rules of the game. Luther and the tragic harshness of his attack sufficed to prove the seriousness of the contest. The issue was nothing less than knowing whether Christian supernaturalism was going to take up ancient naturalism to complete it or destroy it irrevocably to put itself in its place.

These are the stakes of the Reformation. Luther sees perfectly what has been done and what he wants to do. Is there room in Christianity, yes or no, for nature and free will? If nature is corrupted by sin, free will is too. What remain is then a *will* that is not *free* and cannot become so again. Man is immutably fixed in evil by original sin. No doubt he conserves a will, and this will is free of any constraint. We can no longer do anything but evil. However, we do so voluntarily. If grace comes to change the course of our willing, it is still the will that wills, and it does not undergo any constraint by this fact. Will is now like nothing so much as a watch about which two gentlemen dispute, which can only go where sin and grace lead it. Its spontaneity is no more than radical impotence. *Qui est vis inefficax, nisi plane nulla vis?*[30] If this will can no longer do anything of itself except to let itself by guided, why say it is free? Let us say rather that it is a slave, submitted to a *necessitas immutabilitatis* that holds it *immutabiliter captivum*. In short it is an empty word: *res de solo titulo*, whose usage ought to be permanently banned from theology.

Considered from this viewpoint, the theses against scholastic theology, which Luther caused to be maintained in 1517, less famous among historians than his theses against indulgences, nevertheless had as profound an impact. Instead of simply shaking up a medieval ecclesiastical institution, Luther's attack aimed at one of the vital organs of its thought. This might be denied by floating a kind of neo-Pelagianism. That is just what would have happened if the Renaissance had been that exaltation of ancient naturalism of which we have heard. In fact, in the measure in

---

30. Luther, *De Servo Arbitrio*, 634–39. These pages are essential for the Lutheran theology of the slave will.

which the Reformation expresses one of the profound tendencies of its time, it wanted to do exactly the contrary. For Luther it is Dun Scotus and St. Thomas who are the Pelagians, and if the Renaissance seeks to kill medieval thought through him, it is in denying, along with nature, the freedom and morality that nature grounds. Henceforth, no more free will: "We are not masters of our acts, but slaves, from beginning to end. Against the philosophers." No more acquired merits: "We do not become just by dint of acting justly, but it is because we are justified that we do just things. Against the philosophers." Now, who persuaded us that our will can accomplish something, acquire justice by practicing it and by justice ultimately acquire merit? It was Greek ethics, which is to say, pagan ethics, to which the medieval philosophers handed over the keys of theology. Let it be expelled from there: "Almost all of Aristotle's *Ethics* is the worst enemy of grace. Against the Scholastics."[31] By lessening sin, they have lessened grace,[32] and pagan nature has taken advantage of the opportunity to introduce itself into Christianity and entrench itself there.

31. Luther, *Disputatio*, 226. Cf.: "Ethica lectio (cum sit plane ad theologiam lupus ad agnum) . . ." Letter to Spalatin, September 2, 1518, I:196. To avoid possible confusion, let us note that the use of the word nature in Luther does not diminish his opposition to the medieval tradition in the slightest. For him corruption is henceforth part of nature and can no longer be expelled from it. Certainly, nature was not originally bad, which would be Manichaeism (thesis 8), but by sin it became naturally bad ("Est tamen naturaliter et inevitabiliter mala et viciata natura," thesis 9), and it remains bad even under grace. The tendency toward sin is now inseparable from nature: "sancti intrinsece sunt peccatores semper, ideo justificantur semper," "simul sunt justi et injusti," whence comes the famous "simul peccator et justus." (Cf. Strohl, *L'épanouissement*, 29). In a word, according to Luther, we can certainly be "reputed" just by God, but not become just, in the Catholic sense of the term (ibid., 27).

32. "Nec movet, quod Latomus me ingratitudinis et injuriae insimulat in S. Thomam, Alexandrum, et alios. Male enim de me meriti sunt . . . Thomas multa haeretica scripsit et auctor est regnantis Aristotelis, vastatoris piae doctrinae." Luther, in Scheel, *Dokumente*, text 85, p. 34. Furthermore, he specifies the point at which the contamination occurred: "Et dicitur [justitia Dei] ad differentiam justitiae hominum, quae ex operibus fit. Sicut Aristoteles 3 Ethicorum manifeste determinat, secundum quem justitia sequitur et fit ex actibus. Sed secundum Deum precedit opera et opera fiunt ex ipsa." Scheel, text 243, 101. Cf. the *Commentary on the Epistle to the Galatians*, 2:21, 503: "Vide ergo . . ." and 504: "Jam sequitur . . ." Accordingly, Luther essentially accuses St. Thomas of having ruined theology of grace by accepting Aristotle's doctrine in *Nicomachean Ethics* III, 7, 1113 b 19ff. as true. Needless to say, St. Thomas never admitted that the justice of grace is the product of our acts. On the contrary, well before Luther, he taught that Aristotle's thesis does not hold in what concerns the acquisition of grace, which is instantaneous: "tota justificatio impii originaliter consistit in gratiae infusione; per eam enim et liberum arbitrium movetur, et culpa remittitur. Gratiae autem infusio fit in instanti, absque successione." *Summa Theologiae*, Iᵃ IIᵃᵉ, 113, 7, respondeo. How could St. Thomas believe

There is no point in pretending that the claim that there was medieval hostility to nature and the world was false or even exaggerated. That is true, and it can hardly be exaggerated, but it is one sided. The problem, in fact, is still to know who condemned nature in the Middle Ages, and which nature. When the question is posed, names tumble out by themselves: Peter Damian, Bernard of Clairvaux, all those who became the apostles of the strictest religious reforms that the twelfth century witnessed. As these personalities conceived it, their peculiar function was to recall ceaselessly the existence and omnipresence of sin, the corruption of the soul and of nature effected by the original fall, the danger of forgetting the wounds that the divine creation had suffered and that reopen at any moment if we neglect to remedy them. The world against which they incessantly write and preach is, as Boussuet would later say: "those who prefer visible and passing things to invisible eternal ones." To depict the Middle Ages without these formidable ascetics would be to disfigure it, and no one dreams of doing that. But to turn them into competent interpreters of medieval philosophy would be an equally serious error. If they have a place in the history of philosophy, it is despite themselves, because they never desired it. Everything in them goes against philosophy. They do not stop reminding us that reason runs dangers when it pretends to be sufficient. However, confronting the greatness of St. Bernard there was another great, Abelard, whom the ascetic of

---

that we justify ourselves? In one sense the justification of the sinner is a divine work that is *greater than that of creation itself.* Cf. *Summa Theologiae* I^a II^{ae}, 113, 9, respondeo. The difference therefore is elsewhere. According to St. Thomas, it consists in that, although gratuitous justification precedes our free choice, it does not happen without it (*Summa Theologiae*, I^a II^{ae}, 113, 3, respondeo). Whence it follows, first that free choice participates in its own justification ("Unde oportet quod mens humana, dum justificatur, per motum liberi arbitrii recedat a peccato et accedat ad justitiam." *Summa Theologiae*, I^a II^{ae}, 113, 5, respondeo). Next, that in the measure in which man is justified and where God has so decided, a certain relation of justice and merit can re-establish itself between man and God. It remains true that it is God who gave man the strength to act well, but it is man who acts well: "quia creatura rationalis seipsam movet ad agendum." *Summa Theologiae*, I^a II^{ae}, 114, 1, respondeo. Thus the Aristotelian notion of merit due to the exercise of free acts retains a positive value in St. Thomas, even under grace that modifies its meaning. It can be said that for him grace is precisely what permits free choice to enter a sort of relation of justice with God. What Luther opposes, although it is not what is sometimes imagined, is thus no less a historical reality.

Clairvaux never tolerated, who was no less real and who greatly benefited not only philosophy, but also theology itself.

Let us go further: if we insist on considering respect and love for nature as essentially alien to the Middle Ages, how many things in the art and literature of the period become incomprehensible! Is it not this distortion that condemns so many historians to regarding men as heterodox, because of their exaltation of nature, who would only have been heterodox if they had despised it? Saint Bernard condemns sculpture, but the buttercups, clover, and broom decorate the walls of our cathedrals. May, with its flowers and its birds, is seen smiling on those walls. July whets its scythe there with measured elegance. The whole round of works and days, veritable mirror of nature, unfolds in the porch of Notre Dame.[33] That is exactly what we see there; it is exactly there that we see it, and all these things are in their place, grateful ex-votos of nature created, ransomed, doubly fulfilled. Peter Damian can rise up with vigor against those who think of earthly things, but our French writers think of them without interruption, and they are right when they think well. They gladly write with Pliny: "Hail, Nature, mother of all things!" In fact, they say that, and if they add that nature has everything it is from its author, that is not to diminish nature but to ennoble it. In *De Mundi Universitate*, Bernardus Silvestris makes nature God's highest decree, *suprema decreta Dei, natura*; the blessed fecundity of the Word, *tu natura, uteri mei beata fecunditas*.[34] In his famous *De Planctu Naturae*, Alan of Lille invokes nature with the same fervor:

> O Dei proles, genitrixque rerum,
> Vinculum mundi stabilisque nexus,
> Gemma terrenis, speculum caducis,
>   Lucifer orbis.
> Pax, amor, virtus, regimen, potestas,
> Ordo, lex, finis, via, dux, origo,
> Vita, lux, splendor, species, figura,
> Regula mundi.[35]

33. Mâle, *L'art religieux*, 69–70.

34. Gilson, "La cosmogonie," 22.

35. de Insulis, *Liber de Planctu*, column 447. The subsequent texts are found in columns 445 C–446 A. Cf. Faral, "Le Roman de la Rose," 430–57. Auerbach, *Dante als Dichter*. In a very remarkable essay Erich Auerbach has proposed the expression *Vulgärantique* (with no pejorative meaning) to designate this survival of Antiquity in the Middle Ages. The phrase matches *Vulgärlatein*; see "Dante und Virgil," 126–44.

However, Nature herself tells us that she does not want to arrogate the prerogative of power for herself to the point of derogating the power of God. She professes to be the humble disciple of the supreme master: "certissime summi magistri me humilem profiteor esse discipulam." Even more, after joining such humility to such magnificence, she admits to being the stage for works that enormously surpass her power: "Consult the authority of theological science, because more confidence must be placed in its fidelity than in the firmness of my reasons. What its faithful witness attests is that man owes his birth to my action, his rebirth to the authority of God. He is called by me from non-being to being. By God he is led to better-being. Indeed man is engendered by me, for death. He is recreated by God, for life." And let us not believe that such notions are peculiar to medieval poets who wrote in Latin. Nature is no less great in the *Romance of the Rose*:

> He [Zeuxis] found no fault, but even with such aids,
> And though he had great skill in portraiture
> And coloring he failed to imitate
> Nature's perfectionment of pulchritude.[36]

But nature is still mindful of her source:

> For God, whose beauty is quite measureless,
> When He this loveliness to nature gave
> Within her fixed a fountain, full and free,
> From which all beauty flows.[37]

> When God, who in all beauties so abounds,
> First made so beautiful this lovely earth,
> Whose foreseen form of fairness in His mind
> He had before He gave it outward shape.[38]

The poet does not need the Renaissance to show him Nature's splendor, because he affirms it four times in four verses. But nature, as he conceives it, finds all its glory in the service of the master who made it and who still takes it as his collaborator.

36. [Translator's note: Guillaume de Lorris and Jean de Meun, *Romance of the Rose*, 345 lines 58–61, verses 16199–16202 in original.]

37. [Translator's note: *Romance of the Rose*, 346, lines 188–191, verses 16231–35 in original.]

38. [Translator's note: *Romance of the Rose*, 359, lines 18–21, verses 16724–32 in original.]

When He, according to his fixed design,
Had thus His other creatures all disposed,
With His own grace God honored me so much—
Held me so dear—that He established me
As chamberlain of all, to serve Him thus
Permitting me, as e'er He will permit
While it shall be His will. No other right
Claim I to such a bounty, but I thank
Him for His love of such unworthy maid
And for His prizing me so much that He,
Great lord of such a vast and fair estate,
Appointed me His constable indeed,
His steward and His vicar-general—
A dignity which little I deserved
Except through His benign benevolence.
God honors me so much that in my ward
He leaves the golden chain that binds
The elements which bow before my face.[39]

If Jean de Meun is looking back at Boethius from whom he takes his inspiration in the Christian past, among his contemporaries Jean belongs to the party of the masters who taught Aristotle's philosophy in the Faculty of Arts of the University of Paris. How could it be otherwise? If there is one nature, there certainly must be one philosophy, and if there is one philosophy, from what other master would we ask its secret but "that Aristotle who took the measure of natures better than anyone since Cain" (verse 18032)? This is why medieval nature has no reason to envy grace. It is also why, when Christian Wisdom converses familiarly with Aristotle in our old poets, instead of seeing naiveté to be excused with a smile, we would do better to realize that a specifically medieval conception of nature is expressed in such passages:

Amis, dit-elle qui me claimes
Amie, pour ce que tu m'aimes
—et en ce n'as tu rien perdu,
Car par ce t'est tout bien venu.[40]

When we muse about it, is not the reciprocal affection of grace friend of nature and nature friend of grace, an example of what gives its

39. [Translator's note: *The Romance of the Rose*, 359–60, lines 49–66, verses 16768–88.]

40. In Cohen, *Mystéres et moralités*, 107–8.

deepest meaning, for example, to the medieval novel in prose, *Lancelot*. Not that the world into which the novelist introduce us lacks pitfalls everywhere. The Devil tends his snares everywhere in behalf of sin. Humans live in danger of mysterious charms, and since man left nature to enter into the city, the weak are oppressed by the injustice of the strong. But Lancelot, Bors, Percival, Galahad come. The redemption of nature is achieved in the presence of the knights of grace. Monsters expire. Hearts wounded by the lance of love heal by the lance of a still stronger love. Like the ruin of some haunted castle, the kingdom of the Devil crumbles. "Evil customs" are abolished. The weak reestablish their rights against the strong. Justice reigns. We might say that the branch of the tree of paradise, cut off and planted in the earth by Eve, finally comes to life and bears fruit. This renovation of the Celtic lands in the springtime of grace has such vigor that it survived the Middle Ages. It sings in all our memories, even if we no longer recognize its message. When he came to the end of his life, Richard Wagner surveyed his work to ask for its last lesson. The mirages of Venusberg have vanished. The accursed gold has returned to the Rhine. The song of the master singers has been sung. Even the long lament of Isold and Tristan has been quieted, but Parsifal's blessing descends on the ransomed world. Nature enters into the enchantment of Good Friday forever.

By helping us feel nature as they did, medieval poets help us conceive it as medieval philosophers thought about it, and not only philosophers but medieval theologians and mystics. St. Bonaventure does not believe that natural knowledge is the highest knowledge, but he is far from holding it in contempt: *cognitio rerum humanarum magna pars est nostrae notitiae*.[41] No one insisted on the impotence of the natural will more than St. Bernard. However, after he has extensively described everything grace can do within the will, when he comes to ask himself what free will can still do, what a cry of triumph! "Free will," responds St. Bernard, "is saved."[42]

41. ". . . cognitio rerum humanarum magna pars est nostrae notitiae, quamdiu sumus in statu viae; et pro tanto ponitur in definitione sapientiae." St. Bonaventure, *In III Sententiarum*, 35, dub. 1, p. 787.

42. St. Bernard, *De Gratia et Libero Arbitrio*, I:2: "Quid igitur agit, ais liberum arbitrium? Breviter respondeo. Salvatur. Tolle liberum arbitrium, et non erit quod salvetur. Tolle gratiam, non erit unde salvetur. Opus hoc sine duobus effici non potest, uno a quo fit, altero cui vel in quo fit. Deus auctor est salutis, liberum arbitrium tantum capax; nec

With even more reason, the legions of dialecticians, physicians, moralists, and metaphysicians who inhabit medieval universities see things this way. It is neither an unconscious absurdity, nor a childish illusion that attaches them to Greek thought. They became philosophers not despite their religious faith, but because of it. If Aristotle's nature conquered them easily, it is because their Christianity needed it: they were waiting for it. Consequently, there is a certain shared feeling that makes all the medieval thinkers so many members of one family. From the patristic period, when medieval speculation is prepared, until the thirteenth century and even the Renaissance, the various expressions of Christian thought bear witness to a remarkable continuity.[43] Certainly, we could not maintain

---

dare illam, nisi Deus, nec capere valet nisi liberum arbitrium. Quod ergo a solo Deo et soli datur libero arbitrio, tam absque consensu esse non potest accipientis, quam absque gratia dantis."—"Ita tamen quod a sola gratia coeptum est, pariter ab utroque perficitur." *De Gratia et Libero Arbitrio*, XIV, 47.—"Verum haec cum certum sit divino in nobis actitari spiritu, Dei sunt munera. Quia vero cum nostrae voluntatis assensu, nostra sunt merita." *De Gratia et Libero Arbitrio*, XIV:50. The whole doctrine supposes something St. Bernard, moreover, affirms explicitly, even more strongly than any other medieval theologian: "Verum libertas a necessitate aeque et indifferenter Deo, universaeque tam malae quam bonae rationali convenit creaturae. Nec peccato nec miseria amittitur, vel minuitur . . ." *De Gratia et Libero Arbitrio*, IV:9.

43. On this subject, see the fundamental testimony of Karl Barth, "Der heilige Geist und das christliche Leben," 58–62, which shows the existence of a doctrinal continuity between St. Augustine and St. Thomas Aquinas, founded on their common acceptance of a stable nature, persisting under the action of sin as well as under the action of grace: "Und ihr Hintergrund ist jener Begriff eines Gottes, zu dem das Geschöpf als solches, in ruhend gesicherter Kontinuität steht . . . ," 60. "Auf disem Boden steht die mittelalterliche Rechtfertingungs oder vielmehr Heiligungslehre, auf disem bodem auch die des Tridentinischen Katholizismus," 60. With this both Lutheranism and Calvinism contradict to St. Augustine, despite so many attempts to utilize him. Of course, Lutheranism is just as opposed to the Catholicism of Erasmus ("Quid autem aliud est Christi philosophia, quam ipse renascentiam vocat, quam instauratio bene conditae naturae?" *Paraclesis*, vol. V, column 141 F). Finally whatever the differences that distinguish them, Augustinianism and Thomism are henceforth united, even on the level of pure philosophy, by this common acknowledgement of a nature *sanabilis*, which sets them in opposition to the Reformation.

On this point, Alphons Viktor Müller seems to be mistaken, unlike Karl Barth. He thinks the agreement of Luther with Augustine can be proved by piling up quotes whose literal agreement can be maintained, but their disagreement in meaning escapes him. It is true that for St. Augustine and all the scholastics, as for Luther, justification only begins here below; true that on this earth, we are always *justificandi* without being fully *justificati*, therefore true also that sin always coexists in us with justice, although it no longer is imputed to us, etc. (Müller, *Luthers theologische Quellen*, 174. But for a disciple of St. Augustine, the sin that coexists with grace in us is not that from which grace justifies us, it is that from which grace has not yet justified us. No doubt, something always remains to be healed in our life, and that is why the formulas agree, *semper justificandi* . . . But at the point where Luther demands that the soul should conserve in itself the very sin of which it is justified, the Catholic tradition holds that, in so far as it is justified, the soul is no longer sinful. In other words, medieval grace becomes the soul's quality, once conferred by God on the soul. That is why the nature of the soul is healed. The "restauratio liberi concilii" is of course only partial here, but it is real (St. Bernard, *De Gratia et Libero Arbitrio*, VIII:26), because its infirmity is really although imperfectly healed: "Sane infirmitas ejus a seipsa est, sanitas vero non a se, sed a Domini spiritu. Sanatur autem, cum renovatur," ibid., XII:40. For St. Thomas justification takes place through a change of state: "transmutatio qua aliquis transmutatur a statu injustitiae ad statum justitiae per remissionem peccati . . ." *Summa Theologiae*, I^a II^{ae}, 113, 1, respondeo. For this, non-imputation of sin does not suffice: "et hoc quod est Deum non imputare peccatum homini, importat quemdam effectum in ipso cui peccatum non imputatur," *Summa Theologiae*, I^a II^{ae}, 113, 2 *ad primum*. Such is the effect of grace: "per gratiam, macula cessat" (I^a II^{ae}, 86, 2, respondeo, 87, 6, respondeo, and 109, 7 respondeo. This is exactly what Luther seems to me to deny.

Accordingly, Müller has not understood the issue. Doubtless Luther admits that justice belongs to a Christian in so far as he is justified. Many texts could easily be quoted to this effect. Lutheran faith thus guarantees the Christian the possession of justice. However, the question is still to know whether justice becomes his in so far as imputed or in so far as incorporated into his nature. Now it can hardly be doubted that the first hypothesis is right, not only because it alone seems to be in agreement with the spirit of the doctrine, but on account of the parallel between what we receive from Christ and what Christ receives from us in the justifying act. Luther often says that Christ's justice becomes ours and that our sins become his. The sense of this double imputation seems clear with each one clarifying the other. Our sins cannot overcome Christ's own justice in Christ. His holiness permits him, and permits him alone, to assume them without thereby perishing. Inversely, his grace becomes that of the Christian without eliminating the corruption of fallen nature, because, even in us, the justice of God remains his, it justifies us—without which it would lose its efficacy; because, even in Christ, the sins he makes his remain ours, it is we who are justified—not "having been justified," but "being justified." Cf. "Peccata sua jam non sua, sed Christi sunt. At in Christo peccata justitiam vincere non possunt, sed vincuntur; ideo in ipso consummuntur. Rursum, justitia Christi jam non tantum Christi, sed sui Christiani est. Ideo non potest ulli debere aut a peccatis opprimi tanta fultus justitia." *In Gallatas*, 2:21, 504. "Igitur, mi dulcis Frater, disce Christum et hunc crucifixum, disce ei cantare et de te ipso desperans dicere ei: tu, Domine Jesu, est justitia mea, ego autem sum peccatum tuum; assumpsisti quod non eras, et dedisti mihi quod non eram." To Georg Spenlein, April 8, 1516, Weimar ed. *Briefwechsel*, I:35. In Luther this "fiducialis desperatio sui" is strictly opposed to the Thomist's confidence in what God has made of him through the grace that renders him capable of acquiring merit again. For the Thomist, and just as much for the Augustinian, because it is true that by crowning our merits God only crowns his gifts, the gifts that he makes to our free will have become no less *our* merits. In a word, in medieval Catholicism it is just as true as in Lutheranism to say that all our justice is *a Deo*. In both cases, it is true to say that justice comes wholly from him. In patristic and medieval Catholicism alone justice produces "an effect in him to whom sin is no longer imputed," a "real [change] of state," (St. Thomas) a "renovation" and a "cure" of being itself (St. Bernard), which Erasmus splendidly defines: *instauratio bene conditae naturae*.

that a common philosophical system existed then. On the contrary, the medieval doctrines are surprisingly diverse, and history has the duty to respect that. But this diversity, the real doctrinal opposition that can be discerned in it, unfolds against a background of real unity.

To be convinced about this, it is enough to make a quick comparison of the three leading positions that dominate the schools in the thirteenth century: Averroism, Thomism, and Augustinianism. To prove that Averroes and his disciples took the order of nature and of rational philosophy seriously is too easy a game to win for it to be worth playing. Indeed, radical Hellenism characterizes them and distinguishes them from the other contemporary schools. In their ardor to seek the causes of nature, they do not forget the first cause, God, but how tranquilly their reason approaches him!

> The first principle is to this world what a father of a family is to his house, the general to his army, or the common good to the city ... Also, knowing that all goods come to him from this first principle and are conserved for him by this first principle, the philosopher dedicates the highest love to it, according the command of both the rule of nature and the rule of intelligence. And as each one finds his joy in what he loves, and the greatest joy in what he loves most, as the philosopher loves the first principle with a great love, as has just been said, the philosopher also finds is greatest joy in the first principle, in the contemplation of its goodness, and it is the only legitimate joy. Such is the life of the philosopher, and he who does not have it, does not follow a straight path. Now, I call philosopher, every man who, living according to the order that nature proscribes, attains the last end and the best of human life.[44]

We should think about this well: the philosopher's delight in the exercise of reason according to rule of nature is the ideal that Boethius of Dacia, master of arts in the University of Paris, proposes to the men of the thirteenth century. Was Erasmus wrong to complain that the Gospel had sometimes been forgotten for Aristotle? He would have had Étienne Tempier on his side, who did not like Boethius of Dacia, and St. Thomas Aquinas who did not agree with either one. But I doubt that Erasmus himself, despite the respect that he sometimes professes for St. Thomas,[45] was in agreement with him.

44. Grabmann, "Die Opuscula," 306–7.

45. ". . . et ipse neotericorum omnium, mea sententia diligentissimus Thomas Aquinas." Erasmus, *Ratio seu Methodus*, column 78 E.

For it is true that St. Thomas was a resolute adversary of Averroism and its disinterest in the supernatural order, but at the same time he defended Aristotle, whose physics, metaphysics, and ethics, in themselves, precede the Christian revelation that completes them. Nature has its rights, and nothing will hinder it in exercising them, provided only that nature keeps to its place. St. Thomas never supported the schemes that dissolve nature into the supernatural. For him, nature is neither what sin has made out of us nor what it destroyed in us, because sin can neither constitute nature nor destroy it. The essence of man is his nature, and to say that sin has corrupted it, would be to say that man has ceased to exist.[46] Thus, if St. Thomas attacks the Averroists unceasingly, it is not because they admit the subsistence of natural beings, recognizing the existence of an order of nature and reason. For him as for them, the highest natural life is that of the philosopher. True temporal happiness is that of the sage. The life of the sage is to follow nature and reason. St. Thomas's reproach is that Averroists forget that for Christians, which they claim to be, the order of nature depends on a divine order that is at the same time its end and origin. After that how can we be surprised when, tranquilly assured in his clear vision of the distinction and harmony of the two orders, St. Thomas in his turn should pass for a pagan and see himself accused of Averroism by certain Augustinians.

However, we now know that for consistent Lutheranism the Augustinians themselves are only pagans and Greeks.[47] It is true that the malleability of nature in the hands of God attains its maximum limit in them. It would be impossible to go a step further without destroying nature, but they never took exactly that step. By affirming that our nature is corrupt, their doctrine certainly does not stop at the perfections gratuitously added by God to our essence. Precisely what man became through sin, it seems, is what now constitutes his definition. It might be said that in St. Augustine and his disciples, metaphysical *essences* are not clearly distinguished from *statuses* willed by God, as if beings were defined rather by statuses than by natures, or at least as if the states of being were really integrated into their nature and indiscernible from it.

46. Aquinas, *Summa Theologiae*, I^a II^{ae}, 85, 2, respondeo.

47. It would be interesting to find out to what degree Luther himself was aware of his opposition to authentic Augustinianism (see Baruzi, "Le commentaire de Luther," 468–70) and even, more generally, to take up the overall problem of his Agustinian interpretation. The same problem presents itself concerning his interpretation of St. Bernard (see above 29–30 n. 43).

It is no less true that St. Augustine's God is the *naturarum auctor*, and that according to a frequently quoted formula, "He administers natures in such a way that they keep the power of carrying out their peculiar operations." Nothing more logical than the wholesale condemnation leveled against medieval philosophy by the Reformation: a strong tie binds Augustinianism to Thomism, beyond their technical differences, and Luther attests for us to its firmness. Every medieval theologian admits the persistence of nature and of free will under grace as a necessary initial thesis. The Averroists often seem to forget grace. The Augustinians often seem to forget nature, but St. Augustine himself always remembers in time that God does not save man without man: *nec gratia Dei sola, nec ipse solus, sed gratia Dei cum illo*.[48]

If there is a break between ancient naturalism and modern times, it cannot have been the work of medieval philosophy, which Erasmus and Luther alike reproach for its failure to consummate such a rupture. It is the thirteenth century that promulgated the value of the *Nicomachean Ethics* rather than the sixteenth, and it is the sixteenth century that made it a crime for Christians to use the *Ethics* rather than the thirteenth. The Middle Ages may have put the Averroists on guard against imprudent or premature use of Aristotle's ethics. Grosseteste, Albert the Great, St. Thomas Aquinas nonetheless translated, commented, and taught it. We have to wait until the Reformation for the naturalism of the Ancients to be rejected as incompatible with Christianity. If it is true that the philosophy of the Middle Ages was, as it were, mortally wounded the day when Greek ethics were publicly decreed to be the enemy of grace, it must be recognized that medieval philosophy had lived off Greek ethics and that it is at the time of the Renaissance when Christian thought is seen to reject the right to live off it. This is a radical break, and in what concerns the Reformation, it seems an inevitable one, but it was a rather surprising break on Erasmus's part, which nothing made necessary either on his side or on that of the theologians whom he opposed. Because of his resounding controversy with Luther, it is fairly well known that Erasmus always remained the champion of the rights of nature and of free will against the Reformation. Heir to a more indulgent theology, not only than that of Luther but of St. Augustine himself, he agrees with Justin in saving Socrates and the masters of ancient ethics.[49] How would he deny

48. See above 21 n. 26.

49. Luther's doctrinal opposition to Erasmus began at the very start, even before their personal relations were established. See Luther's letters to Spalatin, October 19,

that Greek thought is in deep agreement with Christian thought? And if it is in agreement, by what right would he rise up against the thrusting of Hellenism in Christian thought, where it is rightly at home, when one recognizes that agreement?

Here, Erasmus's argument has the advantage over Luther's of making us look not only at the existence of medieval Hellenism, but into its very nature. Twelfth-century Chartres humanism was suffocated, as it were, by the proliferation of philosophical and theological studies. In the fifteenth and sixteenth centuries, it is very true that University teaching fell prey to a withering dialectic, which did not facilitate any serious study of the science nor even of letters properly speaking. We are faced not with an opposition of principle but a collision of acquired mental habits and vices. "Literary" men mounted an assault upon the chairs held by philosophers. The latter defended their chairs both with good reasons, as when they affirmed their right to exist, and with bad, as when they denied the teaching of literature the right to exist. To explain the fratricidal struggle that put medieval humanism and philosophy at odds, we should certainly not forget human stupidity, which never loses its prerogatives, or routine and laziness, which are formidable forces. The theologians no longer knew either classical Latin or Greek, and they did not trouble to learn them. Erasmus never understood much about philosophy, and he had no taste for an opacity for which it pleased him to make philosophy responsible. In that, both sides only appear human. However, through much hesitation and repentance, at the cost of mutual concessions that were to lead into that great Jesuit pedagogical reformation to which we owe several of our greatest seventeenth century classics, theologians and humanists present two fixed attitudes, equally legitimate, both necessary, close enough so that they should have ultimately understood each other, distinct enough to be eventually able to be opposed. Luther's opposition to medieval theology is the condemnation of any humanism. Thus it had to touch Erasmus himself some

---

1516 *Briefwechsel*, Weimar ed., I:70–71; to Johann Lang, March 1, 1512, I:96. The most interesting letter, because it explains why Luther refrains from publicly expressing their disagreement (they had the scholastics as common enemies), is addressed to Spalatin, January 18, 1518, I:133–4. We cannot examine here the purely Erasmian conception of a theology founded on the union of the Gospel and "bonae litterae," instead of on the union of the Gospel and Greek philosophy as in the Middle Ages. The question has been raised elsewhere, in different ways but with a good sense of the nature of the problem, by Humbert, *Les origines*, ch. IV, "Philosophia Christi," and Renaudet, *Érasme*.

day. The struggle of Erasmus against the theologians and the theologians against Erasmus is only the accidental collision of two humanisms that only needed to acknowledge each other to agree.

In effect, Erasmus and the humanists worked for the creation of a very different and, in a sense, even opposed Hellenism to that of St. Thomas. Passing through whatever medieval hesitations and reminiscences one pleases, the Renaissance directs itself to an Antiquity that the Middle Ages did not know or which did not interest them as such. Erasmus did not dream of making Antiquity revive in its entirely. He too would only retain from it what could be harmonized with Christianity. In Universities, his *praeparatio evangelica* will progressively replace sterile dialectical discussions, so alien to the spirit of the Gospel and of little or no benefit for the moral life. At least, in this way, what he retains of Antiquity will truly be what it was in the past, and its whole value will come to be its being treated as past. Not certainly as outmoded, because it is precisely by treating the past as such that history calls it to life. But the life that history gives the past is both fertile and fixed. What the past delivers to us only instructs us because it is offered to us as a form of life gone forever, and that nothing now can make different from what it was. To Erasmus we owe scrupulous research methods, critique of texts and documents that nowadays we put at the service of India, Greece, and Rome, of medieval literature itself. We owe him more still. Humanism is not only history. Humanism, above all, is the sympathy of man for man that animates history, the taste that guides it, finally, the joy that rewards it, when at the end of patient research, it grasps a fragment of the human that was lost and has just been recovered.

Except that by a necessary compensation, history only renders the past for itself in forbidding it to change. Now to change is to endure, to live. Medieval Latin was no longer Cicero's but that is exactly why that Latin still lived. Humanism made it into a dead language. It buried it in its triumph. Wouldn't it be the same thing that occurred then in the philosophical order? Rather than the discovery of Greek thought, was not Humanism rather an attempt to remove Greek thought from the jurisdiction of philosophy and submit it to history, at the risk of thereby making it a cadaver. Like Luther, Erasmus does not fight against a phantom. He attacks the same adversary, although he does not attack it for the same reasons. It has often been said, and in a sense it is true, that the Middle Ages were almost completely alien to history, at least as the Renaissance was going to understand it and we still understand it today. Medieval humanism is very different from the historical humanism about the past that characterizes the Renaissance. It is a humanism of the present, or if we prefer, of the intemporal. When he looks back at medieval philosophy, Erasmus no more recognizes Greek philosophy in it than he does Latin in the language that medieval philosophy uses. He is right: Plato, Aristotle, Cicero, Seneca are no longer what they were. But Erasmus is wrong because they are certainly themselves, as if they were still alive and by living changing. It is even because they are not yet dead that they are so difficult to recognize. What Albert the Great or St. Thomas asked of them was not so much to say what they had been formerly, in Greece or Rome, as to say what they were still capable of becoming, what they would have become themselves, if they had lived in the thirteenth century, in Christendom. What should I say? There they are; there they survive. The historian who meets them again is continually divided between admiration for the depth with which medieval thinkers interpret them and an archeologist's unease before a bas-relief that suddenly comes alive and changes. If Plato and Aristotle are suppressed, what will remain of medieval philosophy? But just as Alexander in the *chansons de geste* is Charlemagne leading his barons into battle, thus and still more deeply do Plato and Aristotle survive in St. Bonaventure and St. Thomas, because they adopt their faith and their principles. Absorbed in the intensity of the present, the medieval thinker has no time to be interested in the past as such. He only retains the eternal present of antiquity and its very permanence that he lifts out of time. "What difference is there, then, between pagans and Christians?", the pupil Charlemagne asked master Alcuin one day—"None, save faith and baptism," responds the master. And indeed, as to the rest, they are men.[50]

If I am not mistaken, here is what Erasmus's passionate taste for historical difference rebelled against, and here also is the question that is posed in the light of the facts that have just been analyzed. To say that the supernatural has been substituted for nature, is a contradiction in terms, because something supernatural is *over* something natural. To say that Greek philosophy has only been a superficial disguise of theology, is to deny Erasmus and Luther, that is to say, to annul the witness of

---

50. That medieval "state" of Antiquity seems to me to match exactly the "Vulgärantike," which Erich Auerbach so clearly defines in the remarkable article quoted above, 25 n. 35.

Humanism and the Renaissance at the same time as that of the Middle Ages. The only way to pose the problem, taking all the facts into account, is thus to ask ourselves whether medieval philosophy might not be the final flowering of Greek philosophy, transplanted into Christendom, before its transition to its historical condition.

Erasmus ended by asking himself the question. Aged, horrified by the unforeseen development of what he called the Lutheran "tragedy," he came to understand where his true allies had to be. In calling with more vigor than ever for an alliance between a simpler, more literate theology and a more speculative humanism, he perceived that if Greek thought is not yet dead, that is due to medieval Christianity: *nam quod Aristoteles hodie celebris est in scholis, non suis debet, sed Christianis: periisset et ille, nisi Christo fuisset admmixtus.*[51] What finer program of studies than to salvage Aristotle for the philosophy of Christ? I am happy to receive it from the hands of Erasmus. *De Transitu Hellenismi ad Christianismum*, what finer title could there be for such a program? Guillaume Budé offers it to me, and I accepted it gratefully. Nothing remains henceforth but to get to work, to climb down from the overviews to the humble detail of facts, to discern in the Antiquity that endures the Christian who works on it from within and transforms it. Since the humanism of our teachers Erasmus and Budé today generously opens itself up to medieval philosophers and makes room for them, may it be capable of teaching me to make them relive as they were. But may they themselves be able to teach me to rejoin the permanence of pure ideas under time and in this chair of the history of philosophy to betray neither history nor philosophy.

51. Erasmus, *Letter to Henry VIII*, Allen ed., number 1381, V:319, lines 302–3.

3

The Meaning and Nature of
St. Anselm's Argument

Per fidem enim ambulamus et non per speciem.

1 Corinthians 5:7

Denique quoniam inter fidem et speciem intellectum, quem in hac vita
capimus esse medium intelligo, quanto aliquis ad illum proficit, tanto
eum propinquare speciei, ad quam omnes anhelamus, existimo.

St. Anselm, *De Fide Trinitatis*, preface

THE ONLY EXCUSE THAT might be invoked for adding a new interpretation of St. Anselm's argument to all those we already have is
the impossibility of resisting the temptation. I have resisted it for many
years, contenting myself with teaching St. Anselm as I thought he
should be understood, but at least conserving the attitude that where
everyone is in disagreement, an isolated individual has little chance to
achieve the truth.[1]

---

1. The pages that follow contain the last four lectures of the course delivered at the
Collège de France in 1934 on "The Doctrine of St. Anselm."

I do not boast today of having discovered the truth, but such important contributions to the study of the question have appeared recently, notably those of Karl Barth and Fr. Anselm Stoltz, that it seems more useful than formerly to propose my hypotheses. Indeed the question has never been studied as closely as it has just been. Karl Barth has submitted St. Anselm's text to as scrupulous an exegesis as if it were an inspired scripture. To discuss his book one would have to write another twice as long, which would simultaneously consider the theology of St. Anselm and Karl Barth. Fr. Anselm Stoltz has criticized Karl Barth, and one can only appreciate his work fairly making it the object of another work. I do not believe that either has spoken the last word on the question, but both have surely made certain essential elements of Anselm's thought stand out, which had been too neglected until now.

It seemed to me that the conclusions I had reached on my own, partly in agreement with theirs, let me do justice to what is true in their interpretation without going to the extremes to which both allowed themselves to be led. I will set aside what has been already said and done a hundred times. I will not even reproduce yet again the text of the famous argument (which, moreover, cannot be reported exactly without being literally reproduced) in order to devote my whole effort to bringing out what seem to me to be the sense of the argument. By "sense of the argument" I understand a meaning as close as possible to what St. Anselm himself gave it.

EXISTENCE AND TRUTH

The classic objection against St. Anselm's argument is that it makes existence come from thought. That objection even explains the epithet "ontological," generally used since Kant to designate the argument. The objection is valid from the point of view of any theory of knowledge that requires sense experience as its necessary ground. Now this is a question that St. Anselm did not pose because he has no theory of knowledge properly speaking. On the contrary, in the absence of a noetic analysis, he has an epistemology, and the most serious flaw in the refutations that are inspired by a noetic analysis alien to his thought, is that they turn our attention away from the epistemology which is the only thing that allows us to comprehend his proof, because it grounds it.

Thus, for an instant let us forget the classical question of knowing whether we can get the existence of a thing, for instance God, from the idea of the thing, and let us ask painstakingly what St. Anselm himself thought he was doing. However we interpret the argument, everyone agrees that its immediate object is to force us to recognize the impossibility of thinking of God as not existing, and thus also the necessity of thinking of God as existing. Whatever reservations we please can be formulated about the probatory value of such a method, but it cannot be denied that Anselm used it.

For example, it can be denied that we have a concept of God upon which to construct the proof, but St. Anselm's whole argument supposes that he had such a concept himself, or believed he had one, so that such an objection does not clarify for us the sense that he attributed to his proof. To understand it as he understood it, we must place ourselves in the perspective that was familiar to him. Now Anselm only knows two kinds of dialecticians, those who reduce the content of thought to *voces*, and those who find *res* there. They are what we call today nominalists and realists. As he says himself in *Proslogion*, chapter IV, when we think about "fire" or "water," by that we can understand either words or things. If they are only words, nothing stops us from saying that fire is water or the reverse. If we think about the things that these words signify, that is impossible. The same occurs in our notion of God. If we express it without thinking about what the words signify, we can say that such a being does not exist. But if we think about what the words mean, what is in our thought is no longer a *vox*, it is a *res*, and it is of the thing that it becomes impossible for us to not posit its existence as real, outside thought. At bottom the fool thinks like Roscelin. He is a nominalist.[2] To be concerned with knowing whether Anselm had the empirical "concept" demanded by Gaunilo and his successors, it would have been necessary for St. Anselm to accept their noetic analysis, which is precisely not the case.

As for objecting that if we do not have an empirical concept of God, we do not have something from which we can get his existence, that

2. It seems undeniable that in this sense, the *Proslogion*'s argument presupposes Anselmian realism. We would need to object to it, if it were understood by that that this *res* possesses its own existential reality in thought and that the proof consists in transforming this existence *in intellectu* in an existence *in re*. Nothing of the sort. But St. Anselm notes that there are contents of thought independent of any choice, which thought can neither make nor unmake at its pleasure, and which it can only accept just as they are. One might say that these are "essences" endowed with an irreducible, intrinsic, necessity. Fire, water, and the notion of God are of this type. See *Proslogion*, Chapter IV, column 229 A.

would be to forget precisely that St. Anselm has at his disposition an intelligible meaning of the word *God* that suffices for him to establish his proof. When we examine this meaning, it is in our thought exactly because of that, and the content of our thought is a *res* from which it comes. We certainly have not encountered a proper concept of God in sense experience, but neither have we arbitrarily fabricated the notion we have of him. As we received the notion of fire from fire, the notion of water from water, we receive our notion of God from Revelation. Faith is what teaches us, and we have only to accept it. Gaunilo does not have the right to say he lacks this notion, because he is a Catholic and cannot be a Catholic without having faith. Even supposing that a person does not have this notion of the faith, it could be formed from experience, since St. Paul affirms that God can be known from his creatures.[3] Therefore believers and unbelievers can, and therefore they must, possess this notion. Once it is admitted that we have the notion, its origin counts for nothing in the demonstration drawn from it, and the analysis of its content suffices to demonstrate the existence of God. But is it really a question of demonstrating?

Certain historians have gone so far as to dispute this point. We have to look for the reason why, because it is not enough to observe such an error nor even to prove that it is an error. It is still necessary to explain how it could occur. For the moment we may content ourselves with re-calling how clear the expressions that St. Anselm uses are: "et solum ad astruendum quia Deus vere est . . ."—"da mihi, ut, quantum scis expedire,

---

3. On this subject, it has been claimed that the *Proslogian* proof presupposes the *Monologium* proofs. St. Anselm says nothing of the sort. In itself the *Proslogion* argument only supposes that the notion of God furnished by faith. Could we obtain this notion other than from faith? Yes, and it is true that it then might be obtained by arguments analogous to the *Monologium* proofs. But let us note well that if, in order to prove God by reason alone, the faith that the *Monologium* requires is eliminated from the *Monologium* itself, the argument of the *Proslogion*, would then be developed not from the proof of the existence of God so obtained, but solely from the idea obtained by that proof. This would thus be *another* proof (like that of Descartes's *Meditation* V after the proofs of *Meditation* III). Moreover, we can ask *if* St. Anselm could not have established his proof outside of faith and answer that he could have and say how (cf. *Liber Apologeticus*, ch. VIII, column 258 B), but what matters above all is to observe that he did not do that. St. Anselm simply said that seeing things would be enough to let us "conjecture" the something "quo majus cogitari nequit," and that from that notion, even conjectural notion, the proof could be completely developed. In short what he said (*Liber Apologeticus, loc. cit.*) is that reason suffices by itself to conjecture the notion, from which the proof comes, but this is not what he did in the *Proslogion*.

intelligam quia es, sicut credimus . . ."[4] What St. Anselm thought he had proved is certainly that this *aliquid quo majus cogitari non valet* exists and that it exists not only *in intellectu* but *in re*.[5]

If we approach these texts without a preconceived scheme into which we want to force them, we will no doubt judge that, unless we are completely mistaken about his intentions, St. Anselm thought that proving the rational necessity of affirming God's existence or the rational impossibility of not affirming it, is to have really proved his existence. Moreover, if we grant Anselm the minimum logical coherence that it is permissible to expect from a philosopher, we also will doubtless admit than in his thought the necessity wherein the reason for affirming his existence is found fully guarantees the fact of this existence, or else his whole argument is useless. Now that observation obliges us to formulate a hypothesis that, if true, will allow us in its turn to give the argument a positive sense. For a philosopher to admit that the necessity of affirming existence guarantees the reality of the existence, he necessarily must also admit that the necessity of his affirmation supposes that of his object. Unless the *Proslogion* argument has no meaning, it must necessarily be situated in a doctrine of the truth such that the existence of truths always presupposes that of their objects.

This is precisely the case. Besides the *Proslogion*, St. Anselm wrote *De Veritate*, a little discussed dialogue, which is nonetheless the epistemological ground of his whole doctrine. Whether he is dealing with God or human freedom or knowledge, we must always return there to understand his thought. Let us therefore ask what clarifications it brings us about the *Proslogion* argument.

Through many and varied applications, *De Veritate* develops two essential ideas. The first is that every truth is "rectitude." The second is that in the last analysis there is only one truth, by which all other truths are true, which is God. By saying that every truth is *rectitudo*, he means that thought is true when it exercises the function for which it is made. Now it is made to say that what it is is and what is not is not.[6] If we do not admit this internal finality of rational knowledge it is useless to wish

---

4. Anselm, *Proslogion*, Proemium, column 223 C. *Proslogion*, ch. II, column 227 C.

5. Proslogion, ch. II, column 228 A. Besides, the matter already stands thus in the *Monologium* proofs, which are self-sufficient, just as the *Proslogion* poof is sufficient without them. See in the contrary sense, Carmelo Ottaviano, *Anselmo*, vol. I, p. 49.

6. Anselm *De Veritate*, ch. II, column 470 A.

to follow St. Anselm's reasoning. We have become separated from him at the point of departure.

So let us suppose that this position is granted: *Vere et recta et vera est [significatio], cum significat esse quod est.* For this to be, it is further necessary that truth always be a relation: that which connects a correct signification to what it signifies. This rectitude that makes truth is found in thought (because it is thought that is true), in so far as the thought thinks as it should. But the *cause* of this rectitude and this truth, on the contrary, is found in the object, because the latter measures and determines thought. Without a thought that does what it should there would be no truth. But without an object in relation to which thought behaves as it should and upon which it is determined, there would no longer be thought. "Is the thing stated the truth of the statement?" the Master asks his Disciple. And the Disciple answers: "No." But he adds, "If the thing stated is not in a true statement and consequently is not its truth, it must be said that it is the cause of its truth."[7] *Sed causa veritatis ejus dicenda est.*

Let us keep this conclusion present in our minds. There is no true thought without an object to which it conforms and that thought states just as it is, because its proper function is to state it thus. I think that this sort of comment, formulated in function of the problem we have defined, allows its implications to be perceived rather easily. There will never be a God because there are proofs of the existence of God, but there are proofs of the existence of God because there is a God. For we cannot join the second conclusion of *De Veritate* to the first without seeing the generality of the thesis: there is a single truth of all that is true, because there is only one Truth, cause of all that is true.

St. Anselm clearly described the universe in which his thought moves and outside of which it could never be fully itself nor freely develop. Let us reduce this description to the traits that are essential for us. There are propositions stated in discourse. To be true, they must do what they are made for, that is to say, exactly convey what the thought is whose expression they are. There are thoughts formulated by these propositions. To be true they must do what they are made for, that is to say, express things as they are. Besides, there are things that these thoughts express. To be true, these things ought to do what they are made for, that is to say, remain faithful to their essences, be conformed

7. Ibid., ch. II, column 469 C.

to their ideas in God. Then there is God, the Word, and the divine Ideas, which are not conformed to anything, because they are the cause of everything else; then things with the truth proper to them, which, being caused in them by God, causes in turn the truth of thought and of the propositions that express thought. As for the truth that is found in the proposition and in thought, it is the reflection of the previous truths. Caused by them, it does not cause any other in its turn.

This hierarchy of causes and effects in the order of knowledge has always seemed to me to be the central piece in the framework of the Anselmian proofs of the existence of God.[8] Karl Barth had the great merit of marking their importance, and if I am not mistaken, of being the first one to do so. In adding that I have taught this for many years, I have no intention of claiming a right of precedence, which in any case, would revert to St. Anselm, but to underline the fact that starting with such different concerns and in disagreement about the consequences that he draws from it, we have independently arrived at the same conclusion on this point.

Thus Karl Barth is completely correct in writing: "There can be no question in any sense of the human *ratio* having a creative and normative relation to truth."[9] Let us say further with him, in a language unknown to St. Anselm but faithful to his thought: "*Ontic* necessity precedes noetic,"[10] but let us not forget to apply this rule, whose value in St. Anselm is universal, to the particular case of the existence of God. If the argument's conclusion is true, God exists in understanding and reality both. But to be true, its conclusion ought to be a *rectitudo*. To be that, its truth must be caused by its object. Now, in the present case the object of thought and of the statement is God. In fact, we began with the word "God" to pass from the word to its meaning, and from the examination

8. "Vides etiam quomodo ista rectitudo causa sit omnium aliarum veritatum et rectitudinum, et nihil sit causa illius? —Video et animadverto in aliis quasdam esse tantum effecta; quasdam vero esse causas et effecta: ut, cum veritas, quae est in rerum existentia, sit effectum summae veritatis, ipsa quoque causa est veritatis quae cogitationis est, et ejus quae est in propositione: et istae duae veritates nullius sunt causa veritatis. —Bene consideras: unde jam intelligere potest quomodo summam veritatem in meo *Monologio* (capitulo XVIII) probavi non habere principium vel finem, per veritatem orationis." Anselm, *De Veritate*, ch. X, column 479 A. I have added the end of the text to show that the *Monologium* itself and not only in the *Proslogion* is answerable to the epistemology of *De Veritate*. Cf. in the same sense Ottaviano, *Anselmo*, I:42–43.

9. Barth, *Fides querens intellectum.* 45.

10. Ibid. 49.

of this meaning, "something greater than which cannot be thought," we concluded that this something exists, not only in thought but also in reality. Since nothing intervenes here between thought and God except the meaning of the word, the cause of the truth of our conclusion cannot be sought in the nature of external things. It can only be God, and he must cause it immediately.

Indeed such is the conclusion towards which the whole *Proslogion* argument is directed. It first establishes that God exists by showing that his definition, *aliquid quo nihil majus*, is of such a nature that it is impossible for thought to not affirm the real existence of its object. The demonstration is well known, but enough heed is not paid to the fact that it presupposes at least two conditions. The first is that every necessary proposition be true. It is the consequence of the conception that sees in the content of thought irreducible and resistant *res*. Because if the reason we cannot think of fire as water is that fire is not water, each time that we collide with an irresistible resistance of the same type, we will naturally conclude that we are colliding with the resistance of a *res* in thought. Such is surely the case when we cannot refuse to attribute a predicate to a subject without violating the principle of contradiction. Thus we have good grounds to say that at the end of this analysis, *aliquid quo nihil majus* cannot help being posited as existing in reality.

The second condition is that every true thought implies the reality of its object, that is, its existence. Thus existence must be a predicate like others, and thought's *rectitudo* concerning existence presupposes its reality, exactly as thought's *rectitudo* concerning what things are presupposes that they are. Thought cannot be the cause of truth any more in one case than in the other, it must always be caused. The difficulty, in the case of *aliquid quo nihil majus* is that the argument deals with existence, precisely because it cannot be the object of any experience for us. Instead of apprehending the object of truth at the same time as truth, we must infer the existence of its object in the name of truth. That is why the *Proslogion* proof, although it already attains its object in chapter II, only possesses full intelligibility in chapter III. We have a truth, what is its cause?

We are certain of the real existence of *aliquid quo nihil majus*, because there is an absolute impossibility for us to not affirm it. But why does the affirmation have this necessity? Here again, the cause can only be found in its object. It is a necessity of thought to affirm the existence of God because in itself the existence of God is necessary.

That is why chapter III of the *Proslogion* must not be considered separable from chapter II under any pretext, nor inversely chapter II from chapter III. It suffices to read its first phrase to understand what role St. Anselm gives it. To observe that existence is "true" in God is to see at the same time what makes the whole previous argument true. It is objected against St. Anselm that the necessity for thought to affirm God's existence does not make God exist, but what Anselm wants to make us understand is precisely that the necessity of affirming the existence of God is only an imitation, by mode of knowledge, of the intrinsic necessity of the real existence of God.

What in fact does he tell us? That *aliquid quo majus cogitari non valet* exists *et in intellectu et in re*. But he also adds that this something exists so truly (that is, its existence is such a *true* existence) that we cannot even think that it does not exist: *Quod utique sic vere est, ut nec cogitari possit non esse*. Thus it is exactly the proper nature of divine existence that makes it impossible even in thought to not affirm this existence outside thought. Besides, St. Anselm continues, we can think something that it is impossible to think as not existing. That something is evidently greater than what it is possible to think as not existing. In other words, God is greater than the creature, and he is greater in the special sense that existence belongs to him in a unique mode: *Et quidem quidquid aliud est praeter solum te, potest cogitari non esse. Solus igitur verissime omnium, et ideo maxime omnium habes esse; quia quidquid aliud est, non sic vere est, et idcirco minus habet esse.*[11] Thus there are things that might not exist and about which we consequently think that they might not exist. But there is one thing, a unique case, for which we cannot even think its non-existence, it is the *aliquid quo majus*. How does that happen? It is precisely that it cannot not exist. Thus the necessity of its existence imposes itself on our thought, and by somehow making itself acknowledged that is what obliges thought to affirm it.

I do not overlook how paradoxical such an interpretation is. The reproach ordinarily leveled against St. Anselm is that his proof does not attain existence; will it not be necessary to say here that the proof supposes existence and that instead of proving God, it is God who proves it? No, it is not God who proves it, because it is certainly it that proves him;

---

11. Anselm *Proslogion*, ch. III, column 228. On the meaning of *vere esse*, see St. Augustine who directly inspires St. Anselm, *De Moribus Manichaeorum*, ch. I, number 1, column 1345.

but he grounds it. Taken by itself and just as it is developed in chapter II, the argument indeed proves, starting from the word "God," that God exists *in intellectu* and *in re*. But we know that in his doctrine neither the truth of the statement nor that of thought "create any truth." Thought only thinks the true by conceiving and stating the things that are as they are. If the fool can say that God does not exist, it is precisely because he does not think truly about what God is, in saying that. Let the fool conceive of God as *aliquid quo majus*, and he will no longer be able to say that.[12] Thus here as always, to think the truth consists in subjecting thought to the necessity of an essence, to oblige it to "rectitude," that is to say, to recognize that what is is and what is not is not.

Therefore, St. Anselm's argument is neither mere verbalism nor a vicious circle. He does not deduce existence, because from the start he moves in the existential order, as the dialogue *De Veritate* has defined it. It is no longer a vicious circle, because the argument does not presuppose the existence of God, it finds it. It finds it precisely by shedding full light on the rational necessity of affirming existence about God, a necessity that according to *De Veritate* can have no other cause than the very necessity of its object. From there come those frequent expressions of St. Anselm: *Quod qui bene intelligit, utique intelligit idipsum sic esse, ut nec cogitatione quaeat non esse. Qui ergo intelligit sic esse Deum, nequit eum non esse cogitare.*[13] Or again, those expressions that strongly bear witness to the presence of a God determining and submitting thought to himself: *Sic ergo vere es, Domine, Deus meus, ut nec cogitari possis non esse, et merito. Si enim aliqua mens posset cogitare aliquid melius te, ascenderet creatura super Creatorem, et judicaret de Creatore, quod valde est absurdum.*[14]

To reject this interpretation, we would have to maintain that the epistemology of *De Veritate* should not enter into the *Proslogion* explanation. Unfortunately, it suffices to compare the two texts to realize that each often recalls the other and that in the whole opus of St. Anselm, there is only one doctrine of truth. Or else it would even be necessary to maintain that in this doctrine God is the cause of all truth except what relates to himself. We might prudently suppose that St. Anselm never imagined anything like that, but he expressed himself clearly enough for

12. Anselm, *Proslogion*, ch. IV, columns 228–29.
13. Ibid., ch. IV, column 229 B.
14. Ibid., ch. III, columns 228 BC.

us to dispense with even such a legitimate hypothesis. However many things there are, there are as many possible "rectitudes" of thought toward them, as many possible truths; but whether thought conceives this rectitude" or not, it nonetheless exists, because in God it preexists our thought. This "rectitude" that is the truth does not begin existing with the statement that signifies it. On the contrary, *significatio tunc fit secundum rectitudinem, quae semper est.*[15] That is why *De Veritate* concludes by reducing all rectitudes or truths to the sole rectitude or divine truth: "The supreme Truth that subsists by itself is not the truth of any thing, but when any thing is according to it, we attribute truth and rectitude to it."[16] Therefore, to eliminate the truth of the argument to divine causality, we would have to admit that the only case where the subsistent Truth does not determine our thought is the one where it is involved itself. How much more simple is it to admit, by contrast, that the necessity of the thing never determines our thought more completely than when we are dealing with that unique case in which, according to the expression Malebranche will later borrow from St. Augustine, if we think of God, it is necessary that he is: *si vel cogitari potest esse,* necesse est illud *esse . . . Si ergo potest cogitari esse, ex necessitate est . . . Si utique vel cogitari potest, necesse est illud esse.*[17] If the mere fact of thinking God implies his existence, then it is that case indeed that if he did not exist, the most impossible of all things would be for us to think that he exists or what amounts to the same thing, to think of him.

What makes it difficult to accept such an interpretation is not only that we are reading Anselm through epistemologies that are different from his nor even that we isolate him from the spiritual family to which

---

15. Anselm, *De Veritate*, ch. XIII, column 485 b.

16. Ibid., ch. XIII, column 486 C.

17. Anselm, *Liber Apologeticus*, ch. 249 B. Cf. Malebranche: "If we think of God, it is necessary that he is." *Entretiens*, II, I:67. "Thus if we think of him, it is necessary that he is." *Recherche*, book IV, ch. 11, art. 3, I:442. These expressions translate those of St. Anselm's so literally that it is difficult not to see one of the points of departure of Malebranche's reflection in the *Proslogion*.

The confused desire to recur to causality to complete Anselm's argument is no doubt the origin of the well known interpretation Dom Adloch gave it in a series of articles in *Philosophisches Jahrbuch*, vol. VIII, IX and X. Carra de Vaux, who is sometimes much less inspired, is completely right in objecting that the argument rests on the principle of non-contradiction; it does not rest either directly or indirectly on the principle of causality or on tradition. *Saint Anselme*, 311. I see nothing in Dom Adloch's reply that disproves this conclusion ("Glossen," 163–70 and 300–309).

he belongs, but also that, even within that family, his thought presents original characteristics that we tend to ignore. For it is very true to say that the necessity of the existence of God in Anselm's doctrine is cause of the necessity of affirming his existence, but Anselm nowhere says and he evidently does not even think that proving the existence of God consists in showing how his necessity causes the necessity in which we are situated of affirming his existence. And in that, St. Anselm's case is almost unique.

The matter is all the more curious because everything invited him to embark on the road of causality. St. Anselm is and calls himself a faithful disciple of St. Augustine.[18] Now there are many proofs of God's existence in St. Augustine, but St. Anselm certainly is not ignorant of the *De Libero Arbitrio* proof that demonstrates God as the cause of truth in thought. Nothing would be easier for him than to reason as follows: Reason cannot not affirm the existence of God. Now that necessity, which is unique, requires a cause. That cause cannot be in thought itself that is contingent. Thus it must be located in God, whose light illuminates thought and forces it to recognize that evidence. It is by joining Augustinian illumination to the *Proslogion* argument in this way that St. Bonaventure will incorporate it into his own teaching.[19] But there it is a new synthesis that cannot be attributed to St. Anselm. Later on Descartes will choose a similar route by proving God as the cause of the idea we have of him.[20] Malebranche in turn will try to establish the existence of God as cause of our general notion of being.[21] By contrast, St. Anselm does nothing

18. St. Anselm affirms that his *Monologium* agrees entirely with the teaching of the Fathers "et maxime beati Augustini," *Monologium*, preface, column 143 C. When Lanfranc his master directed an *admonitio* to him after reading the *Monologium*, Anselm answered that nothing he said was his own invention, but that he had only proved with briefer arguments what Augustine said in *De Trinitate*. See *Epistula ad Lanfrancum*, book I, epistula LXVIII, column 1139 B. Regarding the *Proslogian*, the chapter devoted to the Augustinian sources of Anselm's argument should be consulted in Koyré, *L'idée de Dieu*, ch. VII, "The Idea of God in St. Augustine." See especially the well known expression, 172 n. 3: "Summum bonum omnino et quo esse et cogitari melius nihil possit, aut intelligendus, aut credendus est Deus, si blasphemiis carere cogitamus." St. Augustine, *De Moribus Manichaeorum*, ch. XI, number 24, column 1335.

19. Gilson, *La philosophie de Saint Bonaventure*, 132–33.

20. Gilson, *Études sur le rôle*, ch. IV, "Descartes et saint Anselme," 215–23, and ch. V, "*Une nouvelle idée de Dieu*," 224–33.

21. Malebranche, *Récherche*, book III, part 2, ch. VI, I:327–28.

of the sort,[22] and that is why his argument gives every philosopher the impression of floating in a void. He does not prove God as the cause of a sensible effect, nor as cause of an idea, nor even as cause of the necessity of the reasoning that affirms God's existence. He simply posits that existence as necessary in itself, because it is so for thought, adding that it is because God's existing is necessary in itself that it is so for thought. But he only adds that because he already knows that God exists and in order to tell us why he knows it.

THE *PROSLOGION* AND THEOLOGY

We are not at the end of our difficulty. When we consider all the texts of the *Proslogion*, the problem is not only to show that the proof does not presuppose the existence of God already known by reason, but also to understand why, presupposing this existence by faith, Anselm can still claim he proves by reason that God exists. For nobody is unaware that the *Proslogion* starts from faith in the existence of God. The work's original title was *Fides Quaerens Intellectum*, and the restoration of the title was well done. Not only does Anselm believe in order to understand, but he believes that very thing that he must believe in order to understand. His *nisi credideritis non intelligetis* obliges him to admit by faith that he must begin by faith if he wants to reach intelligence: *Neque enim quaero intelligere, ut credam; sed credam ut intelligam. Nam et hoc credo, quia nisi credidero, non intelligam.* The very beginning of the proof is another appeal to faith: *Ergo, Domine, qui das fidei intellectum, da mihi ut, quantum scis expedire, intelligam quia es, sicut credimus, et hoc es, quod*

22. The most precise text of St. Anselm on this point is still very imprecise. It is found in *Proslogion*, ch. 14, columns 234–35. There, St. Anselm says and repeats that we see all truth in the light of God, and particularly his existence (cf. 235 A). But how does the divine light illuminate? Anselm does not tell us. Perhaps he accepted St. Augustine's teaching, but he did not say so, and even if he thought it, that idea has no role in his argument. No doubt, he thanks God for having found it, "te illuminante," but this pious expression is vague and only occurs when every thing is finished. The same is true of the expressions of the *Proslogion*, ch. 16, columns 236–37. They have an Augustinian tone: "quicquid video per illum video, sicut infirmus oculus, quod videt, per lucem solis videt, quam in ipso sole nequit aspicere." But that does not teach us how the divine light acts on our spirit. All we know with certainty is that for him created truth is an *imitatio* or *similitudo* of the Word, which is the only *vera essentia* properly so called, *Monologium*, ch. 31, columns 184–85. Cf. ch. 33, columns 188 BC and ch. 34, columns 189 AB: "Etenim in seipsis . . . ." That is exemplarism, common to all Christian philosophers. It is not illumination.

credimus. Faith provides him with the concept of God from which he draws his proof: *Et quidem credimus te esse aliquid quo nihil majus cogitari possit*. Finally the proof ends with thanksgiving to God who grants understanding of faith to him who seeks it: *Gratias tibi, bone Domine, gratias tibi, quia quod prius credidi te donante, jam sic intelligo te illuminante, ut si te esse nolim credere, non possim non intelligere*.[23] What else is necessary to establish that we are completely within theology?

It is true that in this way many difficulties would be eliminated, and first of all the difficulty that has just detained us for so long. Instead of troubling ourselves to understand in what sense the *Proslogion* argument is a proof, it would suffice to admit that it is a theological explanation. Starting from faith, we would go by reason to the understanding of the faith, but not to the conquest of truths only falling under reason. This is the interpretation of St. Anselm that Karl Barth proposes to us and that certain neo-scholastic philosophers would gladly grant him. Consequently, it is important to examine it with care. Let us first posit a point on which everyone should be in agreement. The argument of the *Proslogion* is the work of what St. Anselm calls *intellectus*.[24]

---

23. Regarding the original title, see *Proslogion*, preface, columns 224–25. The texts in order quoted are from: *Proslogion*, ch. I, column 227 C; ch. II, column 227 C; ch. V, column 229 B. The expression "te illuminante" of this last text is the only one I know where we might be tempted to see Augustinian illumination. If there is really a trace, it is very vague, because none of the exact ideas that correspond to this term in St. Augustine play the slightest role in St. Anselm's argument. What is Augustinian in his thought is the idea that the restoration of fallen intelligence is a restoration in us of the image of God obscured by sin (*Proslogion*, ch I, column 226 AB), and that is very important, but it is not the doctrine of illumination in the technical sense of the term.

Elsewhere I have indicated the necessity of taking into account the role that faith plays in the *Proslogion* argument; see *Philosophie au moyen âge*, vol. I:42–43, 47. *Études de philosophie*, 15–18. I can only feel confirmed in this opinion by reading Barth, *Fides Quaerens Intellectum*, where an almost exhaustive exegesis is found of St. Anselm's texts on this theme, 19–59. I deeply regret that this pre-established harmony has not been extended from the role of the texts in the proof to the interpretation of the nature of the proof.

Lastly, let us note that for St. Anselm, to start from faith does not necessarily mean to start from Scripture, but also from dogma, and even dogma must be understood in a very broad sense: what is impossible to not believe if one wishes to be Christian. For example *aliquid quo nihil majus* does not come from Scripture but from St. Augustine (see n. 18 above) who declares to the Manichaeans that it is sacrilege to fail to admit it.

24. St. Anselm is inspired here by St. Augustine. The fact is indisputable, but a careful—and very difficult—discussion would be necessary to determined the nature of the connection that links him to his master.

Let us agree to translate this term by "understanding," and indicate by that the act of the intellect apprehending truth. It must be said then that, in the economy of Anselm's doctrine, understanding is a mode of knowledge that presupposes faith and that tends toward the beatific vision: *inter fidem et speciem intellectum quem in hac vita capimus esse medium intelligo.*[25] Thus understanding will be acknowledged to result

---

1. There is no doubt as to the fact. Before St. Anselm St. Augustine teaches that understanding is the reward for faith that seeks, because it is informed by charity. As Martin has shown, *St. Augustin*, 122, the immediate antecedent of *fides quaerens intellectum* is the Augustinian expression "fides quaerit, intellectus invenit" (*De Trinitate*, XV, 2, 2, column, 1058; cf. our *Introduction à l'étude de saint Augustin*, ch. I, 37). It even seems that in what concerns the *Proslogion*, *De Libero Arbitrio* played a particularly important role. St. Augustine wants to prove the existence of God. Now, a) he believes that God exists, but he does not see him: "Etiam hoc non contemplando, sed credendo inconcussum teneo." b) What is he to do then about the *insipiens* who has said in his heart "non est Deus"? He wants not *credere*, but *cognoscere*. Will we leave him without knowledge? c) He is invited first to purify his heart and to believe upon the authority of Scripture. d) But then, why are not we ourselves content with believing? Because "nos id quod credimus, nosse et intelligere cupimus." "Nisi enim aliud esset credere, et aliud intelligere, . . . frustra propheta dixisset nisi credideritis, non intelligetis" (*Isaiah*, VII, 9, Septuagint), St. Augustine, *De Libero Arbitrio*, book II, ch. 2, 5–6, columns 1242–43. The parallelism is striking, not in the proofs, which are different, but in the nature of the knowledge sought and the method followed to obtain it.

2. Does it turn out from this that St. Augustine and St. Anselm belong to exactly the same family of Christian thinkers? I would not make bold to affirm it. It is hardly possible to deny that St. Augustine bequeathed to St. Anselm the model of this manner of thinking. But St. Anselm cultivated the genre much more exclusively than St. Augustine, and the rationality of the plane on which his thought moves, above all when he comes to the Trinity, seems much more accentuated than that to which Augustine himself aspires. Both consider faith, but I do not remember that Augustine ever declared the intention of proving something regarding the Trinity or the Incarnation without appealing to the authority of Scripture. In short, without speaking of "Christian rationalism," since reason moves completely within faith and is submitted to it fully, it seems appropriate to say that St. Anselm underwent a powerful influence of contemporary dialectic, and that he envisaged a more independent rational knowledge than what St. Augustine's wisdom entailed. But the whole question remains to be studied.

25. Anselm, *De Fide Trinitatis*, preface, column 261 A. Anselm here invokes "nisi credideritis non intelligetis" (*Isaiah*, VII:9). On the "eschatological" role of understanding, see Barth, *Fides Quaerens Intellectum*, 15–18. Here again, I observe agreement between the conclusions that I had reached and those to which Karl Barth has come on his part. Perhaps there might be room to nuance his conclusion. It is true to say that, aiming at the beatific vision, understanding the faith is a duty. St. Anselm says so: "idei rationem post ejus certitudinem debemus esurire." But to translate that *debemus*, this duty, by an imperative, is, if not an inexactitude, at least a hardening, of Anselm's thought, perhaps unconsciously Calvinist. *Debemus esurire*: if there is an order, it is not that of obeying but of loving.

from an effort to anticipate the beginning of the beatific vision by reason starting from faith.[26] The *Proslogion* argument is a particular case of this understanding. The question is to know whether knowledge of this sort should be considered theological or purely rational.

Of all those who consider this kind of knowledge theological, Karl Barth has expressed himself most forcefully. The eminent theologian correctly saw that to resolve the problem by limiting oneself to saying, "Since we start from faith, we are in theology," is an overly simplistic solution. Why would a purely rational reflection not be inspired by faith? Granted that it is not deduced from faith, that is to say does not borrow premises or logical conclusions from theology, it is still rational. Karl Barth conceived the possibility of this hypothesis and formulated it forcefully, not, however, without including in his presentation the motives of its condemnation:

> Or should Anselm have thought of it all quite differently—at least parts of it occasionally? Should he really have sought the law of the existence and particular existence of the object of faith in the human capacity to form concepts and judgments (as identical with its laws) and therefore assumed as possible and necessary an independent knowledge alongside that of faith, able to draw from its own sources? Should he therefore have begun *quaerens intellectum* with nothing, that is with the rules of an autonomous human reason and with the data of general human experience, and therefore of his own account as *inveniens intellectum*, that is by means of certain universal "necessities of thought" (comparable to Pharaoh's magicians), not so much have found but rather have created a kind of shadow *Credo*?[27]

Anselm's complete thought is the following: First, we believe God by faith. Second, if this faith is not dead faith, we love its object. Third, from that, in the soul comes the *desire* of penetrating the object of faith by understanding: *sed desidero aliquatenus intelligere veritatem tuam, quam credit et amat* cor meum (*Proslogion*, ch. I, column 227 B). Fourth, therefore it is love that applies reason to the content of faith to obtain a certain understanding of it. The nuance has its importance. The fact that Karl Barth neglects it here is in line with his interpretation, as the fact of emphasizing it is in line with mine.

26. About the fact that in St. Anselm "no part of the entire edifice of the Church is for a single moment in jeopardy," see Barth, *Fides Quaerens Intellectum*, 61. None of his writings, the same author strongly insists, is even "apologetic" in the modern sense of the word, that is to say oriented "*directly* to those outside" (62). The readers of whom he thinks are Christians, theologians, and even Benedictine theologians.

27. Barth, *Fides Quaerens Intellectum*, 53–54.

It would be impossible to more skillfully place his adversaries in a difficult situation. But if this passage from Karl Barth admirably shows what he understood about St. Anselm, it also shows what perhaps escaped him. Let us then try to discern both in order to know what must be conserved and where there is room for additions.

Let us agree, since we have always said it, that the *Proslogion* argument presupposes faith. Let us add with Karl Barth the important specification that Anselm considers the truth of faith to be independent of the rational speculation that it motivates. Faith does not seek understanding to be grounded as faith: *neque enim quaero intelligere, ut credam.* But it is posited as faith to permit understanding: *sed credo ut intelligam.* All that is certain. Let us add the third and similarly fundamental point that reason can never be conceived as capable of *creating* its truth from nothing, that is to say, of engendering a *doppleganger* of the Creed, which would be composed of rational necessities instead of beliefs. To sustain the contrary is to directly contradict St. Anselm, who only recognizes faith's duty to submit to its objects. But does it follow from that that the *Proslogion* argument is a fragment of theology?

Let us first note what is the key point at stake, because one might not think of it. Karl Barth is rightly careful to maintain the independence of theology, but I believe that philosophy interests him very little and for a reason.[28] That is even why we see him so worried about showing that in the *Proslogion* argument there is no "ontologism"; and there again he is right, but in a sense that is not at all philosophical. If in his eyes the argument is not ontological, it is because, conceiving it to be purely theological, he refuses to see in it any proof whatsoever of the existence

---

28. It would be inexact to say that Karl Barth is not concerned about the independence of philosophy. On the contrary, he is too concerned about it, but for him, that is to absolutely deny the access of theology. Philosophy exists. It falls under the order of the "world." As such it must be as completely *mundana* as possible, that is to say, as completely as possible, alien to God and to what is of God. It is at this price that philosophy will be itself and that theology will be free of it. For theology, God speaks, the theologian listens and repeats what God has said. That is all. From the strict Calvinist viewpoint, philosophy must be separated to be itself and to be damned. This is the fundamental principle that seems to me to control Karl Barth's whole interpretation of St. Anselm. His St. Anselm is a theologian for whom not only is reason unable to justify Revelation and Scripture (which St. Anselm would admit), but cannot even achieve recognition of faith by reason, which, completely deficient in relation to the object that it recognizes, will claim to owe its certitude only to its own rationality. But, if I am not mistaken, that is what St. Anselm wanted to do.

of God. In short, since we begin as theologians with faith, there is no longer any question of proving that God exists. We know it from the beginning. "On the assumption that it is true to say: God exists, God is the highest Being, is a Being in Three Persons, became man, etc.—Anselm discusses the question of how far it is true."[29] Thus, the question is not at all to *prove* God. The whole problem is reduced to *recognize* that he exists, it being given at the point of departure that the truth of his existence is not in doubt. This is not a philosopher's work.[30]

29. Barth, *Fides Quaerens Intellectum*, 61. Karl Barth has rightly seen and repeats several times with his habitual energy that St. Anselm wants to "prove" [59 and *passim*, Trans.]. He is no less correct in saying that faith constitutes the self-evident basis of discussion (60). But in what sense must *Grundlage* be understood? Karl Barth does not seem to conceive of an intermediary between making faith and reason equal (which Anselm clearly refuses to do), and subordinating the certitude of reason to that of faith. He thus opts for the second hypothesis. Now, it may precisely be that there is a third possibility, if not from Karl Barth's point of view, at least from St. Anselm's. Faith would possess the *object* of understanding, and in this sense faith would certainly be the ground of the discussion, but the certainty of that object given by faith would in no way be the principle of the certainty that understanding as such obtains from it. In this sense, understanding would certainly give a *doppleganger* to faith, but it would not create it from nothing, since faith would be the obligatory point of departure for the operation. Let us add that it would be a very imperfect *shadow*, but that seeing it would be accompanied by a specific joy that justifies its existence, and that further is eschatologically ordered to the last end of the Christian, not *fides* but *species*. That this is inadmissible for Karl Barth is all too clear, and it is even why he did not dream of attributing it to St. Anselm. The question is to know whether it is admissible for St. Anselm, and if he did admit it.

30. Karl Barth has the merit of drawing the conclusions that we must reach if we consider the *Proslogion* as a theological work. But it is completely classical to consider *fides quaereens intellectum* as one possible definition of the theological method, for example, Josef Becker, "Der Satz," 115–27 and 312–26; see especially 117; it is "der Grundprinzip der theologischen Spekulation über die Glaubenswahrheiten." De Wulf, *Histoire*, I:137: "Such are Anselm's principles. We see that they involve the believer and not the philosopher . . ." etc. It is appropriate to remark that every time the *Monologium* and *Proslogion* are considered theological works, Anselm comes to be accused of more or less accentuated rationalism (see numerous confirmations in Grabmann, *Die Geschichte der scholastischen Methode*, I:276–78). That is all too natural. If St. Anselm truly intends to de theological work, he errs in wanting to demonstrate truths of faith rationally; but if he intends to leave faith intact and see what he can re-encounter by reason alone, there is no other rationalism in his case than what every exercise of pure reason implies by definition. In short, he reasons upon faith, but he does not rationalize faith at all, because faith is not engaged in the adventures of reason, whose conclusions faith no more guarantees than do the conclusions of reason guarantee positions of faith. The fierce respect that Anselm professes for the independence of faith ought to suffice to show that the wrong road has been followed when the *Proslogion* is considered

Each time the thought of a philosopher or theologians is forced, we feel the resistance that his texts then present, first unvoiced, but growing unceasingly. The wise thing is then to renounce the hypothesis. But who can boast of always having wisdom? I believe that in the event, Karl Barth lacked it from the outset of his exegesis. He does not overlook any text. He considers them all. But I do not think that he can have made some of them pass through the mill of his theology without feeling some unease about it.

First, St. Anselm says and repeats that he wants to establish that God exists: "meum argumentum . . . ad astruendum quia Deus vere est . . ."[31] What sense do we give to *astruere* here? We all agree that it is not a matter of confirming faith, since faith does not expect this from reason. *Astruo*, the dictionaries tell us, is: "to build nearby, to add a wing to a house." Does the specter of a rational *doppleganger* of faith reappear here? Might St. Anselm wish to build within faith a rational wing that he would add to the edifice? I think so, but that is what Karl Barth means to deny. So let us try other meanings indicated by the same dictionaries, which we are told are precisely medieval ones: "to support by proofs, prove." But consequently the matter is then certainly a proof of the existence of God. We are no longer seeking *how* it is true to say that God exists, but rather why it is rationally true to say he exists. I do not believe that the most subtle exegeses can honestly eliminate this difficulty.

It is true that Karl Barth recalls the argument's very point of departure, the "name of God," and that this name is taken from Revelation. No doubt it is, but in what sense? Our theologian warns us with remarkable skill that the question is certainly about the name of God, *Der Name Gottes*. However, a difficulty arises at the outset. What is this name: God is called *aliquid quo nihil majus cogitari possit*. Now it is not necessary to be a great exegete to know that Scripture never gives God a name like that. It gives him many and of all sorts. Medieval theologians collected them and commented on them following Dennis, in their *De Divinis Nominibus*. That one is never found among them.

But what is more remarkable here is that Karl Barth, who has not found it in Scripture either, has not even found it in Anselm. Because St. Anselm does not say that he starts from the "name of God." He simply

theological, since by that very act one is committed to accuse a man of rationalism who placed faith above any justifications that reason might attempt.

31. Anselm, *Proslogion*, Preface, column 223 C.

declares: *Et quidem credimus te esse aliquid, quo nihil majus cogitari possit.* There is not the least trace of a *nomen Dei* in the whole argument. The only text that Karl Bath finds to cite in favor of his hypothesis is taken from the last chapter of Anselm's response to Gaunilo, but we must ask ourselves how he translates it: *Tantam enim vim hujus probationis in se continet significatio* (that simply means the Name of God that is presupposed) *ut hoc ipsum quod dicitur ex necessitate, eo ipso quod intelligitur vel cogitatur et revera probatur existere, et idipsum esse quidquid de divina substantia oportet credere.*[32]

It is difficult to see what Karl Barth gets out of that to support of his thesis. First, St. Anselm says as clearly as possible that he wanted to *prove* God's existence: *et revera probatur existere.* Then he does not speak at all of any name whatsoever of God. *Significatio* does not relate to a *nominis*, which appears neither in this sentence nor in the preceding one, but to *probationis*. Let us translate, as Koyre has done quite rightly: "Indeed the meaning of this proof contains [in itself] such force that real existence . . ." etc.[33] The issue is always a certain *cogitatio*, not a *nomen* of God here. I wonder what might have induced the illustrious exegete, so meticulous about texts, to assume such a responsibility? Could it be, *horribile dictu!*, that he let himself be corrupted by St. Thomas Aquinas: *sed intellecto quid significet hoc nomen, Deus, statim habetur, quod Deus est*?[34] That is not impossible. St. Anselm has been so much repeated through St. Thomas! In Karl Barth's case, however, I believe there is something else.

If we admit that the argument starts with the name of God, we are dealing with the name of a person. God is thus accepted from the start as existing, and the argument is not a proof of his existence. If we admit, on the contrary, that we do not start from the name of God as a person, we start from "something" other than God to conclude his existence, and consequently we prove it. In what an impasse Karl Barth has placed

32. Anselm, *Liber Apologeticus*, ch. X, column 260 A, as cited by Barth, *Fides Quaerens Intellectum*, 73 n. 1. It is quite true the *Dominus* to whom the believer directs himself (*te esse*) is a person. For the believer and the theologian *Dominus, Deus* are certainly "names," and St. Anselm would have reasoned as a theologian, if he had chosen to consider them as such. But we find in the *Proslogion* precisely that, instead of asking faith what these names teach us about God as a person (in the usual sense of "name of a person"), he asks it what these words designate. It is because he goes from that "something" to the existence of God that the argument proves it; and it is because the argument proves it, that it is not theological.

33. Anselme de Cantorbury, *Fides quaerens intellectum*, 97.

34. Aquinas, *Summa Theologiae*, Iᵃ, q. 2, article 1, obj. 2.

himself! By not wanting to translate *astruendum* and *probare* like everyone else, he has had to completely invent a *Name Gottes*, which would be the point of departure of the proof and of which St. Anselm never spoke.

Here again, Karl Barth would have been well inspired to yield to the counsels of his text. Let us suppose, *dato non concesso*, that St. Anselm had wanted to ask Scripture for the name of God. What is God called? He is called "aliquid quo nihil majus . . . ," that is to say, that this *person* is called *something*. Often, Karl Barth specifies, *aliquid* is replaced by *id*, or even simply disappears. A praiseworthy scruple, but how would we deduce from there that St. Anselm intended to define thus not *that* God is, nor *what* God is, but *who* he is?[35] No doubt his argument really starts with the meaning of *Deus*, but the word *Deus* is not then considered by him as a name, it is a word. Not the name of an *aliquis*, but a word that signifies *aliquid*. He tells us himself a little further on, as a grammarian who knows his trade, in what category the word *Deus* must be placed here. As it figures in the argument, it is a *vox*, a word,[36] and this word means *something*, precisely, starting from which the existence of God is going to be proved.

Thus, it is necessary to take a stand. St. Anselm certainly intends to prove *that* God exists, and not only to tell us *how* it is true that God exists. But, if his argument is truly a proof, it does not depend, as such, on the certainty we have by faith about the existence of God. In a revealing expression, Karl Barth wanted to push his reader to the contrary conclusion: "Thus his conception of *intelligere* must obviously, if he does not want to contradict himself completely, be his conception of *probare* as well."[37] Yes, in a Barthian perspective; no, in an Anselmian perspective. By writing this phrase, Karl Barth has so marvelously skirted the obstacle that he has not even grazed it.

Intelligere is the result of *probare*, and *intelligere* presupposes faith because it is faith itself that searches for understanding, and it is faith itself again that tells the understanding what there is to comprehend. *Probare*, by contrast, to be itself, must not rest upon faith. It cannot do that without thereby even ceasing to exist. Let us always remember St.

35. "It does not say that God is, nor what he is, but rather in the form of a prohibition that man can understand, who he is." Barth, *Fides Quaerens Intellectum*, 75.

36. "*Aliter enim cogitatur res, cum vox eam significans cogitatur; aliter cum idipsum quod res est, intelligitur. Illo itaque modo potest cogitari Deus non esse; isto vero, minime.*" Anselm, *Proslogion*, ch. IV, column 229 A.

37. Barth, *Fides Quaerens Intellectum*, 62.

Anselm's conclusion: "Even if I no longer wanted to believe that you are, I could no longer not understand it." Thus, without faith, understanding would neither be sought nor found, and the certainty it brings does not replace at all that of faith itself, but, inversely, the certainty of faith does not descend at any instant into that of *intellectus*, as we have defined it. This certainty is exclusively the work of the *probatio*, which is exclusively the work of reason. *Fides quaerit, intellectus invenit.* If understanding were sure about what it finds solely because faith guarantees that to understanding, faith would have sought in vain, because it would not be understanding, it would be faith itself that would have made the find.

Thus between the two interpretations of the *Proslogion*, there is all the distance that separates Catholicism from Calvinism. There is a Catholic way of maintaining that the *Proslogion* is the work of a theologian. It is inspired by the concern to safeguard the rights of God, by safeguarding the rights of reason that God has created. But there is a Calvinist way of maintaining the same thing. It is inspired by the care to safeguard the rights of God by refusing any right to man, or any other duty, except that of repeating the word of God. Karl Barth, who did not make this mistake about St. Augustine,[38] certainly seems to have dragged St. Anselm over to his side, and this error is all the more surprising because St. Augustine himself invites him to not fall in to it.

Karl Barth has seen clearly the eschatological function of understanding in St. Anselm. Now St. Anselm owed that idea to St. Augustine: "It is again Our Lord himself, who by his acts and words, exhorted those whom he called to salvation, to first believe. But next, speaking of the very gift he was going to give to those who believe, he did not say: Believe, that is everlasting life, but rather, 'Now this is everlasting life, that they may know thee, you the only true God, and Jesus Christ whom thou hast sent, that is everlasting life' (John 18:3). And to those who believed already, he then said: 'Seek, and you shall find' (Matt 7:7). Because if something is believed without knowing it cannot be called found, nor can anyone become suited to find God, unless he has believed first, what he is then going to know."[39] In this life no doubt, the best already see him better than others, and after this life, all will see him in a more evident and perfect manner. St. Augustine himself adds

38. See chapter 2 n. 43 above.

39. Augustine, *De Libero Arbitrio*, book II, ch. 2, 6, column 1243. It is quite remarkable that Malebranche should have inscribed precisely this text of St. John as the epigraph of *Méditations chrétiennes et métaphysiques*, 1. Here is yet another family resemblance.

that, but how do we not see that to fulfill that eschatological function, the knowledge thus obtained, although impossible without faith, must be other than that of faith? Since faith does not find its object, intellectual knowledge must find it, and find it in the sense in which beatific vision will find it. Between faith and understanding there is a difference in kind. Between understanding and beatific vision, there is a difference of degree that is strictly infinite, but is only a difference of degree. That is why, despising all else, we must already desire and cherish this knowledge here below,[40] and that is also why, when we achieve it we will be filled with such joy.[41] It is not only a question of repeating the word of God here, but having repeated it, to race before what it announces to us. And no doubt, this magnificent intellectualism may horrify Karl Barth, but his semi-Manichaeism would have no less horrified St. Augustine and St. Anselm. We have no right to impose it on them.

THE *PROSLOGION* AND MYSTICISM

While teaching simultaneously Cistercian mysticism and St. Anselm's doctrine at the Collège de France, I could not help observing how

40. See the last lines of chapter II. Perhaps it is not superfluous to observe that the *ipso demonstrante* that precedes, does not signifies that God "demonstrates" what we find (for how then would it be our reason that finds it?) but that he "shows" by faith what we have to find. "*Demonstrare*: show, indicate, designate, make gestures." God acts like Clement of Alexandria's Pedagogue, but it is good for the pupil to understand and find by reason the truth that the unique Teacher indicates to him.

41. The difference between this attitude and that of Thomism is seen in that in St. Augustine and St. Anselm, we continue to believe what we know. That is why St. Anselm can demonstrate everywhere, since he does not cease to believe, while St. Thomas is forbidden to demonstrate where the result of the alleged demonstration is not the equivalent of faith. For, if it were that (as in the case of the existence of God), we would know instead of believing. But if it is not that (as in the case of the Trinity), we cannot pretend to demonstrate without deluding ourselves about the value of the proof and without endangering faith, for which, the proof, supposing that it is really demonstrated, ought to be able to be substituted. Thus, St. Thomas knows that God exists; he does not believe it. He believes in the Trinity, and does not know it. St. Augustine and St. Anselm believe and know at the same time that God exists and at least St. Anselm believes in and knows the Trinity at the same time. From there comes the delight that their proofs give them. Augustine, *De Libero Arbitrio*, book II, ch. 15, 39, column 1262, after *Est enim Deus*. St. Thomas has an exact notion of what philosophy and theology are, and if he is far from being unaware of those delights, he knows that to obtain them, it is necessary not only to renounce the comprehension of mystery, but even its demonstration: "dummodo desit comprehendendi vel demonstrandi praesumptio." Thus what is *jucundissimum* is theology, whose conclusions do not only draw their content from faith, but also their certainty. *Summa Contra Gentes*, book I, ch. 8, 7.

Anselm's project resembles that of the mystic. Not only is he a spiritual author of the first rank—we know that even if we only read the first chapter of the *Proslogion*—but in him intellectual effort clearly seeks a goal analogous to what the mystics' ascesis aims at. Like St. Bernard, St. Anselm moves *inter fidem et speciem*. St. Bernard gets a foretaste of the beatific vision through ecstasy. St. Anselm gets a foretaste of it through understanding. The first wishes to be already united to God in the joy of charity. The second wants to enjoy him already through the joy of contemplation. Thus I said that on the level of understanding St. Anselm's *fides quaerens intellectum* was the methodological equivalent to St. Bernard's *Nosce te ipsum* on the level of love.

But how would I have dared imagine that the *Proslogion* might be considered a mystical work properly speaking? I believe that the idea never would have come to me without my encounter on the Aventine Hill with Fr. Anselm Stoltz, and his gift to me of his recent work on St. Anselm.[42] I mention the incident to situate the discussion that is to follow under the sign of friendship from the start.

Fr. Stoltz's work is very remarkable. It is certainly one of the most original studies, perhaps the most original, that has been devoted to the *Proslogion*. By the rigor of its analysis and solidity of its conclusions, it immediately proved to be worthy of Karl Barth's book whose conclusions, it declared, could not be completely accepted. But since Barth had said that whatever we think about his interpretation, it will at least be recognized that he is on the right track, Fr. Stoltz responds: "But it is just this acknowledgement that Barth will not and cannot find."[43] In effect, if he admits with Barth that the *Proslogion's* content is theological, he reproaches him for not having seen that it is a well defined

42. Stoltz, "Zur Theologie Anselms," 1–24. As may be seen, I do not dispute what could very vaguely be called the *Proslogion's* mystical tone. We have to find out whether it is a work of mystical theology in the strict sense, that is to say, "knowledge of God obtained by a mystical approach," which must itself be an "experience of God." In this sense, neither faith nor "religious life in the nakedness of faith, however deep it may be, however intimate the relations of the believer may become with the invisible whose omnipresence he acknowledges," suffice to define the mystical order. The latter only begins where God is "experienced," by knowledge or love. See Fonck, "Mystique," in *Dictionnaire de théologie catholique*, vol. X, column 2600. The issue thus is to learn whether the *Proslogion* is theological knowledge derived from personal experience of God that St. Anselm would have achieved. That is what I think I must dispute.

43. Stoltz, "Zur Theologie Anselms," 2. [Trans. Note: My thanks and acknowledgement are owed to my Fitchburg State College colleague and friend Prof. John Burke for his assistance in translating these and subsequent Stoltz quotations.]

kind of theology, mystical theology: "It is essentially a bit of mystical theology."[44] Supposing that matters are thus, what is going to become of St. Anselm's argument?

On many points, particularly where he too does not allow himself to be a captive of his system, Fr. Stoltz demonstrates remarkable penetration. He sees perfectly and says that chapters I–IV of the *Proslogion* cannot be interpreted without admitting that the issue is the existence of God.[45] Perhaps we will find that he is satisfied with too little there, but the more interpreters of St. Anselm one reads, including oneself, the less fussy one becomes. Thus Fr. Stoltz concedes that in those chapters the issue is really, *somehow* the existence of God. He even adds that *astruendum*, which was discussed above, implies "that something actually should also be proved of the existence of God." But this valuable concession is immediately limited by the conditions in which it is granted. According to Fr. Stoltz, what St. Anselm wanted to prove is not strictly that God exists, but only that God exists *as faith teaches that he exists*, and to establish further that he is indeed *quo nihil majus cogitari potest.*[46]

We must proceed with caution here. That St. Anselm did not want to prove the existence of God in general, but that existence of God which faith teaches us; that furthermore he wanted to establish the existence of *quo nihil majus cogitari possit*, it seems to me these are indisputable facts, because they are explicit in the very letter of the *Proslogion*. But let us take care of the consequences that supposedly follow from them.

The first and not least important brings us back to Karl Barth. Since St. Anselm wrote the *Proslogion* as a Christian and believer, its author is not a philosopher: "Nothing is more perverse than to view *Proslogion*'s composer as a philosopher."[47] Since, at the end of the day, that consequence does not force itself on us as evident, Fr. Stoltz sets out to prove it. How would Anselm know as a philosopher that God is not only his creator but his savior? That Adam possessed the knowledge of God to which Anselm aspires? That we ought to have inherited Adam's happiness? That without God's help the soul cannot attain the end to which

44. Ibid., 4. It would be much more exact to say that Anselm is "between the mystic and the philosopher." Levasti, *Sant'Anselmo, vita e pensiero*, 41.

45. Stoltz, "Zur Theologie Anselms," 14–15.

46. Ibid., 15. "Von der Existenz Gottes im allgemeinen ist nicht die Rede, nur von seiner speziellen Daseinsform und der Berechtigung der Formel quo majus cogitari nequit in ihre Anwendung auf Gott."

47. Ibid., 6.

God has destined it? "Anselm thus rests entirely on the foundation of his Christian faith."

Who denies that? But also, what does that prove? All these texts are taken from *Proslogion* chapter I and the admirable meditative prayer that is developed there. For my part, I never proceed to the argument in chapter II, without analyzing that prayer in the greatest detail, and I never disguise the fact that it is a prayer. How could I? But how does that prove that what follows is not philosophy? Where does this really leave us? If I pray to God as a Christian and believer before beginning the work of rational reflection or while I pursue it, does the product of my reflection lose all probative force? Therefore, if by chance it had happened, although good historians claim to be unaware of it, that St. Thomas prayed to God to enlighten his reason, his reasoning would be disqualified in the eyes of philosophers and changed into theology! Such conclusions do not seem to impose themselves.[48]

But, it will be objected, it is not just a question of prayer, but of dogmas, and these dogmas are not cited only in the opening invocation. They reappear throughout the work up to the end where the blessed Trinity is introduced with no transition. Anselm wants to grow closer to God much more than to prove him, and he wants to approach him by the understanding of the faith, "through the knowledge of dogma about God."[49]

The objection must be completely accepted, because it is true. To answer that Anselm is a philosopher when he speaks of the existence of God but becomes a theologian again when he speaks of the Trinity, would not be a serious answer. Chapter I is a prayer. The prayer reappears several times throughout the work, always when reason tries to master the understanding of faith that deals with the existence of God, of his nature, or even of the blessed Trinity. Anselm maintains only one and the same attitude, employs only one and the same method. If what he says of the Trinity is theological, what he says about God's existence is too. But if what he says of God's existence is philosophical, what he says about the Trinity is too. Now, for the moment the proposal is to consider everything as "mystical theology." What should we think?

Although the problem affects the whole *Proslogion*, we have to discuss it only in function of the argument, the object of our research.

48. Like the *Proslogion*, Malebranche's *Meditations* begin with an ardent prayer (6–8). Yet it is not a treatise of mystical theology.

49. Stoltz, "Zur Theologie Anselms," 8.

The first question is to know whether St. Anselm himself presents it as constituting or leading to mystical contemplation. The point has fundamental importance, because in the last analysis, if the *Proslogion* is claimed to be a book of mystical theology, it must be interpreted like St. Bonaventure's *Itinerarium* and considered as a guide toward mystical states strictly speaking. That would not be at all impossible. Except that in St. Bonaventure's case we are warned from the beginning that the whole book is a guide toward the ecstasy for which that of St. Francis on Alvernia is the model. In St. Anselm's case I fully see that some want to make him say something similar, but not that he said it.

One of Fr. Stoltz's greatest merits is having shed light on the *Proslogion*'s specific character. What distinguishes it from all of St. Anselm's other treatises is that it expresses the thoughts of someone "who tries to elevate his thought to contemplate God and to seek to understand what he believes." The expression *ad contemplandum Deum* is found in the text, and the interpreter is thus on solid ground in seeing in the treatise "an attempt by the soul to elevate itself to a kind of divine manifestation"[50] The question is simply to discover what kind of contemplation St. Anselm wants to talk about. It is evidently not that of the beatific vision, which is impossible in this life, but exactly, as we are told in the same place, "the contemplation of God to which we can arrive by understanding what faith tells us about God." Is that, strictly speaking, mystical contemplation?

As far as I know, St. Anselm has not left us any other indication about what he understands by "contemplation," than what we could get out of the *Proslogion*. The term appears in the *Homilies* several times, but Dom A. Wilmart advises us to regard these texts with great suspicion.[51] Thus we ought to address ourselves to our text. Fr. Stoltz speaks generally of "experience of God" to designate the goal to which St. Anselm tends in our treatise. "All is subordinate to the desire for experience of God . . ."—"As he wants to come to the experience of God . . ."—". . . he has found the knowledge of God, the experience of God . . ."[52] These are

---

50. Ibid., 3.

51. Wilmart, "Les Homélies attribuées," 11–12.

52. Stoltz, "Zur Theologie Anselms im *Proslogion*," 8–9. "Dem Willen nach Gotteserfahrung ist demmach alles untergeordnet . . ."—"Wie er zur Gotteserfahrung kommen will . . ."—"er hat die Gotteserkenntnis, Gotteserfahrung gefunden . . ." Cf. 10: "Die Seele will Gotterfahren."

very strong expressions, which undoubtedly refer to strictly mystical states. St. Bernard uses precisely the terms *experiri, experientia*, to designate an ecstatic union with God. It is thus easily understandable that Fr. Stoltz should use them. Unfortunately, St. Anselm himself does not use them. To my knowledge, he never designates the contemplation of God, as he describes it in the *Proslogion*, as an experience of God, and, in all the texts cited by Fr. Stoltz in support of his theses, I am unable to find a single expression where the word is employed by St. Anselm. To know that a thing is somewhere is much easier than knowing that it is not. To say that it is there let us at least wait either to find it or for someone to show it to us.

Instead of this missing "experience," there will be no lack of substitutes. There have been many, but they are only substitutes. St. Anselm is unquestionably a person of great spirituality. He meditates, and his meditation, rational or not, is animated by the liveliest piety. He seeks for God: *quaere eum*. He seeks for the face of God (but that is with Ps 27:8).[53] He has never seen the visage of God, who is present everywhere, and, more than everywhere else, in his heart. Made to see God, he has not yet seen God, etc. The whole initial invocation is full of expressions of this type, but we must see what they signify. They mean exactly that original sin has deprived man of the knowledge of God that Adam enjoyed before the fall and that the soul asks God to show himself to it as he once showed himself to the first man. But are we going to encounter that "bread of angels" with which Adam was nourished in its plenitude? Anselm never said so. He even said the opposite: *Liceat mihi suspicere lucem tuam, vel de longe, vel de profundo.*[54] Now in what does this view of the light consist? To look for God in love and find him in joy through the understanding of what faith teaches us in this regard. Thus, instead of saying that for the *Proslogion* contemplation is a mystical experience, therefore the famous argument is a fragment of mystical theology— which St. Anselm does not say—we must simply say with him that the object of the *Proslogion* is to restore to us that contemplation,[55] that vi-

53. [Trans. note: Following the Vulgate enumeration, Gilson says Psalm 26.]

54. St. Anselm, *Proslogion*, ch. I, column 227 B. It must be added that Fr. Stoltz is not unaware of this text. On the contrary, he explicitly quotes it (7 n. 27). We are dealing with different interpretations.

55. The word *contemplandum* can be misleading, but it must be remembered that St. Anselm speaks the language of St. Augustine. Now the latter uses this very word to refer to the knowledge through reason of the existence of God, which we obtain from

sion of God, which remains possible to us after original sin, that which we found in the understanding of faith.[56]

Supposing that these general difficulties are not enough to detain us, it still remains to prove that the argument itself is mystical contemplation of God rather than a proof of his existence. I confess that Fr. Stoltz's procedure on this point surprised me a little. I do not reproach him for having held back from a new analysis of chapter II, because it

---

faith. Thus, if it is admitted that the contemplation to which we are referring is mystical in St. Anselm, the proof of the existence of God in St. Augustine's *De Libero Arbitrio* would have to be called similarly mystical. In both cases, *contemplatio* is only a Latin equivalent of the Greek θεώρημα. It is a vision of truth by the intellect. The fact that the word is found in a text of Augustine that is the immediate source of the *Proslogion* (see above, n. 24) and is employed by him to refer to the knowledge of God's existence by reason starting from faith as in St. Anselm, makes it particularly difficult to deny of the one, the source, the mystical character attributed to the doctrine that is patently inspired in it. "Quanquam haec inconcussa fide teneam, tamen quia cognitione nondum teneo, ita quaeramus quasi omni incerta sint." An unshakeable faith is thus compatible with uncertainty of reason. Now what is the nature of the desired *cognitio*? "Illud saltem tibi certum est, Deum esse.—Etiam hoc non contemplando, sed credendo inconcussum teneo." St. Augustine, *De Libero Arbitrio*, book II, ch. 2, 5, column 1242. Therefore, to contemplate simply refers to the vision of truth by the understanding that results from a demonstration by reason. Cf. the immutable rules of wisdom are "omnibus qui haec intueri valent, communes ad contemplandum," *De Libero Arbitrio*, book II, ch. 10, 29, column 1257. On one occasion St. Augustine carried this contemplation to a mystical state, in the "extasis at Ostia," but the contemplation of ideas required by his proofs of the existence of God cannot be said to be a mystical intuition of the existence of God.

56. Fr. Stoltz insists that this contemplation is accompanied by intense delight, ("Zur Theologie Anselms," 8–9). Karl Barth already drew attention to this point, *Fides querens intellectum*, 4–6. But the delights of rational contemplation can be very intense without being mystical. Even the intellectual contemplations of a saint like Anselm, however fervent they maybe and recompensed by the most pious delights that can be conceived, are not mystical states on account of that. This contemplation cannot be proved to be mystical because it is accompanied by delight. On the contrary, this contemplation would have to be proved to be mystical for us to have the right to consider the delight that accompanies it as mystical. Furthermore, it would be useful to begin by defining what a mystical state, an *Erfahrung* of this type, would be. It is not an attempt to reach God by love *in caligine*. It is not *docta ignorantia*, but a vision of God by the understanding in this life. Chapters II–IV of the *Proslogion* in particular would have to lead to an intellectual vision of the existence of God that would at the same time be a mystical experience of his existence. Is not that truly a great deal to ask of them? Perhaps they take on this value in St. Bonaventure's *Itinerarium*, ch. V, number 3, 332), but if St. Bonaventure himself places this milestone on the road that leads to mystical experience, he never claimed that it was one. When the instant of mystical experience arrives, dialectic ceases and understanding itself ceases to see, only love remains. We are far from *fidens quaerens intellectum*.

was not necessary here, but, if he thought it was true, he might at least have affirmed that St. Anselm here proves neither the existence of God in general nor that of the revealed God in particular. Instead of that, he chose to analyze chapter fourteen, less burdened with completely elaborated exegeses, and which sums up everything that precedes it. I quote the opening of this summary following Fr. Stoltz: *Quaerebas Deum et invenisti eum esse quiddam summum omnium, quo nihil melius cogitari potest*, etc.[57] Here is the interpreter's commentary: "It is not the existence of God that is the question here." That is surprising!

First, even if, when summing up twelve or thirteen chapters, St. Anselm forgot to say he proved the existence of God, that does not authorize us to say he did not, if he did so in chapters where we can still read it. But above all, if that phrase does not mean that he found the existence of a sovereign good, such that one can conceive nothing better, what does it mean? To find yet another meaning, *esse* must be deprived of its existential signification to conserve only an attributive function. That is what Fr. Stoltz valiantly does, and he arrives at the result that, because Anselm does not say he "found" that God exists, he did find three things "as a result of the investigation," the first of which is: "that God is the *quo majus cogitari nequit*." In short, the first result of St. Anselm's search would be, not that a sovereign good exists, than which nothing greater can be conceived, but that God is that than which nothing greater can be conceived. Now we know perfectly, and Fr. Stoltz better than anyone, that this thesis is not the conclusion of any search. It is what faith teaches him and what he takes as the point of departure of his argument. If, in order to maintain this interpretation, Fr. Stoltz must hold that the first of Anselm's conclusions is his point of departure, that is proof by *reductio ad absurdum* that the position is false.[58]

57. Stoltz, "Zur Theologie Anselms," 12.

58. Fr. Stoltz approaches Chapters II–IV in the light of this unfortunate exegesis. Naturally, he comes up against the "da mihi ut . . . intelligam quia est, sicut credimus." In the German original, Karl Barth (*Fides quaerens Intellectum*, 111) translates following the obvious meaning: 'dass du da bist . . ." Koyré (St. Anselme, *Fides quaerens intellectum*, 13) translates in the same sense "that you are, as we believe." Fr. Stoltz, who dreads encountering a poof of God's existence in the *Proslogion*, translates: "dass du bist wie wir glauben" ("Zur Theologie Anselms," 13). "Quia es, sicut credimus" would now no longer simply mean that you exist, as we believe, but rather that you exist as faith teaches us that you exist. It would be the mode of divine existence revealed by faith that would control the object of the contemplation rather than existence itself, which would control the object of a proof. I admit that I do not see grammatical impossibility here,

Must we then despair of finding a solution? I do not think so. At bottom, no one, not even Fr. Stoltz, dares to deny that St. Anselm's argument looks in some sense to existence, but Stoltz asks us to see in it mystical contemplation of divine existence, not its demonstration. For his part, Karl Barth certainly wants to admit that St. Anselm supplies us with a demonstration (and not contemplation), but he holds that it is a theological demonstration. Reason thus does not prove that it is true, because it is faith that posits it, but reason permits us to show *how* what faith posits as true is true. Both agree in denying that the argument is a rational proof of the existence of God. But the discussion of their arguments also makes us see how difficult it is to harmonize their theses with the texts. How does it happen that so many sincere efforts, conducted with total concern for probity and exactness, should conduct historians to so opposed conclusion? The only conceivable explanation is the presence of some hidden confusion in the very framing of the question.

THE NATURE OF THE *PROSLOGION*

The first thing behind these difficulties is that the historian is never content with the philosopher's answers to the questions he has posed—supposing that he takes interest in them—but wants at all cost to get from that philosopher answers to questions that he himself poses. And if the questions are not in the doctrine he studies, the answers will be equally absent. But someone wants to find them there, and that is where we begin to do bad history.

That is precisely what has just occurred before our eyes. It is clear that if Karl Barth, Fr. Stoltz, and I can be made to behave ourselves with common sense, there would be no fundamental difficulty. We all agree that Anselm's argument presupposes faith, that it is an intellectual vision, and that it precedes beatific vision. We read the same text, and we interpret it in the same way as to its literal meaning, up to the moment when, instead of deducing from the text what St. Anselm thinks,

---

and this grammatical non-impossibility of a single phrase is the only positive thing that can be alleged in favor of the interpretation. It is not much against the rest, and that does not even stand up against the words that follow: "quia es, sicut credimus, et hoc es, quod credimus." Because if *quia es* does not designate existence, it is the manner of existing, and how would the manner in which God exist not fall under *hoc est*? What are eternity, necessity, immutability but his attributes. A thesis that is maintained at the cost of such expedients is like a hypothesis that does not succeed in "saving the phenomena." It would be better to abandon it.

we make it say what St. Anselm was understood ahead of time to have thought. If it is resolved that it is about philosophy, this is a proof, and *est* means one thing. If we are convinced that it is about theology, or mysticism, *est* means something else. From that point on, all is lost. The interpretations of St. Anselm will never be so many that they cannot be increased by one more.

Therefore, the first thing to do will be to not impose on St. Anselm the structures to which we have become accustomed, but within which he never thought. We thereby will avoid unsolvable quarrels, and we will win the necessary freedom of spirit to study the questions that he posed as well as their answers, which will be history. This observation is not in the least negative. It simply supposes that perhaps in St. Anselm's time the problem of classification of these modes of knowing did not present itself to his thought as it would present itself in the thirteenth century, but above all it summons us to ask St. Anselm what was the exact nature of his treatise, as he conceived it.

Of all the treatises he wrote, St. Anselm considered one, *De Grammatico*, to be a useful introduction to dialectic: *non inutilem, ut puto, introducendis ad dialecticam.*[59] He cites three others, *De Veritate, De Libertate Arbitrii, De Casu Diaboli* as *pertinentes ad studium sacrae scripturae.* Personally, I must confess that I would never have doubted this regarding *De Veritate*, but I now see very clearly what Anselm meant in chapter I of this work, where he writes: *Quoniam Deum, veritatem esse credimus, et veritatem in multis aliis esse dicimus, vellem scire an ubicumque veritas dicitur, Deum eam esse fateri debemus.*[60] The nature of this work is quite similar to that of the *Monologium* and the *Proslogion.* The issue is, believing a truth of faith, to come to know something. *De Veritate's credimus-scire* is, I do not say identical, but similar to the *fides-intellectum* of the other two treatises. The danger begins here.

De Veritate "relates to the study of holy Scripture," St. Anselm tells us. Therefore, Karl Barth translates, it is theology. I do not know about that at all. St. Anselm does not tell us this. For Karl Barth, any study that relates to holy Scripture is theology, but was it so for St. Anselm? The word did not come to the world with a completely finished meaning. Through Fr. Chenu's studies we know what great difficulty it provoked

59. Anselm, *De Veritate*, prologue, column 467 A. The text concerning the three other treatises is found in the same place.

60. Ibid., ch. I, column 468.

in the thirteenth century, and the last word has not yet been uttered on the question. Even if St. Anselm had written that *De Veritate* is a theological treatise, that would leave untouched the question of what he understands by the word, and we would still have to extract it from his text. But he has not even said it was a theological treatise. Karl Barth finds a "theological program" in St. Anselm. He makes Anselm prove "the necessity of theology," the "possibility of theology," the "conditions of theology," the "method of theology," etc. To read this succession of chapters, which are very suggestive, we would think St. Anselm had left us a *De Natura et Subjecto Theologiae*. Now, to my knowledge, he never used the word. Perhaps *theologia* is found in his works, but I have never managed to find it. In any case, Karl Barth does not cite a single example of it. The word does not appear in the Gerberon edition's index. In short, by attributing it to Anselm, we foist a term on him about which the least that can be said is that it was unfamiliar to him, and a concept of which we have no means of telling whether he used it, nor what sense he gave to it. After that, how can we be surprised that his texts resist our analyses, when, using the term in our fashion, we want to make the texts prove that St. Anselm wrote the *Proslogion* as a theologian? Or that every argument taken from the texts in favor of this thesis provokes a counter argument, equally drawn from the texts, which annuls the first? The game could be continued for a long time, but it is not clear that history would gain by it.

The same problem presents itself in regard to the expression "mystical theology." What in fact does St. Anselm tell us? That the *Monologium* is an example of "meditation on the divine essence," while his *Proslogion* represents "the effort of someone to lift his thought to the contemplation of God and seek to comprehend what he believes."[61] It follows from that that the first is meditation, the second an impulse toward contemplation, or even contemplation itself. But is it *mystical* contemplation? Here again, I don't know at all. For Fr. Stoltz, every contemplation is, *ipso facto*, mystical, just as for Karl Barth, every meditation on holy Scripture is fully theological. But St. Anselm never applied the word "mystical" to the contemplation of the *Proslogion*. I am unaware that he employed it elsewhere, and I know still less what sense he would have given it. In

---

61. Anselm, *Monologium*, Preface, columns 142–43. *Proslogion*, prooemium, columns 223 A and 224 B. Cf. Stoltz, "Zur Theologie Anselms," 3. Stoltz's remarks on these texts are very appropriate, but not perhaps the conclusions he draws from them.

St. Bernard there is a problem of mystical, or rather let us say ecstatic, contemplation, and we have splendid data to discuss it. But nothing of the sort is found in St. Anselm, and it is a hopeless endeavor to want to get the proof that the *Proslogion* is a treatise of mystical theology from his texts, where the issue is neither of mysticism nor of theology. If, after decreeing that we are in mystical theology, we go on to establish what the texts of the *Proslogion* ought to mean, we enter into the zone of exegetical catastrophes, and it cannot be surprising that they have occurred.

Let us test a third and last temptation, my own. St. Anselm says in *De Veritate* that he wants to know (*scire*) whether there is one truth or several. At the beginning of the *Monologium*, he announces that his "meditation" upon the divine essence does not involve any conclusion based on the authority of Scripture: *quatenus auctoritate Scripturae penitus nihil in ea persuaderetur*. His only means of proof are *rationis necessitas* and *veritatis claritas*. As for the *Proslogion*, he himself declares that the original title of this contemplation was faith searching for understanding.[62] I agree that each of these treatises has its peculiar character and ought to be interpreted as such. Nonetheless, they offer many common traits and resemble each other like the children of a common father. Is not the most striking thing that, starting from faith, all of them tend toward rational knowledge (*exemplum meditandi de ratione fidei*), an intellectual contemplation (*intelligere quod credit*)? In short, does not St. Anselm simply want to write philosophical treatises?

I would like this very much, but here again I must respond that I am not at all sure. St. Anselm did not tell us that the *Proslogion* was philosophical. I am completely ready to examine the texts where he used that word, if they are to be found, because I have not combed his works with the intention of looking for it. But I do not recall having found it there, and therefore I do not know the meaning that he would have given it. If I dared to risk a hypothesis, I would imagine that in his eyes philosophy was the way in which illustrious pagans, whom faith had not yet enlightened, had of reasoning about things divine and human. But I repeat that I am not at all sure, and I am prepared to beat a retreat before the first exact text that might be advanced.

Accordingly, as far as we know, the *Proslogion* is neither a treatise of philosophy nor of theology, nor mystical contemplation. Some will

62. Anselm, *Monologium*, Preface, column 143 A; *Proslogion*, Proemium, columns 224–25.

find this conclusion discouraging, but it seems to me, on the contrary, that it is the point where the problem begins to becomes interesting. For we thought we knew in advance what the *Proslogion* is, and we discover that we knew nothing about it. Thus it is that history has something to teach us. As history of philosophy is often practiced, it resembles a mail car, where the historian would be the postal worker. Around him the walls are covered with pigeonholes, each of which have names: theology, philosophy, idealism, realism, pantheism, nominalism, with all their divisions and subdivisions. Just as the postal worker knows that there is a pigeonhole for each letter, the historian knows that there is one for each doctrine. The only problem is to read the envelopes and distribute the letters by their addresses. A mail car is a very useful instrument, but as a means of geographical exploration, its value is slight.

Why do we not ask history what pigeonholes we must provide to house doctrines rather than asking for doctrines to distribute in our pigeonholes? The only issue is really there, because many difficulties must be overcome before finding a response to it, and the chief difficulty involves the fact that philosophers and historians do not move on the same level, although they speak of the same things. The pigeonhole approach belongs to philosophy when it invades history. Now, although history of philosophy belongs to philosophy, it is not philosophy. These two orders of knowledge do not have exactly the same object.

Philosophy deals principally with essences, and since essences are general, it is a science. History, even history of philosophy, deals with the particular, and that is why, even where it reaches certainty, it is not a science. Thus it is possible, as a philosopher, to give definitions of philosophy, of theology, of mysticism, expressing the essence of each of these disciplines, valid for all of philosophy, all of theology, or all mysticism generally. It is not easy, but the philosopher has the right and the duty to attempt it. On the contrary, the historian only considers a *certain* philosophy, a *certain* theology, a *certain* mysticism. Thus he grapples with the problem of the "mixture of ideas" in particular. Essences are not presented to the historian in their purity, but in a multiplicity of possible combinations, a great number of which were unforeseeable and which he has the duty to respect when he describes them. He therefore must find expressions, perhaps surprising for the philosopher, all the more because they consist of philosophical terms, but apt to describe the particular, contingent, concrete state in which these combinations of distinct essences are presented to him.[63]

The study of St. Anselm is a particularly notable case in this regard. The very difficulty of classifying him is most instructive. The *Proslogion* argument presupposes faith. It will be said that it is theological. But then a new kind of theology must be imagined, of which I know no other

---

63. No doubt here is one reason for the resistance sometimes made to the expression "Christian philosophy." Van Steenberghen, for example, admits that "Christian Revelation exercised a real and historically discernable influence on the evolution of western thought" ("Hommage," 505). So we have an agreement in principle on the reality of the fact. It only remains to know if we ought to refuse to give a name to the fact or to give one and which. It is permissible to not designate this state of philosophy with a name, but it is not convenient. If we want to give it a name, it is necessary to accept the one I propose or to find a better one. Now it is remarkable that nobody has succeeded in finding another. And for good reason. If we refuse to label as "Christian philosophy" that philosophy which owed Christian Revelation the admirable lights on divine things that faith supplies to it in addition to its liberation from error and its confirmation in truth (Denzinger, *Enchiridion*, text 1635, p. 437), we must despair of ever being able to name it.

So the question is posed a bit differently from what has been claimed. Van Steenberghen reproaches me with "having wanted to introduce *Christian philosophy* into the "technical language of philosophy" (L'Hommage," 506). That is not at all the same. The thing to be named has been known for a long time. There are philosophers (and scholars) who only trust to their reason. There are others who, besides their reason, keep "divinam Revelationem veluti rectricem stellam" always present to their sight (*Enchiridion Symbolorum*, text 1681, p. 455). These are two distinct attitudes, so distinct that Pope Pius IX expressly condemned the first and approved the second. It is no surprise that many authors have used a special label to designate an attitude that is *obligatory* for the philosopher as a Christian, and, to designate the philosophy that the Christian philosopher's obligatory attitude engenders, they have chosen the expression "Christian philosophy." More than a hundred years ago Sanseverino published his *Philosophiae Christianae Compendium*. Heinrich Ritter's *Histoire de la philosophie chrétienne* dates from 1843 [Trans. note: In German, 1841]. The encyclical *Aeterni Patris*, dates from August 4, 1879. Immediately after its publication, the future Cardinal Ehrle commented on the encyclical in a long series of articles, "Die päpstliche Encyklika." Far from thinking that the thing whose restoration the encyclical prescribed is merely an expression without technical value for philosophers, Ehrle sustains that Revelation ought necessarily to engender a "Christian philosophy," whose development starting from the nucleus of Revelation, alongside theology and under its protection, has been pursued without interruption during centuries ("Die päpstliche Encyklika," 21). I could cite several provincial councils in the same sense. Thus I am not the one who wants to introduce this expression into the technical language of philosophy. It is its adversaries who wish to expel it. How does one wish to institute "Christian philosophy" in the schools according to the spirit of St. Thomas Aquinas, if the expression itself does not have technical value? What kind of thing is a school of philosophy founded to institute "Christian philosophy," where it is taught that "Christian philosophy" has no sense for a philosopher? I apologize for going here, but I have no other way of discharging a responsibility that does not correspond to me, than to show who assumes one and what it is.

example, a theology whose conclusions are not based on the authority of Scripture. Because St. Anselm says, at the beginning of the *Monologium*, that nothing—*penitus nihil*—will be proved in it by the authority of Scripture, but that everything will be established solely upon the "necessity of reason." As for the argument of the *Proslogion*, it is clear that the certainty of the conclusion owes nothing further to the authority of Scripture nor to that of faith. St. Anselm says it himself, and what he says here can have only one meaning for any unprejudiced mind. He began by believing in the existence of God (*quod prius credidi*), but now he understands it (*jam sic intelligo*), and he understands it in such a way that even if he no longer wanted to believe that God is, he could not fail to understand it: *ut si te esse nolim credere, non possim non intelligere*. One must be deeply committed to a system to not recognize that we are dealing with the existence of God here—*te esse*—and that at the end of the argument, the conclusion no longer depends on faith, because if faith ceased, the conclusion would not cease to be sound. And thus I ask the historians: are we going to place under the rubric of theology a conclusion that prides itself on not owing its certainty either to Scripture or to faith? The question holds for the *Monologium* and the *Proslogion* in their entirety, but we pose it in the context of this precise point.

I have no intention to answer in the name of everyone nor is it my place to do so, but it is not inappropriate to attempt a first and completely provisional response, submitted to a discussion that this time would be useful. Thus I state, *salvo meliori judicio*, that these two treatises, doubtless just like *De Veritate*, but setting aside the others, are not theological treatises. The "family" of theologies doubtless has many species, when one pursues its history further, because that history has hardly begun, but I doubt that it could ever make room for writings that by their deliberate intent declare that the certainty of their conclusions is not based on that of Revelation. *Argumentari ex auctoritate est maxime proprium hujus doctrinae, eo quod principia hujus doctrinae per revelationem habentur.* Now St. Anselm refuses to have recourse precisely to what is "proper" to this science. He expressly excludes it from his method. Thus one cannot classify within theology, which is a science whose characteristic is to argue by authority of Scripture, treatises that declare that the "truth" of their conclusions owes nothing to this authority.

We are not dealing with an abstract discussion with no historical import. The whole interpretation of the *Proslogion* is involved. To admit that this composition is a theological work, two serious obstacles must necessarily be overcome. Certain historians, surrendering to the evidence, admit that St. Anselm really wanted to give rational demonstrations, not only of God's existence, but even of the Trinity. Since this second ambition is inadmissible for a theologian, it is now concluded that St. Anselm's theology is stained with rationalism. Yes, if it is theology. But if, by chance, it is something else, the reproach only proves the historian's error of perspective about the work he is studying. Now, to attribute rationalism, even Christian rationalism, to a doctor who places faith above any rational justification, is to go a bit far, and we should look twice before formulating such a reproach. We can try to get around this obstacle, as Karl Barth and Fr. Stoltz have done, by saying that St. Anselm did not really want to demonstrate all that by reason alone, but then we come up against another obstacle: the formal and reiterated affirmations of St. Anselm himself. Whether we like it or not, he proceeds exactly as St. Thomas says one must not proceed in theology, *comprehendendo et demonstrando*. Except, and this is why his attitude escapes St. Thomas's reproach, it is not at all faith as faith that he demonstrates, and what he understands from it does not authorize him to eliminate it. Thus that in no way proves that he practices theology in a way opposed to the one St. Thomas understands. That can simply mean that the *Proslogion* is not a theological treatise.

If we agree with this conclusion, a new problem cannot be avoided, whose mere shadow has no doubt been enough to push many historians toward the solution that has just been criticized. To deny that the *Proslogion* is a theological treatise is implicitly to admit that it is a philosophical work. Is it then truly philosophical?

One can only answer yes or no to a question posed this way. Here the issue is no longer to know whether St. Anselm himself used the term philosophy, or if he had the intention to do philosophical work, but rather whether, in fact and whatever his intentions might have been, the *Proslogion* is or is not the work of a philosopher. Now, I think we must answer no. Doubtless, the method that St. Anselm follows is purely rational, that is why the *Proslogion* argument can be so easily grafted onto philosophies that do not remit to faith—but the *object* to which it applies is posed by Anselm himself as transcending reason. More remarkably still, it is necessary for this speculation to be applied to faith and to it alone. If it only ignores everything else, it will be nothing. Possibly, we can say that philosophy includes, among so many others, a group of thinkers who choose the content of faith as the object of their reflection. But these are thinkers who doubtless would raise objections themselves, because the essence of the knowledge that they pursue demands that it should select faith as its object.[64] Let us say, further, that if this knowledge can only be concerned with faith, it is that faith itself, in seeking understanding, gives birth to it. Can knowledge be considered part of philosophy, which, if only to be engendered, demands an act of faith? What if it is knowledge that at each instant of its development, *and even if it is not deduced from faith*, demands the presence of this act of faith? Finally, what if it is rational knowledge, where the act of faith survives, however necessary that knowledge's conclusions may be? One can try to maintain it, but it will be hard to believe, and I think it is better to renounce it.[65]

64. This is why the thinkers with whom we are dealing here, and St. Anselm in particular, although very important for the history of philosophy and especially of Christian philosophy, cannot simply be classified as "Christian philosophers." The purely rational nature of their methods of demonstration allows many of their conclusions to be incorporated without modification into philosophy, and that is why they are part of its history, but the object of "Christian philosophy" is very different from what St. Anselm proposes. A Christian philosopher knows that he can rationally "demonstrate" nothing regarding the Trinity or the Incarnation ("dummodo desit comprehendendi vel demonstrandi praesumptio," Aquinas, *Summa Contra Gentes*, book I, ch. 8). However, for St. Anselm, since the quest for understanding starts from faith, it starts from all of faith. Hence, its "proofs" and its" "necessary reasons" not only attain the existence of God, but also attain the Trinity and the Incarnation. Do we want to understand a genuine disciple of St. Anselm? "However, the truths of faith being supposed undeniable, one can and even one ought to meditate on my law day and night, and humbly ask me for light and understanding." Malebranche, *Méditations*, Meditation III, 5, 41. Part of Malebranche's work (but not all of it) is constructed on this Anselmian plan.

65. This desire to keep within faith is nowhere expressed more clearly than in Anselm's reply to Lanfranc's "admonition." He certainly thinks he has established by reason what he teaches in the *Monologium*. But his reasons, however necessary they might seem to him, would never have convinced him to the point of giving him the boldness to publish them, if St. Augustine had not said the same things before him: "Etenim ea quae ex eodem opusculo vestris litteris inseruistis, et quaedam alia quae non inseruistis, nulla mihi ratiocinatio mea, quantumlibet videretur necessaria, persuasisset ut primus dicere praesumerem . . . Quod dico, non aliquid eorum quae dixi apud vos defendendo, sed ea mea non a me praesumpsisse, sed ab alio assumpsisse ostendendo" (*Ad Lanfrancum*, book I, 68, column 1139 B). Assuredly, that is not the normal attitude of a philosopher. Is it necessary to add once more that it is likewise not that of a theologian. A theologian would prove what he says by the authority of Scripture or by that of St. Augustine as authoritative interpreter of Scripture. For St. Anselm, St. Augustine's authority is not involved in proving his conclusions, but in authorizing their publication: "ut eadem, quasi mea, breviori ratiocinatione inveniens, ejus confisus auctoritate dicerem" (*Ad Lanfrancum*, column 1139 B).

Thus, with Van Steenberghen ("L'Hommage," 504), I reject the expressions I have used on occasion, although I no longer know where: Christian philosophers move

Thus the *Proslogion* is not mystical contemplation of God. It is not theology. It is not philosophy. Many will say it is the confusion of the three; let us place St. Anselm and his kind, because there are such, in the class of the confused. I too would like that, in order to get out of the impasse, but that is difficult precisely because we are dealing with St. Anselm, one of the clearest and most rigorously precise minds that can be found. There is no confusion in his case. We are told that there is a little mysticism in his mix, but there is none at all. What this passionate lover of understanding seeks, even in the ardor of prayer, is *unum argumentum, quod nullo alio ad se probandum, quam se solo indigeret.* In truth, a strange mystical contemplation that is obtained by a unique argument that suffices to demonstrate itself! There would be a little theology there, someone adds. There is none at all, since nothing—*penitus nihil*—is grounded in the authority of Scripture, but everything in the necessity of reason. By chance, will this then be part of philosophy? But it is not philosophy at all, because this search, however purely rational it is, rejects any other object than that of faith and conforms to it completely. What keeps itself outside of the three types cannot be defined as their confusion, nor can we define as their mixture that in which none of the three is found. What is it then?

To know that, it is necessary to make the concern to describe precede the concern to name. Here are the principal traits:

1. Sought by faith itself, the speculation is properly applied to faith and only faith.
2. The faith that seeks this knowledge remains independent of it, because this knowledge has neither the right to contradict it nor the power to ground it.

---

within a faith. There are grounds also to correct the expression in *L'esprit de la philosophie médiévale* (I:37) that seems to admit that *fides quaerens intellectum* defines the method of Christian philosophy. The history of Christian philosophy will never be written without St. Anselm, nor without many other thinkers, the majority of whom were theologians (including St. Thomas Aquinas), but if St. Anselm greatly enriched Christian philosophy, I believe that there is an ambition and an exclusive limitation in his expression that prevent our seeing the definition of the attitude of a Christian philosopher in it. I take this occasion to thank Van Steenberghen for his most courteous criticisms. I would respond to them if I believed in the efficacy of controversy, but it would be almost useless, because the task that falls to us is not to prove that others do not understand us, but to make ourselves understood by others. Let us work as best we can on it; time will do the rest.

3. Faith remains transcendent to this knowledge, which, where it terminates, can only contemplate its object from afar, and where it fails, can only incline itself before faith.

4. On the other hand, what this knowledge sees in faith is the part of it that is possible to know by reason and to see by understanding.

5. Thus, it will never make an appeal to the authority of Revelation to prove the truth of its conclusions.

6. But this knowledge will proceed by necessary reason towards visions of understanding.

7. These visions of understanding do not eliminate faith but contemplate its intelligibility .

8. Prepared by purification of the heart and sustained by prayer, this knowledge is a source of spiritual delights and consolations that announce the beatific vision.

This first approximation to St. Anselm's position in the *Proslogion* will doubtless require completions and corrections, but overall we can allow that it is sufficiently faithful. Thus it remains to find a name for it. Now St. Anselm himself never proposed one. We are thus equally perplexed when we speak of "philosophy," "theology," or "mysticism," and wisdom invites us first to attend to Anselm's own expressions: it is a *study of Holy Scripture on the intelligibility of faith.* This composite definition, which is not found in St. Anselm, even supposing that it is accepted, is still not a denomination. To find this denomination, since it is not found in the writings of St. Anselm himself, it would be necessary to discover other Christian thinkers whose position is similar to his and who have designated with an acceptable name. That would be to go beyond the framework of this study and to start anew the labor we have just attempted on the *Proslogion* argument on two or three other works.

At least two questions remain to be posed. Are the conclusions drawn from the study of the *Proslogion* argument valid for the whole *Proslogion* and subsequently for the whole work of St. Anselm? I believe that they hold for the whole *Proslogion*, and I do not believe that they hold for the whole work of St. Anselm, but that remains to be established.

To this first question a second would be added. Does a family of thinkers exist with which St. Anselm is related, or at the very least a family of works that could be assigned to the same class as the *Proslogion*, and what should it be called? I believe that such thinkers and such works exist, that they have existed before and after St. Anselm. To only mention one, Clement of Alexandria[66] doubtless resembled him much more than is imagined, and furthermore the same confusions have accumulated about the meaning of his work as about the work of St. Anselm. I believe that his "Christian gnosticism" would have a great deal to teach us about the deep meaning of such an attitude. Perhaps it would even give the name that we are looking for to designate it. I am strongly inclined to believe it, but that too remains to be established.

66. The approximation has already been made. "He [Anselm] uses reason a little bit like the Gnostics, whose unconscious disciple he is" (Filliatre, *La philosophie*, 52). I do not even believe that, as the author adds, "the Gnostic further disdains faith." That is certainly not true of Origen nor of Clement. But above all, this felicitous approximation is swamped among many others that are less so, and completely spoiled by this strange conclusion: "Thus Anselm is a rationalist, perhaps a mystical rationalist" (60). We thus return to Bouchitté's "Christian rationalism" (*Le rationalisme chrétien*, 452), a vague designation that becomes infelicitous as soon as one makes it precise. A little further on (*Le rationalisme chrétien*, 459) St. Anselm becomes a "mystical realist," of neo-Platonic and Augustinian inspiration. There is some disorder in all this—Clement of Alexandria's name is likewise evoked by Levasti, *Sant'Anselmo*, 41.

This conclusion supposes that one recognizes that Clement's "gnosis" is neither a rationalism nor the fruit of mystical experiences. I am persuaded of both, but this is not the place to demonstrate it.

4

Peter Lombard and the
Theologies of Essence

W E RECENTLY DREW ATTENTION to a group of doctrines that, for
want of a better name, we labeled "theologies of essence."[1] Moreover, we are dealing with a well known historical group, but which had
not yet been marked, or perhaps which we had not yet clearly distinguished, as presenting among other well known common characteristics,
that of interpreting Exod 2:14, *Ego sum*, as meaning: I am *essentia* in the
full sense of the word; that is to say, I am the being which never changes.

The main source of this interpretation and of the decisive consequences that it entails cannot escape us. Alexander of Hales and St.
Bonaventure themselves remit us here to St. Augustine and sometimes
also to St. Jerome. Since the latter seemed to us to be of merely secondary importance, we have limited ourselves to completing the information
that these theologians offer us by citing other texts from St. Augustine in
support of their theses. Subsequently, we were brought by completely different paths to a text known to all, which is so classic that our forgetting it
would have been inexcusable in writing these pages, and all the more because it was the very text upon which Alexander and Bonaventure were
commenting: the *Sentences* of Peter Lombard. A fitting punishment for

1. Gilson, *Le thomisme.*

this common fault of failing to reread the text of the Lombard each time a commentary of it is consulted!

However, it suffices to do so here to find oneself in presence of texts in which Augustine interprets the famous passage from Exodus in the language of *essentia*. Since these texts are at everyone's disposition in Peter Lombard's *Sentences*, it is unnecessary to reproduce them once more in their entirety, but we invite the historians to reread them as they are presented there, because their very grouping produces a completely different impression than the same texts scattered throughout the immense corpus of St. Augustine's own works. Seeing them thus assembled we feel how much weight they have exerted on the mind of certain theologians. Furthermore, here is the list of their references, according to the exact order in which Peter Lombard reproduced them[2] in book I, distinction 8, chapter 1 of his *Books of Sentences*.

CHAPTER I, *DE VERITATE AC PROPRIETE DIVINAE ESSENTIAE*

1. Augustine, *De Trinitate*, book V, chapter 2, number 3, column 912. God is undoubtedly *essentia*, which the Greeks call *ousia*. Indeed *essentia* is said from and by reason of *esse*, and who is more than He who said to Moses: *Ego sum, qui sum*? To this Peter Lombard adds the brief commentary: *Ipse vere ac proprie dicitur essentia, cujus essentia non novit praeteritum vel futurum.*

2. Jerome, *Ad Marcellam*. The Quaracchi editors observe in a note that this passage is not found word for word in St. Jerome, but rather in Isidore, *Etymologiae*, book VII, chapter I, numbers 10–13, column 261, and that the Migne edition rightly remarks on its composite state. The first part, up to *non sunt* is taken from Augustine, *De Civitate Dei*, book VIII, chapter 11, column 235. Gregory would enter into the composition of the remainder.[3] Let us dwell on the formula taken from Augustine: *Deus solus, qui exordium non habet, verae essentiae nomen tenuit, quia in ejus comparatione, qui vere est, quia incommutabilis est, quasi non sunt, quae mutabilia sunt.*

---

2. The references to modern editions of these texts are also indicated in the excellent edition of Lombard: Petri Lombardi, *Libri IV Sententiarum*. The passage in question is found in I:57–59; book I, distinction 8, ch. 1.

3. Lombardi, *Libri IV Sententiarum*, I:57 n. 3.

At this point, focusing upon a formula that he just attributed to Jerome, Peter Lombard comments on it at some length, and his commentary strongly emphasizes the connection of immutability to essentiality. Indeed, let us not forget that the chapter in question is entitled: *De Veritate ac Proprietate Divinae Essentiae*. Now, to make the "truth" of the divine essence evident, Peter Lombard starts from the words attributed here to Jerome—*Deus tantum est et non novit fuisse*—to note that they mean: *tanquam non possit dici de Deo fuit, vel erit, sed tantum est*. The rest of the passage simply develops this point.[4]

3. Augustine, *In Joannis Evangelium*, tractate 99, numbers 4 and 5. Another composite text, or rather, an agglomeration of more or less literally borrowed expressions. But this time, Augustine alone finished the essential part: we can speak of God in the past or future as we speak of him in the present. For example, we can say, "God will understand" (John 16:13). But to understand is to know. Now God's science is none other than his essence that never changes. Hence Peter Lombard's conclusion: *Ecce hic dicit Augustinus verba cujuslibet temporis dici de Deo, sed proprie est*.[5] In this regard, returning to the text of Augustine that he had earlier attributed to Jerome, Peter Lombard explains that, whatever the tenses of the verbs we use in speaking of God—*fuit, erit, est, erat*—these verbs then connote neither past nor future, neither imperfect nor perfect, nor pluperfect, *sed essentiam sive existentiam divinitatis simpliciter insinuant. Deus ergo solus proprie dicitur essentia vel esse*.[6] Peter Lombard seems thus to underline the identity of the terms *essentia* and *existentia*, or *essentia* and *esse* even more than the text on which he is commenting does, given, furthermore, that *essentia* is identified in its turn with immutability in being.

Chapter II of this same distinction VIII deals directly with divine immutability. We can pick out other texts there that confirm the previous ones, but it is not necessary to recall them, because Peter Lombard does not use them with a view to establishing the equivalence of *immutabilitas*, *essentia*, and *esse* that we ourselves are seeking to un-

4. Ibid., I:58.

5. Ibid., I:58.

6. Ibid., I:58–59. Here we pass over the short text that Peter Lombard next takes from St. Hilary, *De Trinitate*, book 7, number 11, column 208: "*Esse non est accidens Deo, sed subsistens veritas et manens causa et naturalis generis proprietas*." But St. Thomas adopts it himself in the existential sense in *Summa Contra Gentes*, I, ch, 22 end, and *Summa Theologiae*, I, 3, 4, *Sed contra*.

derline. That equivalence is found in many other twelfth- and thirteenth-century theologians. If there can be interest in noting its presence in Peter Lombard's *Sentences*, it is first because he himself strongly emphasizes the meaning of the Augustinian texts that he quotes to this effect, but also because the place occupied by the *Sentences* in the teaching of theology in the thirteenth century assured the diffusion of this doctrine. So it is appropriate to mention Peter Lombard's work as an important link in the chain that ties Augustinian theology of *essentia* to that of the *Sentence* commentaries of the thirteenth century. As for the reader of St. Thomas Aquinas's commentary on these texts, he will note how much, by this period, its author had already gone beyond the theologies of essence to establish himself on the plane of existence. Having commented on the text of Peter Lombard that we just recalled on "the truth and property of the essence of God," the first thing that St. Thomas makes haste to take from it is that according to the word of God himself to Moses, *qui est maxime est proprium nomen Dei* and that *hoc nomen qui est dicit esse absolutum*.[7] The commentary manifestly bases itself on the text here only to go beyond it. Linking up *essentia* to *esse* from within instead of reducing *esse* to *essentia*, St. Thomas enlarges the traditional theologies of essence with an existential perspective whose necessity and depth had never before been so strongly felt.

7. Aquinas, *In I Sententiarum*, distinction 8, question 1, article 1, *contra* and ad 4, I:194, 196.

5

THE CONCEPT OF EXISTENCE IN
WILLIAM OF AUVERGNE

CONVERGING LINES OF WORK have recently made evident the influence that the religious dogma of creation exercised on the very structure of medieval metaphysics. A world created by God like the Christian world cannot but differ profoundly from a world like those of Aristotle or even Plato, which, although they are in a certain sense and in some measure produced and made, still do not derive their origin from a creation *ex nihilo* properly speaking.[1] Creation has even been presented as "something exclusively Christian."[2] However, history shows no such thing, because the notion of creation is only Christian in so far as Christianity is first Judaism. Inscribed in the first verse of the book of Genesis, it is thus the common possession of the Jews themselves and all those who regard this part of the Old Testament as a sacred book, that is to say, in the first place, Christians, but also Muslims. In fact, at the present stage of our knowledge, it seems that Muslim philosophers were the first to discern the most immediate metaphysical implications of the religious dogma of creation. At least one Jewish philosopher would soon follow them on this path; then after a certain interval Christian philosophers embarked on it in their turn. The history of the problem is

1. On this point see Gilson, *L'esprit*, ch. IV, 67–73.

2. Sertillanges, *Le Christianisme*, I:50.

therefore dominated by the history of Muslim philosophy, which the history of Christian philosophy only continues and deepens on this point.

The Muslim philosophers had the merit of understanding at the outset that the creation narrative as it is read in Genesis cannot be philosophically interpreted unless the fact of existence is made evident and conceived separately. However the creative act is conceived, it is essentially the gift of existence. By that gift, something that was not begins radically to exist. Therefore, henceforth the problem is posed of knowing what existence is and what place it holds in the metaphysical structure of an existent being. To solve the problem, the Arab philosophers started from the Aristotelian notion of being conceived as an essence. Therefore, created being immediately appeared to them as an essence that does not contain the reason of its own existence in itself, because it receives it from the creator. The existence of the created essence is thus added to this essence, and since the existence is a composite with the essence, it is distinct from it. This relation remains to be named, but it can be said that for any philosopher who poses the problem starting with essence, its name is inevitable. That which, in a given being, does not belong to its essence of itself, but happens to or is added to this essence as if from outside, is a kind of accident. So these philosophers reached two important results: first, they brought the fact itself of existence into a state of clear philosophical awareness, and by doing this they introduced it into the history of philosophy to the point that the beginning of a new era in the history of ontology can be dated from their work. Next, they bequeathed to their successors an approach to the problem that applied the primacy of the point of view of essence over existence, since created being was in the situation of being conceived as an essence to which existence happens or is added like a kind of accident.

It seems that Alfarabi (d. 959) was the first philosopher in whom this approach reaches its complete and definitive expression. One of his interpreters tells us that according to him the existence of a created thing is not part of its essence: "For God existence and essence are one, each cannot be conceived without the other because divine essence exists of itself. For other beings existence is only an accident that is added to essence. Therefore for these beings essence is separable from existence and has its own reality."[3] Nothing could better distinguish what "essentialism" implies than this approach to the problem of existence. Furthermore,

---

3. Madkour, *La place d'al Fârabi*, 78.

that is what Alfarabi's own now well-known formula implies: "existence is not a constituent character, it is only an accessory accident."[4] Thus being is already for Alfarabi what it will remain for his follower Avicenna: an essence possible in itself, which becomes necessary by its cause, when the latter confers actual existence on it as an accident.

It is well enough known that this was indeed Avicenna's position. As has been rightly noted,[5] it is true that for him existence is not an accident in the ordinary sense of the term. Historians are completely right to rectify and nuance simplistic expressions of his thought that have sometimes been given, but it is useful to add in rejoinder, first that Avicenna's own expressions are far from being clear; next and above all, that the only way that has ever been proposed to translate them into Latin inevitably entails this simplification of his thought. *Accidit* is the verb that Avicenna's medieval translators regularly used to express the relation of existence to essence in finite being;[6] and not only medieval translators, but his modern translator.[7] In his turn, Alagzel's medieval translator used the same formula,[8] and that is what Averroes later again chose in his critique of Avicenna's doctrine.[9] Finally, the modern translator of Maimonides found no other way to express the relation of existence to essence as he conceived it himself following Avicenna.[10] Thus everything encouraged medieval Christian theologians to conceive the

4. See the whole text quoted by Saliba, *Étude*, 84.

5. Goichon, *La distinction*," for example 130–47. According to Goichon, in Avicenna himself, it is certainly a matter "of a real distinction founded in the very nature of the thing," (138) which is exact, at least in so far as in Avicenna it certainly is other than a matter of a distinction of mere reason. As for knowing whether Avicenna's distinction must be conceived as real in the sense this expression will have in Giles of Rome (*ut res a re*) or even in the sense it can be given in St. Thomas Aquinas, that would be a completely different question.

6. For example, Avicenna, *Sufficientia*, I, 4, folio 16 recto 2.

7. Carame, *Avicennae Metaphysices Compendium*. See book I, tractate IV, ch. 2, article 1, 38. Note, book I, part 1, tractate III, ch. 2 (28–29) for the moment at which Avicenna poses problems of this type as a logician. This point has its importance to interpret William of Auvergne's position correctly.

8. "Et esse de quo quaeritur per *an est*, est accidens ei quod ipsa res est, scilicet ei de quo quaeritur per quid est; omne autem accidens alicui causatum est; si enim esset ens per se, non esset accidents alii" (Algazel, *Metaphysica*, part I, tractate 2, 53, 1, lines 14–17).

9. See the texts quoted by Aimé Forest, *La structure métaphysique*, 143 n. 2.

10. See Maimonides, *Guide*, I:230–31, and 231 n. 1.

relation of essence to existence in finite being as reducible to the relation of essence to accident.

As will be seen, this is the first source of the doctrine we are going to study in William of Auvergne. There is a second, no less important, although its influence is exercised on another level. At the stage of philosophical evolution at which we have arrived, it is one and the same thing to say that existence befalls essence like an accident, and to say that finite being is composed of its essence and of its existence ("really," it is sometimes added), or, what comes to the same thing, that existence and essence of finite being are distinct. Moreover, no one will dispute that the second proposition follows from the first. However, the question remains of finding out whether, speaking historically, all of these expressions appeared simultaneously. Now it certainly seems not. The formula about the accidental character of existence in relation to essence comes from Alfarabi through Avicenna. That is certain. Thus it is equally certain that in the thought of these two philosophers existence is distinguished from essence and forms a composite with it. How could what is "separable" not be distinct? However, the expression "real composition" of essence and existence will be sought in vain in their writings, and it even seems that the pure and simple expression "composition" is not found there. Therefore, it probably has anther source, and as William of Auvergne himself will indicate it us, it is simple to note it straightaway: it is Boethius.

Boethius did not teach the doctrine of the composition of essence and existence in the finite, but he taught another, that of the composition of *quod est* and *quo est*, and since *quo est* is also called *esse* in him, he can be said to have taught the composition of *quod est* and *esse*. And whatever the sense of *esse* may be in Boethius's own terminology,[11] it is correctly translated by "exist," it is almost inevitable that the distinction and composition of essence and existence should be attributed to him. We see that this is what in fact happened in William of Auvergne, where the Avicennist doctrine of the accidental character of existence will be indifferently expressed in terms taken from Avicenna himself (*essentia-accidens*) or in terms taken from Boethius (*quod est–quo est* or *esse*).

The first question that presents itself is to know whether William of Auvergne became aware of the importance of the notion of existence and of the necessity of acknowledging its place in the metaphysical structure

---

11. For the meaning of these expressions in Boethius, see the excellent passages in Roland-Gosselin, *Le De Ente et Essentia*, 142–45.

of the concrete.[12] The texts require an affirmative answer. In fact, in a remarkable passage in *De Trinitate*, William explicitly distinguishes two senses of the term *esse*. In the first sense, it properly means the essence or the substance of each being, that is to say what remains when the layer of accidents that cover it have been removed or even when abstraction is made from its specific determination. In a second sense, it means the fact, distinct from the previous one, that this being exists: "You must know," William says, making an aside to his reader as he likes to do,

> that the term *esse* has two senses . . . the first sense designates what remains after the different accidents that surround it have been removed, and that is properly what is called essence or substance (*essentia sive substantia*); and it is in this sense, with a determination of this type that the notion of each being (*esse omne*) is grasped, or with another determination, when it means merely what is signified by the formula of its definition without the name species. So this is what is called the substance of the

---

12. We quote William of Auvergne according to the following edition: *Guillielmi Alverni episcopi parisiensis, mathematici perfectissimi, eximii philosophi, ac theologi praestantisssimi, Opera Omnia*, 2 vols. in folio, Orléans: F. Hotot, sold at Amiens by Michel du-Neuf-Germain, 1674. Other copies were put on sale by Jean Lacaille, rue Saint-Jacques, *ad insigne fontis*, the same year. The editor was B. Le Féron, Doctor and member of the Sorbonne, canon of the cathedral of Chartres. The text of the *Magisterium Divinale* printed in these two volumes along with other authentic or apocryphal works is from a manuscript belonging to the cathedral of Chartres, about which Le Féron pronounces himself as follows: "Restat ut moneamus Lectorem in iis edendis quatuor tractatibus usos nos fuisse unico codice Carnotensi paulo post annum 1300 descripto, mendis multis, perpetuisque abbreviationibus referto. Quare vix fieri potuit ut editio haec nostra erratis prorsus omnibus careat, praecipue cum exscrita Carnoti ex eodem codice exemplaria Aureliam mittenda fuerint, ut ibidem praelo mandarentur. Ignosce igitur candide Lector, si uno aut altero loco interturbatum sensum reperias. Quaecumque occurrent sive codicis, sive preli vitio errata, non impedient quominus mentem Authoris aliquatenus assequi possis." (II:Preface). Indeed, the text is sometimes obscure or even incomprehensible, but it is generally intelligible. Unfortunately, it is to be feared that Le Féron's copy can no longer be checked against the original, manuscript 475 that contained *De Trinitate* and *De Universo*, since it probably disappeared in the fire in the library of this city in the course of World War II. However, thanks to the outline that Le Féron provided (II:Preface) we know the contents of the three volumes, and the order of the works by William that they contained. Furthermore, comparison of Le Féron's text with that of manuscripts 3476 and 3477 of the Bibliothèque Mazarine confirms that they are very close to each other. The difficulties and *loci desperati* are observably the same. Furthermore, it can be confirmed that the *etc.* found in Le Féron's edition do not indicate any abbreviation of the text by the editor, but are already found in the manuscript itself. In the absence of a highly desirable re-edition of *Magisterium Divinale*, we can already work on the basis of a text that it is possible to check.

thing and its being (*esse*) and its quiddity. And it is the being that
the definition signifies and explains and it is just that which is
called the thing's essence. The second sense of *esse* is what is expressed when we say of anything that it exists, and what is added
to the notion of this thing. Whatever the thing we imagine may
be, a man, a donkey, or something else, to exist (*esse*) is never
included in its notion or conceived as being part of it. That alone
is excepted whose existing is said as something essential, because
his essence can only be conceived as the existing itself, since it
and his existing are one single thing in every way.[13]

For the moment let us set aside the phrase from this conceptually
rich passage that presents a concept of God as the being whose essence
is his very existing, but let us retain the fundamental distinction that
precedes it, between *esse essentia* or *esse substantia*, and, so to speak, *esse
is*. What is obscure and perhaps even a little confused in the definition of
the first of these two types of essences comes from the fact that William
wanted to define at the same time the being of essence determined by its
specific notion alone, without any accident, and being in general, that is
to say essence or substance in general, without any specific determination. In other words, taken in this first sense, *esse* can mean either such
and such an essence (man or donkey for example), or being in general,
taken purely and simple. Whatever we make of the distinction within
this first meaning, its contrast with the second meaning is plain, because
it is clear that William certainly thought of existence *qua* distinct from
essence, when he contrasts with *esse essentia* that about which we think
when we say about any thing that it is.

We must make the meaning of the position that William holds on
this point as precise as possible. Moreover, the limit to that precision is
soon reached, and there are two reasons for that. First, William works as

13. "Oportet autem te scire, quia esse duas habet intentiones, et una earum est re-
siduum a circumvestione et varietate accidentium, et hoc est proprie quod nominatur
essentia, sive substantia, et accipitur in intentione hac, cum hujusmodi determinatione,
intentio quae est esse omne, vel alia, et signficat illud solum quod diffinitiva oratione
significatur sine nomine speciei. Hoc igitur est quod dicitur substantia rei, et ejus esse,
et ejus quidditas; et hoc est esse, quod diffinitio significat, et explicat, et hoc ipsum
dicitur rei essentia. Secunda autem intentio hujus quod est esse, est illud quod dicitur
per hoc verbum, est, de unoquoque, et est praeter uniuscujusque rationem. In nullius
autem ratione accipitur esse, quidquid imaginati fuerimus, sive hominem, sive asinum,
sive aliud, ut in ratione ejus esse intelligamus; eo solo excepto de quo esse essentialiter
dicitur: ejus namque essentia nisi per ipsum esse intelligi non potest, cum ipsa et ejus
esse omnimodo sint una res" (*De Trinitate*, ch. 11, II:2).

a pioneer here. Thus, he employs concepts that have not been tried out by his Latin predecessors, and since he expresses them in terms originally constructed for other concepts, we ought not be surprised by occasional vacillations in his terminology. Besides, we cannot frequent his works for long without becoming convinced that he thought in the measure in which he wrote, and, so to speak, as his pen flowed. Moreover, this is one of the reasons that make reading him so pleasant, because his most exact works retain a vivaciousness, spontaneity, and freshness that contrast agreeably with the usual dryness of works of this types. In compensation, impulsive declarations must be expected, brought forth under the pressure of the moment, made once and for all without any further explanation following to elucidate them. So we cannot expect a higher certainty in interpretation than what the nature of the text itself allows, but we should try at least not to stay below it.

However, that is what will happen if we are willing to define William of Auvergne's position as Stephan Schindele does. "On what is essential," that historian said, "he certainly remains in the terrain covered by Boethius and Augustine, although he is not completely closed to new circles of ideas."[14] That is to say too little, and it would perhaps be more correct to say that William is resolutely open to the new philosophical concept of existing put into circulation by Alfarabi, Avicenna, and Algazel, but that he has not thereby abandoned the terrain of Boethius and Augustine. The Platonic order of essence subsists, just as Augustine and Boethius had defined it, but it is now placed in subordination to that of existence, whose peculiar specificity William has clearly discerned.

It is possible to go further than Schindele and still not go as far as we should. Indeed it is tempting to say that William of Auvergne surpassed the level of Augustine and of Boethius to attain that of Avicenna. Nothing is wrong in that proposition, but it would still not express the whole truth. It is undeniable that Avicenna's influence affected William's thought, and it can even be called decisive. We will encounter texts where the Bishop of Paris speaks of existing as an accident of essence, but they are the ones where he only follows the authority of his guide. At least once, in one of those departures customary in him, William unveiled his true thought by saying that existing is much more than a simple accident. In fact, in his eyes it is the very heart of the real, that which

14. "Der Hauptsache nach steht er freilich noch auf dem Boden von Boëthius und Augustinus, doch verschliesst er sich auch neuen Ideenkreisen durchaus nicht" (Schindele, *Beiträge*," 9).

each thing has first, as if by virtue of a first participation, from the supreme Existing, to which each thing owes existing in its turn:

> It is indubitable that all things exist, either by participation in the first existing, as we have said, or by participation in some thing that flows from it, like a light spread over everything. Here is an indication. Existing is so loved and desired that each thing seems to not care about itself but to run risks in order to exist. For example, the whole loves its parts, but it wraps in a particularly strong love those of its parts where its existence seems to reside more. Thus the hand exposes itself to dangers to protect the head, but if the whole believed that its existing resided in another part, it would certainly also expose the head and even everything it is in order to protect that part. Indeed it risks all its resources in order to conserve its existence or to not lose that part. Thus by comparison to all that exists, existing itself seems as something else (*aliud*) and as better (*melius*) than everything that exists. Therefore existing in itself would not be an accident but it is necessarily above any substance and any accident, since each thing accedes to undergo harm in its essence in order to not lose existing. In fact it is impossible that the totality of beings should be universally mistaken in what is by their nature or of their nature. Thus by their love, by their desire, and by their preference, the universe proclaims that existing is what is best. Since the totality of beings makes everything take second place, one must be incredulous or deaf to not hear its clamor. Therefore since the First is essentially everywhere, it follows indubitably that, since being is everywhere, its existing is necessarily also thus.[15]

15. "Sive autem ita sit sive aliter, dubitari tamen non potest omnia esse, vel participatione primi Esse qualiter diximus, vel participatione alicujus quod ex illo fluit, sicut lumen sparsum super omne. Indicium autem hujusmodi est, quoniam adeo amant et appetunt esse, quod unaquaeque res seipsam negligere videtur et exponere propter ipsum esse: quemadmodum omne totum partes suas, et partes illas fortiori amore complectitur, in quibus videtur magis consistere esse ipsius, ut caput manus periculis objecta tuetur; sed si in alia parte crederet esset [sic, for esse] suum, profecto et caput pro ea exponeret et etiam omne quod est: totam enim possibilitatem suam exponet ut esse conservet, aut ne amittat ipsa [sic, for ipsum]. Gratia igitur et electione omnium quae sunt, et aliud, et melius omnibus his quae sunt ostenditur ipsum esse: non potest igitur accidere esse secundum se, sed necessario omni substantia et accidente melius est, pro cujus amissione unumquodque damnum suae essentiae negligit: universitatem namque in eis quae per naturam sive natura ejus sunt universaliter errare impossibile est. Amore igitur suo, et desiderio, et electione sua clamat universitas hoc esse optimum; cum omnia ipsa universitas postponat, incredibilis aut surdus est, qui clamorem universitatis non audit: quoniam autem et ubique sit essentialiter, ex his etiam non est dubium, cum ubique sit ens, et ipsum illius Esse necesse sit esse" (*De Trinitate*, ch. VII, II:9).

Manifestly, William of Auvergne, in an intuition that to us appears new among the Latins for that time, here discovers a universe composed of beings whose most intimate reality is their very act of existing. Now as we have just seen, to begin with, these beings are acts of existing only because their first cause, as its proper name indicates, is act of existing. It was extremely important to establish this metaphysical connection. Indeed by it the created universe comes to be defined in its most intimate nature by that of its Cause, and bound to it by the closest bond. As is God, such is the universe. Since God is henceforth conceived as *Esse* and since what he creates is a universe of acts of *esse*, God also appears to us as intimately present to the *esse* of everything that exists. Here we are too close to some of the most basic views of Thomism to fail to quote the very words that William uses to express it. The traditional doctrine of the presence of God in the essence of everything that is is deepened here in the most remarkable way, in a doctrine no longer of the presence of Essence to essences but of *Esse* to *esses*:

> Creator vero unicuique creatorum proximus est ac praesentissimus, immo etiam intimus, et hoc apparere tibi potest per abstractionem sive spolationem conditionum omnium atque formarum accidentalium et substantialium. Cum enim ab unoquoque creatorum omnia haec abstraxeris, ultimum omnium invenietur esse, vel entitas, et propter hoc Dator ipsius, Verbi gratia, cum Socratem spoliaveris forma sua singulari, qua est Socrates, et a specifica, qua est homo, et a generalibus quibus est animal, corpus, substantia, adhuc remanebit ens, quapropter remanebit et esse suum, et entitas, quasi intimum indumentum ipsius, et velut interula, qua primo induit ipsum creator, et cum ipsum esse et entitatem ei detraxeris, erunt ei detractae omnes causae essendi et adminicula, excepto creatore. Quare manifestum est quod omnium adminiculorum et adjumentorum essendi, primum est creator et intimum. Haec autem omnia idcirco scripsi tibi hic, ut erigant te quoquomodo ad imaginandum sublimitatem creatoris cujus completa cognitio beatitudo est et gloria virtutis intellectivae nostrae.[16]

We cannot read a text like this without immediately remembering the rightly famous expressions of St. Thomas in *Summa Theologiae* I, 8, 1:

> Cum autem Deus sit ipsum esse per suam essentiam, oportet quod esse creatum sit proprius effectus . . . Quamdiu igitur res habet esse, tamdiu oportet, quod Deus adsit ei secundum modum, quo

16. *De Universo*, Iª IIᵃᵉ, ch. 30, II:625.

> esse habet. Esse autem est illud quod est magis intimum cuilibet, et quod profundius omnibus inest, cui sit formale respectu omnium quae in re sunt . . . Unde oportet, quod Deus sit in omnibus rebus et intime.

The ancestry of these ideas is obvious, and the formulas themselves are not dissimilar. Assuredly, as always, St. Thomas's text carries the Thomist stamp. That *cum sit formale respectu omnium quae in re sunt* could never have come to William's mind, still enmeshed in the Avicennist solution of *esse* as accident. The whole properly Thomist doctrine of *esse* as the highest act of being and of the form itself was yet to be born, but it must be added that the raw metaphysical intuition whose elaboration it will be, is already there, not only recognizable but expressed in terms such that when we encounter it, it cannot be mistaken. Would we perceive its originality and new depth today if what we otherwise know through Thomism did not draw our attention to it so powerfully? Perhaps, but it is at least doubtful. No doubt we would see nothing more there than what William himself saw, a term of speculative thought rather than the origin of a theology and an ontology.[17] However that may be, here William is certainly a precursor of St. Thomas, and if we do not dare to affirm that he is even a source, we wold be rash to deny it.

The last remark goes beyond the limits of our problem, but the previous ones involve it directly. Indeed, we see William bring out the notion of *esse* taken in its existential sense; first, we see him detach it

17. However, William did not lack a presentiment of such developments. Notably, he perceived the connection that unites ontology to etiology and links the efficacy of all secondary causes to the presence of divine *Esse* in them: "Omnis autem substantia est amplectens, si dici fas est, essentiam creatoris intra se, ac si sentiat praesentiam creatoris sustintentem se, ne ruat in non esse, et retinentem in se, ne refluet et vanescat in nihilum, et implentem se non solum ipso esse, quo ipsa est, sed etiam viribus seu virtutibus, et aliis bonis spiritualibius, quibus omnis substantia a creatore impleta est usque ad redundantiam et refluentiam, nec aliud intendo esse vires et virtutes naturales, quae principia sunt operationum, quam fontes quasdam redundantes, velut influentias quasdam, operationes suas, Hujus exemplum evidentissimum in sole, etc . . ." (*De Universo*, I^ia II^ae, ch 68, 1:920). In the passage this internal sense will certainly be remarked of God's presence permanently saving his creature from nothingness, which, *perhaps* obscurely, is linked in William's own thought to that preponderant love of existence that he noted in human nature. A spirituality might emerge from these principles. There are beautiful texts here, which are perhaps inevitably overstated when we collect them, and are still more overstated by organizing them in relation to each other more than William himself does. In their natural state they are tiny islands separated by an ocean of texts. *Apparent rari nantes . . .*

from the notions of substance to which it is still tied in Aristotle and of accident to which it had been tied in Avicenna; finally, we see him affirm the primacy of existing over accident and even over substance. Here we witness the appearance of a metaphysical intuition of the highest importance, which will receive its technical development in the thought of St. Thomas Aquinas. Nothing entitles us to think that William foresaw this development. He does not speak of *esse* as the supreme act of the substance and of the form itself and, to our knowledge at least, he will never speak of it. In this text he does not even pose the henceforth inevitable problem of the relation of *esse* to *essentia* in the created substance, although he posed it elsewhere. Here the issue is still only the raw intuition of the transcendence of existing over the rest of what is real, but it is expressed with such force that it already seems able to make the schemes of earlier metaphysics explode, and consequently, to call forth another. Let us add that the argument on which William supports his thesis, more psychological and empirical than metaphysical, is very original in its style. Unfortunately, this vein will not be worked after him again, at least until the investigations of modern existentialism. The fact is that William's successors, and above all St. Thomas, will be essentially metaphysicians, and in a question of this sort, the last word indeed goes to metaphysics. It remains no less true that if the metaphysical primacy of existing is real, it ought to express itself in facts, notably in psychological experience, in an empirically observable fashion. The violent love of the existent for existing is one of these facts; it may be regretted that William contented himself with noting it, that he did not seek out others, but this particular observation is very much in his personal style, a style that the Middle Ages were to neglect a bit too much after him.

If he did not directly speculate about the notion of existence he had just affirmed with such vigor, our philosophical theologian at least studied it in two cases where he could not help encountering it, those of the divine being and of the created substance.

To take the problem with complete rigor, it does not seem that the notion of existing is directly involved in the structure itself of the proofs of the existence of God, but the proofs certainly lead up to it. They have already been studied,[18] and it is not necessary to our project to recall them in detail, but it would be useful to point out how unusual William's situation is. There is a strange mismatch between the end he pursues and

18. Masnovo, *Da Guglielmo d'Auvergne*, see especially ch. III, 61–89.

the means of which he disposes to attain it. In his very Preface he adverts that his work is completely directed to philosophers, because they are the ones he desires to convince, or at least to persuade of the truth of Christian wisdom. To obtain that result, he must only recur to methods of proof or persuasion that philosophy itself possesses. Now for him these means are reduced to those of Logic. Nothing is clearer than his declarations on this point: "Huic praedae capiendae seu venandae probationum parat venabula, texit retiacula. Huic regno expugnando fabricat et acuit syllogismorum tela."[19] Thus William of Auvergne forewarns us here that he will approach all problems as a logician, as if no proper order of metaphysical argumentation existed that is distinguished from that of logic properly speaking, although presupposing it. Now we have just seen that he has firmly grasped and clearly, although summarily, detached the metaphysical plane of existence from others. Therefore one might expect to see him grapple with this thorny problem: to attain divine existing, that is to say, existing supremely and *par excellance*, with the aid of the resources of logic alone. It is not difficult to foresee that William will not succeed. The technique at his disposal was not adapted to such a new metaphysical intuition that he required it to serve.

From that we at least understand what is so peculiar about the very manner in which William posed the problem of the existence of God. Parting from a pair of contrary concepts, he undertakes to define one in contrast to the other, and, what has more scope but is also riskier, even to establish that positing the object of one implies positing the object of the other. The immediate goal envisaged by William is to establish that the term *ens* is said either in the sense of being through essence or in the sense of being through participation. We already know what *ens* means: a being, that is to say, that which, by reason of the verb, is said to be. The task is uncomfortable because the terms *ens* and *esse* have multiple meanings, as we have seen, and besides, there is no definition.

To escape from this difficulty, we will first argue from a notion that is easier to grasp, that of good (*bonum*). Indeed, it seems that the senses of *ens* and of *esse* are analogous to what is attributed to *bonum*. Like *ens*, *bonum* is said of what is such substantially or of what is such by reason of participation. This, moreover, would still be the case of the term that designates the color white. "White" can signify what is white substantially, therefore, what is white *essentialiter*, because its essence is whiteness; but,

---

19. *De Trinitate*, Prologus, II:1.

as in the phrase "a white wall," it can also signify what has whiteness or participates in it, without being it. In the same way in the case of being, first there is that whose very essence is *esse*, and of which we predicate essence when we say that it *is*. In such a case, the being itself and its *esse*, what we assign when we say that it *is*, are one and the same thing in every regard. Next there is that which is attributed by way of participation, because it has it, but which is in no way identical to the essence of the very substance of the being.[20]

This threshold distinction opens not only the proof of the existence of God, but it characterizes its spirit. It is immediately evident that William is inspired here by Boethius, whom, furthermore, he immediately names. Indeed, the same examples of "good" and of "white" are found in *De Hebdomadibus*, just as the same terminology to contrast the goods *participatione* with the goods that are so *substantia*.[21] It is not surprising therefore to see him refer to this authority immediately afterwards. *De hoc ergo legis in libro De Hebdomadibus Boetii.* What we read is that every simple being is its being (*omnes esse simplex est esse suum*), and that what it has and what it is make only one (*et id quod est unum habet*); otherwise, the simple itself would be divisible into participant and participated, the being itself being then other than *esse*. The participant and the participated would then form a sort of composite of the two, so that the being itself would not be simple in the highest degree. Furthermore, we have the reason for that. Everything that is said of whatever something may be is essential or accidental to it. In other words, it is said of it as being whether its essence or of its essence; or, on the contrary, as other than its essence, which is called "accidental," and which is said of all that which is possessed by participation. Being is then said of a certain subject by reason of substance, of a certain other by reason of participation, "and as it cannot be said of every subject by reason of participation, it is necessary that it be said of some subject according to essence."[22]

20. "Ad hunc modum et ens cujus essentia est ei esse, et cujus essentiam praedicamus cum dicimus est: ita ut ipsum et ejus esse quod assignamus, cum dicimus est, sint res una per omnem modum. Aliud vero dicitur participatione in habendo, scilicet quod nullo modo est idem cum essentia ipsius substantiae entis" (*De Trinitate*, ch. 1, II:1).

21. Boethius, *De Hebdomadibus*, columns 1311–12, notably 1312 A.

22. "De hoc ergo legis in libro De Hebdomadibus Boetii, quoniam omne esse simplex est esse suum, et id quod est unum habet. Alioquin simplex igitur ipsum partibile esset in participans et participatum, cum aliud esset ens ipsum aliud ejus esse. Essent

Some observations must be made about the very terminology of this passage. Influenced by the two sources from which it derives, it lacks unity, and what is worse, it tries to express a particular doctrine, that of William of Auvergne himself, in the language of two thinkers whose doctrines differ both from his and from each other's.

In fact, the text by its own nature falls into two parts: the explanation of a division, and the reason that justifies it. The transitional formula that William uses does not say that the reason in question comes from the same author as the distinction itself: *Hanc etiam divisionem bene leges in eodem libro* [Boetii], *ratio autem quae cogit ita esse haec est*. The division, William himself tells us, comes from Boethius, and it is naturally expressed in Boethius's language. That fact is very important. Indeed it explains the language William employs for a start, in the very positing of the problem over which he lingers. Boethius had divided goods into *bona participatione* and *bona substantia*. In *bona participatione* that which is (*id quod est*) is not the good itself, which is the *esse* or *quo est*, in this case, of the being that is good by participation. In the *bona substantia* (or *substantialia bona*), by contrast, *esse* itself is what is the *bonum*. In other words, since the *esse* is the *quod est*, the *id quod est* here just becomes one with the *quo est* or *esse*. Thus we obtain two intimately connected divisions: first, that of the *simplex* and the *compositum*, and next, second, that of the *ens substantia* and the *ens participatione*; the first where the *id quod est* becomes only one with *esse*, the second where *id quod est* is one thing, the *esse* another thing.[23] That said, it becomes

---

igitur participans et participatum quasi conjunctum ex illis duobus, hoc est, ipsum ens non esset simplex in ultimo. Hanc etiam divisionem bene leges in eodem libro, ratio autem quae cogit ita esse haec est: omne enim quod de quocumque dicitur, aut essentiale eidem est, aut accidentale: hoc est aut essentia, aut de essentia, quae [sic, for *quod?*] est pars essentiae aut praeter essentiam, et hoc est quod vocamus accidentale, quodque secundum participationem haberi et dici dicimus. Ens igitur de unoquoque aut substantia aut participatione dicitur. Dicitur autem de quodam substantialiter, de quodam participatione dicitur: et quoniam non potest dici de unoquoque secundum participationem, necesse est ut de aliquo dicatur secundum essentiam" (William of Auvergne, *De Trinitate*, column 1, 1–2).

23. "Omne simplex, esse suum et id quod est unum habet. Omni composito aliud est esse, aliud ipsum est" (Boethius, *De Hebdomadibus*, column 1311 C). In the light of this division, Boethius next wonders "quemadmodum bona sint," that is to say, "utrumne partipatione, an substantia" (1312 A), and answers regarding substantial goods: "Non igitur participatione sunt bona, sed substantia: quorum vero substantia bona est, id quod sunt bona sunt; id autem quod sunt, habent ex eo quod est esse. Esse igitur ipsorum bonum est" (ibid.).

evident that the two members of the division are not exactly comparable, because there is a plurality of goods by participation, but there can only be one single good by substance, the *Bonum* itself, in which all the other goods participate in so far as they are good. In fact, if everything these other beings are were identical to the Good, they would be the Good itself, that is to say, no longer things, but the principle of things. Now, here, there is only one single and unique thing: *Unum enim solumque est hujusmodi, quod tantum bonum, aliudque nihil sit.* In short, goods are not and could not be simples. Even more, they could not be at all unless they were willed by Him who is none other than the Good. Thus, that is why they are and are goods: *Idcirco quoniam esse eorum a boni voluntate defluxit, bona esse dicuntur.*[24]

What could William find in such a text? Not a proof of the existence of God, because Boethius himself there says that is taken for granted,[25] but a division of the concept of good such that it requires that all beings be posited as so many participated goods, whose existence implies that of a single substantial good, who is precisely God. In taking over Boethius's *divisio*, William thus personally did two things: transport what Boethius had said on the level of the good to the level of being and interpret what in Boethius was only an explanation of the *defluxus* of the being of goods from the will of the Good as a proof of the existence of the Being by essence. Now we do not lack certain indications about the way in which this transformation occurred in his mind. First, we must keep in mind that Boethius's language invites this in *De Hebdomadibus*, that is to say, in the opusculum *Quomodo substantiae in eo quod sint bonae sint, cum non sint substantialia bona* bequeathed to the Latin Middle Ages a formidable ambiguity by identifying the terms *esse* and *quod est*. As long as the problem of existence had not been identified, which is still the situation in Boethius himself, there was no ambiguity; *esse* then meant nothing but the formal cause, that in virtue of which "that which is" is found "to be that which it is." The Good, for example, is then the *esse* of that which is good, just in so far as it is good; similarly Whiteness (*albedo*) is the *esse* of white things, because it is by Whiteness that they are that. Only, from the moment when the meaning of the notion of existence

---

24. Boethius, *De Hebdomadibus*, column 1313A.

25. "Amoveamus igitur primi boni praesentiam paulisper ex animo, quod esse quidem constat, idque ex omnium doctorum indoctorumque sententia, barbararum quod gentium religionibus cognosci potest" (Boethius, *De Hebdomadibus*, column 1312 C).

was grasped as well as the scope of the problems that are connected to it, ambiguity is produced between *esse* in the sense of *quo est* and *esse* in the sense of *is*. Without changing a word, Boethius's old formula can now be read in a completely new sense. Indeed, *diversum est esse, et id quod est*[26] can mean first, in the old sense, that which is distinct from its form; next in a new sense, that which is distinct from its existence. That is not all, because the two senses can be reflected in one another, and thus, in the thirteenth century, we will find many authors who will speak Boethius's language of *quo est* to express their peculiar conception of existing.

When we pass from William's *divisio* to the *ratio* that justifies it, we detect a second cause that might have favored this ambiguity. There in fact, we read the observation: *omne enim quod de quocumque dicitur, aut essentiale eidem est, aut accidentale.* One of Boethius's formulae may in truth still have exerted its influence here, because he categorizes as an accident the fact "of being something" in the mode of simple participation in contrast to "being something" in that which one is, which is substance.[27] This is only an isolated text, but when we recognize with what care each word of *De Hebdomadibus* was weighed and scrutinized in the Middle Ages, especially by William of Auvergne, we must note it. We must do so all the more because it may have established the link in the mind of its medieval readers between the teaching of Boethius himself and that of Avicenna regarding the accidentality of existence in the finite and participated being. Here in fact William changes language, because just as his *divisio* bespoke that of Boethius, the *ratio* he proposes bespeaks that of Avicenna. It is the language of the contrast *essentia–accidens*, founded on the principle that *quod est praeter essentiam, hoc est quod vocamus accidentale.* How will we not recognize here the same reason that had led Avicenna to classify existence in the order of accident? Now, precisely, we have just seen William transform Boethius's whole argumentation about good into a parallel argumentation about existence. Thus everything summons us to see here, at least probably, what we will observe in another case without any possible doubt, a first

---

26. Boethius, *De Hebdomadibus*, column 1311 B.

27. "Id quod est, habere aliquid praeterquam quod ipsum est, potest; ipsum vero esse, nihil aliud praeter se habet admixtum. Diversum est, tantum esse aliquid, et esse aliquid in eo quod est: illic enim accidens hic substantia significatur" (Boethius, *De Hebdomadibus*, column 1311 C). According to Boethius himself, the source of the doctrine is Aristotelian: *In Categorias Aristotelis*, liber I, column 186 AB.

convergence of Boethius and Avicenna, where, moreover, Avicenna is the river and Boethius the tributary.

That allows us to take a different approach to the problem of knowing to what intellectual family we should link William of Auvergne in this matter. Several historians judge that he is in the line of St. Anselm and that his proof of the existence of God, completely foreign to the spirit of the proofs developed in Aristotle's *Physics* and *Metaphysics*, are, on the contrary, related to the *Proslogion*'s so-called ontological argument.[28] That has recently been disputed, if not in what concerns the *Monologium*, at least as it has to do with the *Proslogion*,[29] and, it seems to us, rightly so. In what we have just read from William, nothing suggests the presence of St. Anselm. He does not mention his name. He employs none of his formulas. Furthermore, it would have been impossible for him to utilize them for the simple reason that his treatise follows the inverse path to that of the *Proslogion*. We have already noted it: William avoids mentioning God, whose concept he seeks to construct rationally, starting from that of being, proceeding by gradual determinations. Thus he cannot begin from any concept of God whatsoever, something that is of the very essence of Anselm's position in the *Proslogion*, which in addition he explicitly accepts from faith before arguing rationally upon it: *Et quidem credimus te esse aliquid, quo nihil majus cogitari possit.*[30] Thus William did not start from Anselm's definition of God. He even starts from something other than a definition of God, and even if we wanted to maintain that in fact he applied it at other points, on this one, he did not follow Anselm's fundamental method of *credo ut intelligam* at all. Consequently, we must conclude that William of Auvergne is not an Anselmian in what regards the proof of God's existence.

However, let us recognize that the matter is not exhausted. We still must take account of the reasons why it was believed that William's position approximated that of St. Anselm. The chief reason is obviously what

---

28. Baumgartner writes: "eine Beweisführung, die ganz an das ontologische Argument eines Anselm von Canterbury anklingt" (*Die Erkenntnislehre*, 100). Here is the reason for this judgment: "Seine Argumentation bewegt sich wie die des Anselms von Canterbury in reinen Begriffen. Während aber der letztere im *Monologium* von dem Begriff des höchsten gutes ausgeht, im *Proslogium* von dem des denkbar höchsten Seienden, stützt sich Wilhelm auf die verschiedenen Aussageweisen des Seins" (*Die Erkenntnislehre*, 98). Cf. in the same sense, Schindele, *Beiträge*, 45–46.

29. Masnovo, *Da Guglielmo d'Auvergne*, I:71–78.

30. Anselm, *Proslogion*, ch. II, column 227 C.

Matthias Baumgartner alleged: like St. Anselm's proof, William's is not at all physical after the fashion of Aristotle's proofs. It moves in the order of pure concepts. "His method of argumentation, like that of St. Anselm of Canterbury, proceeded by pure concepts." That has also been denied,[31] but it is not certain that Baumgartner was indeed wrong on this point. Let us at least say that some distinctions are necessary, and the surest way to proceed is to first analyze the texts where William develops his proof of the existence of God.

For him, let us recall, the issue is to establish that there is someone whose "being" is predicated as essence: *necesse est ut de aliquo dicatur secundum essentiam*. The heart of the argument is the idea that, if "being" is said of everything on the grounds of participation, that term would have no sense (*nullus subesset intellectus eidem*), and this is because it would be impossible to ever attain its object (*eo quod nunquam fineretur*). Obscure in itself, this last expression is clarified in the light of the development that follows. To fasten onto the meaning of *ens* is to find an object to which this term can be applied in its plenitude without any qualification. If there is nothing of which it can be said that it is an *ens* purely and simply, this term taken in itself has no sense. To show it, we return to the example of the good. If *bonum* were only said in the mode of participation, this term would always designate something that is good as participating in the Good, but never a Good in which all that is good participates. There would thus be no object corresponding to the term *bonum*, which comes back to saying that this term would have no sense: *si nunquam diceretur bonum, nisi secundum particpationem, nulla esset intentio hujus nominis bonum*.

To establish this point, William first proceeds to a dialectical experiment bearing on two terms. Let us start from object A, good by participation in another good object, which we will call B. If there are only participated goods, A will be good as participating in B, which in turn will be good as participating in A. It is the same as saying that A is good because it possesses what A possesses, or that it is good in virtue of its participation in what participates in it. The goodness of A itself will be the cause of its cause. Indeed, this cause is B, which is only cause of A because A itself is the cause of B. "Therefore, the same is cause of its cause, and it will naturally give to what gives to it before having that very

---

31. Masnovo, *Da Guglielmo d'Auvergne*, I:82–85.

thing to give; it will in fact give it before receiving it," which is absurd and contradictory.

For the moment let us work in the same way, but with more than two terms. A is good because it has B. B is good because it has C, and so on. What does *bonum* mean then? The term designates then an infinite involution of participateds and participants (*est igitur complicata et involuta infinita infinitas partipatorum et participantium in intentione hujus nominis bonum*). In other words, what the term *bonum* signifies is nothing but *bonum* itself repeated an infinite number of times. Now this infinity does not stop. It has no term at which the intellect can pause. Whatever term of the series we may consider, it will never signify *bonum* purely and simply, but a *habens bonum*, which itself will only be such in virtue of its participation in another, which will never be the Good. That is why we say that in such a case the term Good will be devoid of sense, because there will not be any object to which this term corresponds. For there to be a definite sense, it is necessary to posit an object that does not have the good, but is it. "It is thus manifest that *bonum* is said of something by reason of essence, and it is shown in the same way, that *ens* can not be said of everything by reason of participation. It is thus necessary that it should be said of something by reason of essence, for there to be a definite signification and sense (*ut finiatur intentio et intellectus ejus*)."[32]

Whether or not it is a matter of "pure concepts," in any case it is clear that William follows a purely dialectical method. Certainly, the concepts he uses are related to the real,[33] but he relies upon their intrinsic properties

32. William of Auvergne, *De Trinitate*, ch. I, II:2. In this whole development, William utilizes the term *intellectus* without defining it. No doubt, he is employing it in a well-known sense that he holds to be obvious. In fact, he seems to follow Boethius's usage here: "Tria sunt ex quibus omnis collocutio disputatioque perficitur: res, intellectus, voces. Res sunt quas animi ratione percipimus intellectuque discernimus. Intellectus vero quibus res ipsas addiscimus. Voces quibus id quod intellectu capimus, significamus." The *intellectus* is thus the resemblance of the thing formed by the spirit within itself and expressed by the word: "Intellectus vero animae quaedam passio est. Nisi enim quamdam similitudinem rei quam quis intelligit in animae ratione patiatur, nullus est intellectus. Cum enim video orbem vel quadratum, figuram ejus mente concipio, et ejus mihi similitudo in animae ratione formatur, patiturque anima rei intellectae similitudinem, unde fit ut intellectus, et similitudo sit rei, et animae passio" (Boethius, *In Librum De Intepretatione*, column 297 B, cf. column 298 A).

33. Masnovo (*Da Guglielmo d'Auvergne*, I:82) points out that, by contrast with the process of arguing followed by St. Anselm in the *Proslogion*, William of Auvergne takes a "fact" as the point of departure, "this given thing, *aliquid*, being." Undoubtedly being is a fact in a certain sense, but not in the same sense nor in the same degree as Socrates

alone to establish his thesis. For him the question is to know whether the terms *bonum* and *ens* would have a conceivable sense if neither the Good nor Being in itself existed. We have just seen that his reply is negative, but it is grounded on the principle that a concept's intrinsic intelligibility postulates the existence of its objects. In other words, we have the right to affirm an existence if it is required in order that the concept of its object may have an intelligible and definite sense. This is to deduce being from the concept, and in this sense it can be understood that several historians should have situated William of Auvergne in the Anselmian family. The proof of the existence of God constructed by William is doubtless not at all that of the *Proslogion*, and so we have said, but St. Anselm's ontologism, in the Kantian sense of the word is not tied to the form of the argument called ontological since Kant. Under another form, a demonstration like that of William, which posits being as the condition of the conceivability of a concept, is no less "ontological" than that of the *Proslogion*. Not only is it grounded on the internal requirements needed for the concept of "being" to be possible, but it argues in name of what the *modi dicendi* it uses imply. We should not forget that the tools of which this metaphysics disposes are those of logicians. Thus, it suffices for him to establish that the *modus dicendi secundum participationem* implies the *modus dicendi secundum essentiam* to establish that the existence of the participated being implies that of Being. The order of what is *per accidens* demands that

---

or Callias. Furthermore, this observation does not suffice to resolve the problem, because, if it is true that being can be taken as a fact, it is also true that it can be taken as a concept. If William considered it in so far as it is a fact, it would be right to take his method to be an "a priori procedure" (ibid.), but we believe we observe precisely that he argues from being as a notion. Moreover, he says the equivalent in a text that we reproduce below (23 n. 4 [sic]). What he proposed to reach is the existence of the First Thing, the notion of which he identifies with that of pure being. To reach it in itself, we must take the way of intellect, which alone attains being. Assuredly, William will say "per viam sensus cognoscitur utcumque ex testimonio sensibilium," but we see that this secondary method (which leads rather to *Deus et Dominus* than to *Ens*) is imperfect. The true method, which we see him apply right here, rests upon the notion of *ens*, which is the first notion for him. That is why we see him conclude in his own words that if the notion of God is not innate (since as *Deus et Dominus*, it is only known from what is sensible), it is so in as much as God is Being: "Ergo ipsum per se impressum est intellectui nostro inquantum ens, inquantum autem Deus et Dominus, non est ex primis apprehensionibus . . ." Now let us not forget that *ens* and not *Deus* is the proper name of the *First Thing*. There could be no further *a posteriori* aspect of this proof than what is in the notion of being, but, above all, it is not on being as *aliquid* given that the proof rests. It rests completely on being as the first notion, to such a degree that it comes to present the notion of the First Thing as naturally imprinted in our intellect.

of what is *per se*, as the order of *dicendi secundum quid* demands that of *dicendi simpliciter*.[34] Now, let us note well that William does not doubt for an instant that the requirements of thought also hold for reality. The necessary conditions of our concepts exist necessarily. In this sense, it seems indisputable to hold, if not that William argues from pure concepts as if they were detached from any link the sense experience, at least that his whole argument rests directly on the content and relations of certain concepts. If I *state* something *per accidens*, my statement implies another, which is the same statement about the *per se* mode; and, since the real corresponds to the logical, if what I state *per accidens* exists, the corresponding *per se* necessarily exists also.

This logicism is all the more curious in the measure in which it tends towards a more manifestly existential conclusion. William of Auvergne is one of the first Latins to become aware of the immense problems that the discovery of Greek and Arab metaphysics pose for Christians, but one gets the impression that he confronts these problems in his turn with techniques that do not go much beyond those which Abelard already possessed: grammar and dialectic. A deeper study of *Magisterium Divinale* will probably allow us to detect progress in this regard. He learned while writing. In *De Trinitate*, with which this great work commences, we find him no less busied in constructing dialectical machinery where the arguments deal with words, the substitutes for concepts themselves substituted for the real. There is more. In his twelfth-century Latin predecessors, grammar sometimes came to the aid of logic, and William is no more hesitant than they to conclude from grammar—that is to say, from the properties of the *nomen*—to what is most real in the supreme Existent. For we "name" it the Being by essence, but it must be noted that it is precisely because it is by essence that we can give it the name of being with complete appropriateness. Indeed, the names that bespeak essence are the only names properly speaking; as for the names that bespeak accidents, they do not name, properly speaking, they *denominate*. For example, "man" is a name, which names someone,

34. "Scito autem quod modi dicendi quos diximus, videlicet modus dicendi secundum essentiam et secundum participationem necessario sequuntur. Modus enim dicendi secundum essentiam et secundum participationem, ut ostendimus, sine altero esse non potest, sicut neque participans, inquantum participans est, potest esse sine partipato. Ad hunc modum, modi dicendi per se et per accidens sibi invicem obligati sunt, sed modus dicendi per accidens solus esse non potest ullo modo; non enim possibile est, ut aliquid dicatur de aliquo secundum accidens, et de nullo dicatur per se" (*De Trinitate*, ch. I, II:2).

but "white" names nothing and nobody. It can only denominate.[35] The same goes for the name "being," which is only truly a name because it is said of that whose very essence is *esse*.

It is just this notion, so rich in meaning, which William pursues with rather rudimentary means. A new metaphysical intuition bursts the grammatical and dialectical formulas in which he encloses it. We can no longer doubt this, when, after having established the necessity of positing the *ens secundum essentiam*, he tries to make the notion precise, this time not infelicitously. Let us start with grammar. If there is someone whose *ens* is said according to essence, it must be that the word *ens* is truly a "name." We are thus speaking of a true being in the sense that being is its essence, its very substance. Such is the case of him alone, whom William, following Avicenna, names *Primus*, the First Thing, that is to say He whose being is so linked to his essence that his non-existence is at the same time impossible and unthinkable.[36] "Ontologism" in the Kantian sense of the word refuses to pass unnoticed here. The name "being" has a conceivable sense; for it to be conceivable as *nomen*, it is necessary that it be attributed to something by reason of essence. Thus there

35. *De Trinitate*, ch. II, II:3. I do not know the origin of this distinction, which I have not been able to find with this sense in either Boethius or Priscian.

36. "Redeamus ergo, et dicamus, quia postquam ens de quodam dicitur essentialiter, ipsum est proprium nomen ejus, de quo essentialiter dicitur, et proprie nominat ejus essentiam, per quam essentiale est, sive unius, sive multorum communiter. De illo igitur dicitur secundum veritatem, quia secundum essentiam sive substantiam quae in unaquaque re veritas ejusdem rei dicitur. Item inseparabile ab eodem; quoniam de primo dicitur essentialiter, nec actu, nec ratione est separabile ab eodem sive enim essentia illius sit de quo dicitur, sive pars essentiae, inseparabile est actu et impossibile est non esse, sed etiam intelligi non esse." *De Trinitate*, ch. II, II:3. The stages of this grammatical argument are the following: 1) *Ens* is the proper name of that of which it is said by reason of essence. 2) It thus signifies its very essence. 3) As the essence of a thing is its truth, *ens*, which signifies the essence of this being, also signifies its truth. 4) As the essence of a thing is inseparable for it, what the term *ens* designates is inseparable from the being by essence. 5) The being whose proper name is *ens* thus is such not only that it cannot not exist, but it cannot even be conceived that it does not exist.—This argument is not literally that of the *Proslogion*, but it cannot be disputed that their spirit is related. In both cases is certainly is a matter of proving not only that God is, but that his non-existence is unthinkable. "Quod qui bene intelligit, ubique intelligit idipsum sic esse, ut nec cogitatione quaeat non esse" (Anselm, *Proslogion*, ch. IV, column 229 B). Cf. "Sic ergo vere es, Domine, Deus meus, ut nec cogitari possis non esse" (*Proslogion*, ch. III, column 228 C). A little further in *De Trinitate*, 3, William argues in the name of the principle of non-contradiction: it is contradictory to say that Being is not, because an essence cannot accept its contrary: "qua de causa ens hujusmodi non ens, seu non esse, intelligere etiam impossibile est."

is something whose very essence is to be, that is to say, something, which not only cannot not be, but cannot even be conceived as not being.

Such is William of Auvergne's First Thing, and his notion is directly enriched by that of being-*esse* whose importance Alfarabi and Avicenna have just revealed. This being, whose being is inseparable because it is its substance, and whose non-being is unthinkable because the substance of a being is its truth, it of course Existing. We already pointed out the formula in the passage that defines the First Thing as the essence that can only be conceived by existing itself (*ejus namque essentia nisi per ipsum esse intelligi non potest*) because its existing and itself are but one (*cum ipsa et ejus esse omnimodo sint una res*). Let us add only that this expression directly sets William on the road that leads to St. Thomas Aquinas's God, that is to say, not to God in whom existence flows from essence, where it is entailed, but to him, on the contrary, whose essence is merged with existing and is only conceived through it. A God whose essence can only be conceived by existing, because his *essentia* and his *esse* are identical in every regard, is no longer the God of Augustinian essentialism, which at this same period is recognized in Alexander of Hales and in St. Bonventure.[37] A new philosophical conception of the Christian God begins to establish itself before our eyes.

It seems that William becomes more and more aware of it in the measure that his work is elaborated. After having proved by the same dialectical method of the As and Bs that we must arrive at an uncaused First Thing by going back up the series of causes,[38] he proceeds to describe it

37. On this point see Gilson, *Le thomisme*, ch. II, 2.

38. Because, if we argue from two terms, A and B, it is necessary that both of them exist to cause the other one, before existing as caused by it; and if we argue from a longer series, it will go to the infinite. Now, an infinite series of terms escapes our thought, and we will never find the explanation of a series of causes that can only be the first uncaused cause. Thus, in the case of cause, as in that of being, the question is to argue in the name of a requirement of intelligibility. That is what William himself says: "Nos autem cum eis qui intellectum, et finitionem, sive fixionem intellectus destruunt, eoque philosophandi viam obstruunt, et scientiae ipsius principium et radicem, quae vere verus est intellectus, destruunt, dum infinita et inintelligibilia ponunt, et ineffabilia, disputationem nullatenus aggrediemur, dimittentes eos ire in adinventionibus suis, videlicet in immensum erroris, et tenebras infinitatis et incertitudinis ponentes. Quare *necessitas intelligendi* [*our emphasis*] ponere cogit, videlicet quod est, de quodam dicitur secundum essentiam et de quodam non secundum essentiam. Similiter et ens. Et faciemus sciri quod omnes illud de quo dicitur secundum essentiam est non causatum, causatione formata intellige, quam solam viderunt Philosophi; non enim viderunt causationem effectivam intimam, de qua aliquid infra loquimur [*namely, in regard to the*

as the absolutely simple being, despoiled of any accident, supremely one, and separated in being from everything else. Ultimately, that is why He of whom we say that he is being by essence is singular. "To be" is his proper name. Thus there is a reason why he called himself *Qui est*, speaking to Moses, and this testimony suffices to establish the truth of what precedes. Likewise, the book of *Wisdom* calls him *Qui est*, and Job says to him: *Tu enim solus es*. Indeed, he is that thing alone, in the way we have said, because for him alone is being by essence. Without doubt, he is often called "God and lord of the universe," or "God and lord of the ages," but these expressions rather make us understand his praise and his glory according to our manner of knowing and speaking.[39]

There would have been nothing new here, if William were content to cite Scripture and notably Exodus to establish that God is being, but we find more than that. When St. Augustine cited the *Qui est* of Exodus, it was to establish that God was the *essentia* par excellence, that is to say, the Eternal.[40] In William, the same text means that God is *esse* taken in the strong sense of existing, and in that he is a sure predecessor of St. Thomas Aquinas. Besides, there is proof that St. Thomas read William of Auvergne.[41] It is not enough to say that William certainly preceded St. Thomas on this path; he perhaps facilitated the access to

---

Trinity]. Haec enim est quam infra describimus et quoniam de omni creato necesse est ut dicatur non secundum essentiam" (William of Auvergne, *De Trinitate*, ch. II, II:3).

39. "Quis igitur de illo dicitur ens per essentiam secundum hanc intentionem, singulare est et proprium nomen ejus quod quaerimus. Hoc igitur non frustra se nominavit, Exodi 4 ad Moysem, qui est, quod testimonium fieri sufficit ad certitudinem eorum quae diximus. Similter Sapientiae 13 nominatur, qui est, et Job ad ipsum dicit, tu enim solus es. Hoc unum est eo modo quod diximus: ipse namque solus est essentialiter. Frequenter autem ipsum Deum et dominum universi, sive Deum et dominum saeculorum: sed ista magis sonant nobis laudem ipsium et gloriam ex ipso nostro usu loquendi et intelligendi" (*De Trinitate*, ch. IV, II:5). The first of the texts cited by William is well known. It is not found in Exodus 4 but at Exod 3:15: "Dixit Deus ad Moysen: Ego sum qui sum. Ait: sic dices filiis Israel: Qui est, misit me ad vos." The second is read in Wis 13:1: "Vani autem sunt omnes homines, in quibus non subest scientia Dei, et de his quae videntur bona, non potuerunt intelligere eum, qui est, neque operibus attendentes, agnoverunt quis esset artifex." The third is found in Job 14:4: "Quis potest facere mundum de immundo semine? Nonne tu, qui solus es." Of these three texts, St. Thomas will only retain the first in *Contra Gentiles*, I, 22. Cf. *Summa Theologiae*, I q. 13, article 11; In I *Sententiarum*, distinction 8, q. 1, article 1, contra (note the appeal to Avicenna in the solution); *De Potentia*, q. VII, article 5, ad 1, and q. 10, article 1, ad 9. *In Dionysius, De Divinis Nominibus*, ch. V, *lectio* 1, II:489.

40. Cf. Gilson, *Introduction Augustin*, 27–28.

41. Cf. Gilson, "Pourquoi saint Thomas," 59–64.

it. For no hesitation is possible about the meaning of his own doctrine. Although he is far from having understood what a profound revision of the whole of theology that notion of God demanded, and although he even hesitated over his formula, as we will see, he nevertheless grasped it firmly and expressed it in such terms that it cannot be doubted that it is definitely what he means to speak about. He presents *ens* as the name that best expresses the divine essence,[42] but he also recalls immediately afterwards that *ens* has neither quiddity nor definition,[43] which seems to imply necessarily that in his thought the First Thing no longer has any, if not as God, at least as Being. If there is no quiddity, how would there be an essence? But this is precisely what he is, as William has told us from his first and decisive formula, he whose essence is reduced to his existence: *ens cujus essentia est ei esse, et cujus essentiam praedicamus cum dicimus est; ita ut ipsum ei ejus esse quod assignamus cum dicimus, est, sint res una per omnem modum.*

Since such is the place that existing occupies in our notion of God, what place will it occupy in our notion of finite and created being? This second problem has been examined much more closely than the first, but it will be useful to take it up again, that is to say, to take up the analysis of the texts on which the proposed solution rests. There seems, indeed, to be agreement in admitting that, as Stephan Schindele said, "William of Auvergne is one of the first scholastics to teach the real distinction of

---

42. "Ens vero adeo declarat ejus essentiam, ut ipse per ipsum innotescere voluerit filiis Israel, quo uno noto nota sint omnia quaecumeque de essentia ipsius dici possunt," William of Auvergne, *De Trinitate*, ch. IV, II:5.

43. "Item non habet [*namely*, ens] quidditatem, nec difinitionem; omne namque difinibile et quocumque modo explicabile aliquo modo resolubile est et vestitum; per viam igitur intellectus non est natum cognosci, nisi per se; per viam autem sensus cognoscitur utcumque ex testimonio sensibilium. Ergo ipsum per se impressum est intellectui nostro in quantum ens, inquantum autem Deus et Dominus, non est ex primis apprehensionibus, et hic est modus quo errant imperiti intellectu circa ipsum" (*De Trinitate*, ch. IV, II:6). What William says here about *ens* recalls what Avicenna had already said about God, all the more because the notion of *ens* is proposed here as our proper notion of God: "Igitur omne habens quidditatem causatum est, et caetera alia, excepto necesse esse, habent quidditates quae sunt per se possibiles esse, quibus non accedit esse nisi extrinsecus; primus igitur non habet quidditatem" (Avicenna, *Metaphysica*, tractatus VIII, ch. 4, folio 99 verso b). Perhaps William must be placed with Avicenna among those to whom St. Thomas Aquinas alludes: "Aliquis enim [*namely*, modus habendi essentiam] est sicut Deus, cujus essentia est ipsummet esse suum; et ideo inveniuntur aliqui philosophi dicentes quod Deus non habet quidditatem vel essentiam, quia essentia sua non est aliud quam esse suum" (*De Ente et Essentia*, ch. V, initium, 37 n. 1).

essence and existence," to point that his position here will hardly differ (*kaum verschieden*) from the one that most Thomists will adopt later.[44] For his part, in the excellent edition and commentary that Fr. Roland-Gosselin provided for St. Thomas's *De Ente et Essentia*, he declared: "The real distinction between essence and existence is clearly taught be William of Auvergne. Barring further information, it is he who inaugurates this doctrine in Latin theology. He does so under the combined influence—very easily discerned—of Boethius and Avicenna, associated with each other owing to the term *esse*."[45] These last observations contain much truth, perfectly expressed, but for us the question is whether everything they say is true.

In a first text, after having defined, as we have seen, the being "whose essence is existing, and whose essence we predicate saying *est*, so that itself and its *esse*, which we assign by saying *est*, are one single and the same thing in every regard," William adds: "But there is another that is said by participation, because the being it has is in no way identical to the essence of the substance itself of the being."[46] We should not neglect to observe the force of the expression. William affirms of participated being *quod nullo modo est idem cum essentia substantiae entis*. It is impossible to go further, and on the strength of this text it would be legitimate to affirm that William indeed admitted the real distinction of essence and existence, if we did not know otherwise that he does not always keep a close watch on his pen. Endowed with the highest degree of imagination about ideas, he tends to formulate as powerfully as possible what he grasps at the very moment when he expresses it. Here, it is in opposition to the First Thing and the being by essence that he thinks about second and participated being. Since the first being is absolutely the same thing as its essence (*res una per omnem modum*), it must be that the second is not that at all (*nullo modo est idem*).

So far the record, but that does not bind the future. To start, let us recall that it is to explain this thesis that William puts forward the *divisio* proposed by Boethius in his *De Hebdomadibus* between simple being, whose *quod est* is one with its *esse*, and the composed being, where the

---

44. Schindele, *Beiträge*, 23.

45. Roland-Gosselin, *Le De Ente et Essentia*, 160.

46. William of Auvergne, *De Trinitate*, ch. I, II:1: "Aliud vero dicitur [*namely*, ens] participatione in habendo, scilicet quod nullo modo est idem cum essentia ipsius substantiae entis."

quod est and the *quo est* are distinct; then secondly, a *ratio* that certainly seems inspired by Avicenna, because it contrasts what possesses *esse* in virtue of its substance or essence with what only has it by way of accident.[47] Now it is commonly recognized today that the Boethian distinction between *quod est* and *esse* is not a distinction between essence and existence in the Thomist sense of the expression, although it has been utilized to formulate it. Besides, we ourselves have observed that although he speaks here of existence as an accident, because it is *praeter essentiam* in the participated being, he says elsewhere, speaking this time on his own and not as an echo of Avicenna, that existence is above not only accident but substance itself. All that can be concluded from this first text is thus that William had to admit certain distinction between participated existence and its essence, and that he even ought to have a point of view where this distinction must be called total, but nothing tells us yet whether he conceives of it like Boethius or like Avicenna or in a third way that he has not so far defined and that would announce the so-called "real" distinction of St. Thomas Aquinas.

It is true that the problem could be simplified by suppressing one of its terms. Admitting, as seems to be agreed, that William here goes beyond Boethius in giving the latter's *esse-quo est* the new meaning of "exist," it has been held that he connects directly with St. Thomas by making participated existing an accident of essence. Schindele held that for St. Thomas himself existing was only an accident. Firstly, if that were correct, it would be necessary to conclude from it that St. Thomas is behind William since at least once the latter formally declared that *esse* is superior to substance as well as to accident. But the texts of St. Thomas cited by Schindele do not say what he makes them say. In fact, St. Thomas distinguishes two senses of the term "accident." In the broad and improper sense, accident designates everything that is not part of essence, but is added for any reason whatever. In this sense if we wish, it can be said that the existing of a participated thing is an accident; but in the strict sense, essence is not an accident (*et sic proprie loquendo, non est accidens*) because it is the act of the form itself, and because the ultimate perfection of a being is not an accident of it.[48] Nothing is clearer

47. See the text reproduced above 89 n. 13.

48. Cf. Schindele, *Beiträge*, 23 n.3, which remits to two texts of Aquinas: *Quodlibetum* XII, q V, article 5, and *Quodlibetum* II, article III, ad 2. The first of these texts is such a perfect synthesis of Thomist doctrine of this point that we allow ourselves to

than the position of St. Thomas on this point. Whether he accepted the distinction in Boethius's sense, which, to our knowledge, no one holds, or whether he admitted it in Avicenna's sense, which would clash with his refusal to hold existing as a simple accident, the distinction proposed by William would not be what St. Thomas Aquinas will admit.

However, it can still be held that he agrees with St. Thomas, precisely because he refuses to confuse this existing that he holds to be more than a simple accident with the participated essence. Thus, let us see what he himself says about it, weighing each expression that he uses, in the two principal texts that are cited in order to attribute the real distinction between essence and existence to him:

Here is the first of these texts, which is also the shorter:

> Jam ante declaratum est in prima parte primae philosophiae, quia omne hujusmodi causatum est possibile esse per se, et est recipiens esse supra se quod est aliud ab ipso, et propter hoc est in eo potentialiter sive possibiliter, quoniam est ei accidens, hoc est, adveniens ei, et respectum ab ipso supra totam completam essentiam suam. Esse enim omne, quod datur a causa hujusmodi suo causato, separabile est ab illo saltem intellectu, et omne receptum a suo recipiente, et generaliter omne esse cum fuerit aliud a suo ente, separabile est ab ipso, modo quo diximus. Omne autem a quo ejus esse separabile est, non habet illud nisi possibiliter, sive

reproduce it entirely, for a start, despite its length: "Respondeo dicendum, quod opinio Avicennae fuit quod unum et esse semper praedicant accidens. Hoc autem non est verum; quia unum prout convertitur cum ente, signat substantiam rei, et similiter ipsum ens; sed unum prout est principium numeri, signat accidens. Sciendum ergo, quod unumquodque quod est in potentia et in actu, fit actu per hoc quod participat actum superiorem. Per hoc autem aliquid maxime fit actu, quod participat per similitudinem primum et purum actum. Primus autem actus est esse subsistens per se; unde completionem unumquodque recipit per hoc quod participat esse; unde esse est complementum omnis formae, quia per hoc completur quod habet esse, et habet esse cum est actu; et sic nulla forma est nisi per esse. Et sic dico quod esse substantiale rei non est accidens sed actualitas cujuslibet formae existentis, sive sine materia sive cum materia. Et quia esse est complementum omnium, inde est quod proprius affectus Dei est esse, et nulla causa dat esse nisi inquantum participat operationem divinam; est sic proprie loquendo, non est accidens. Et quod Hilarius dicit, dico quod accidens dicitur large omne quod non est pars essentiae; et sic est esse in rebus creatis, quia in Deo solo esse est ejus essentia" (Aquinas, *Quodlibetum* XII, q V, article 5). Here is the second text: "Ad secundum dicendum, quod esse est accidens, non quasi per accidens se habens, sed quasi actualitas cujuslibet substantiae; unde ipse Deus, qui est sua actualitas, est suum esse" (*Quodlibitum* II, article III, *ad* 2). It would be excessive to base oneself on these two concessions to language, withdrawn as soon as made, in order to attribute to St. Thomas the Avicennist thesis that existing is an accident.

potentialiter, et ita non habet illud ea necessitate, qua aliquid
dicitur necessario esse per se.[49]

At first sight a more explicit declaration in favor of the real distinction between essence and existence could hardly be hoped for, all the
more because the text remits us to the first part of the First Philosophy,
that is to say to William's *De Trinitate*, precisely as Fr. Roland-Gosselin
has interpreted it,[50] which indeed contains many texts in this sense. It
cannot be doubted that we are dealing here with a doctrine directly inspired by Avicenna's, and Pierre Duhem rightly maintained that.[51] As in
Avicenna, the domain of being is divided in two here, that of necessary
being and that of possible being. Necessary being is that whose existence
is inseparable; as for possible being, it receives into itself an *esse* that is
"other than it" (*aliud ab ipso*), in regard to which it is in potency, and that
is added to its complete essence as an accident.

The very precision with which William expresses himself here invites us to wonder whether he is really "the one who introduces into
Latin Scholasticism" the distinction between essence and existence
posited by Arab neo-Platonism,[52] or rather, if he is, in what sense he
is. Because it is generally forgotten that the problem is not single but
double. As William poses it here, it amounts to distinguishing the being
whose existence comes from a cause exterior to it from Being uncaused
because necessary. Everything suggests that the question is reduced to
strictly this point, and it is in relation to the question thus posed that the
terms William uses obtain their exact sense. In the caused being, indeed,
existence is received from elsewhere, and it is for that reason that it is
not necessary but possible. It is equally for this reason and within these
limits that it is as an accident, that is to say exactly, as adventitious (*accidens, hoc est, adveniens ei*) or added onto the essence complete in itself.
In other words, the distinction between essence and existence that is
the question here simply expresses the fact that in created being essence
only exists in virtue of the existence that its creator confers upon it. We
are thus sure henceforth that William held at least this first distinction

49. William of Auvergne, *De Universo*, I–II[ae], ch. 3, I:594.

50. Pierre Duhem thought that these words referred us to a *Metaphysics* by William,
whose text would be lost today (*Le système du monde*, V:282). In opposition and rightly,
Roland-Gosselin, *Le De Ente et Essentia*, 160 n. 2.

51. Duhem, *Le système*, V.282–83.

52. Ibid.

of essence and existence, which Albert the Great and the majority of his successors likewise held after him.

Moreover, it does not seem that a Christian theologian could avoid it, because it simply translates into technical language the relation of the creature, whose existence is only possible, to the Creator who made it exist. It is perhaps too hasty to conclude upon finding this teaching that those who admitted it were *ipso facto* teaching the distinction between essence and existence in the Thomistic sense of the expression. The difference is such that many of those who will admit the distinction of essence and existence in the first sense will not admit it in the second. Thus indeed, the question is not to know whether created essence is in potency in regard to the existence that its creator confers upon it in creating it, which all admit, but whether, in the very metaphysical structure of created being, existence forms an element distinct from essence, which many deny. To specify the question thus is perhaps the best means to distinguish Avicennism from Thomism here. If St. Thomas denies that created existing is simply an accident, it is not merely to say *more* than Avicenna, it is to say *something else*. What Avicenna and William ask is whether existence is included in the complete essence of the created. To this, of course, they answer no, whence their conclusion: the existence of the created comes to it from outside. *Advenit, accidit*, and in this sense it cannot be denied that existence is accidental to finite essence, thus, that it is its accident. The question posed by St. Thomas is completely distinct. He asks whether *in the being already created and consequently existent*, received existing is different from essence. In other words, he asks whether the metaphysical composition of the real includes, beyond this term that is essence, another term that is existing (*esse*). To the question thus posed, we know that St. Thomas answers affirmatively. To say that William clearly teaches "the real distinction between essence and existence in creatures," is equivalent to holding that he had already given the same answer to this question. Now there are reasons to doubt that.

Let us recognize first that the language that William uses, taken quite literally, would authorize us to hold this thesis. Indeed he says that possible being and the existing that it does not have by essence are really two (*duo sunt revera*); that one comes upon the other and does not enter into its quiddity; in short, that the being of this type is composed of its possibility and of its existing, and resolves itself into them.[53] The

53. "Quoniam autem ens potentiale est non ens per essentiam, tunc ipsum et ejus

expression is undeniable: *ens igitur secundum hunc modum compositum est et resolubile in suam possibilitatem sive quidditatem et suum esse.* Everything is there: composition (*compositum*), distinction (*resolubile*), real character of these two properties (*duo sunt revera*), no excuse is left to anyone who wants to try to evade it.

We will attempt it no longer. On the contrary, let us recall that it seems indisputable to us that William taught a real distinction of essence and existence, but we wonder what it is, that is to say: what does it distinguish? As can be seen from our text, the distinction about which William is thinking expresses the relation of participated being to being by essence. He conceives essence as distinct from its existence *because essence might not exist*, and the distinction as he conceives it consists in just that. Moreover, that is what this clause of the text clearly suggests: "Indeed, all existing given by such a cause to its effect is separable from it at least in thought [*saltem intellectu*]." And again, a little further on: "Indeed every existing that is other than its being is separable in the aforesaid way [*modo quo diximus*]." Indeed, existence can be separated from the being that receives it by thinking that it does not receive it or that it might not have received it; but it does not follow thereby that, while it possesses it, it is really distinct from it. Quite the contrary, the precision that William brings to bear in formulating his thought here would have no sense if he did not want exactly to avoid our imagining existence as distinct from essence in the very structure of the actually existing being. The possible as such is defined according to him: what contains nothing that renders its existence impossible. Thus one does not find existence there,[54] and consequently our thought distinguishes the possible from it. That is what William of Auvergne says. But this text does not say that, in the possible realized by its cause, *esse* and *essentia* remain distinct so as to form a composite properly so-called, and it rather suggests the opposite. Thus, we cannot base ourselves on

---

esse quod non est ei per essentiam, duo sunt revera, et alterum accidit alteri, nec cadit in rationem nec quidditatem ipsius. Ens igitur secundum hunc modum compositum est et resolubile in suam possibilitatem sive quidditatem et suum esse" (William of Auvergne, *De Trinitate*, ch. VII, I:8).

54. "Esse vero potentiale quod quidem in se et per seipsum consideratum invenitur non prohibens suum esse; verumtamen in hac consideratione nondum invenitur habere esse, sed tamen invenitur prope, ut habeat esse, et haec appropinquatio nominatus in eo possibilitas" (*De Trinitate*, ch. VI, I:6).

it to attribute to William the distinction of essence and existence, as St. Thomas Aquinas was to understand it.

However, that is what has been done, and it is interesting to look for the reason, because, over and above the exegesis of a text, it concerns the heart of the doctrine. "The clause *saltem intellectu* will be noted," Fr. Roland-Gosselin says commending this passage, "but also the term that it comes to attenuate, which is *separabile* and not *distinctum*. The same restriction is found in *Secunda Secundae*, ch. 9, p. 852 at G. If it perhaps signals hesitation in William's mind, it still does not amount to diminishing the realism of the distinction he affirms so vigorously everywhere else."[55]

Our commentator already falls into an insuperable difficulty here precisely because he tries to find in William of Auvergne St. Thomas's real distinction within the essence actualized by *esse*, between essence and the *esse* that actualizes it. Now if William is truly talking about that, it is impossible to maintain that the clause *saltem intellectu* does not diminish the realism of the distinction that some wish to attribute to him. Indeed we then grapple with contradictory texts, some saying that essence and *esse* are *revera duo*, others limiting themselves to saying that essence is separable from its *esse*, *saltem intellectu*. How should we choose? By choosing all, as we should; by thereby refusing to pose the problem on a level where we can only chose some or the others. Another level is precisely that of the relation of participated essence to the cause of its existence. If we interpret the texts from this point of view, they betray no hesitation on William's part, and all are equally valid in their total sense. Indeed, created essence is really distinct from its *esse*, because it does not have it from itself but from its cause. Created essence is separable *actu*, because it does not possess *esse* before the First Thing created it and because it would not possess it if the First Thing annihilated it (this is why, thinking about this problem, William says *separabile*, not *distinctum*). Finally it is separable *saltem intellectu*, in the actually existent *esse* because we can conceive the essence without its existence, although in so far as actualized by its cause it may not be really distinct. That the question is really of separability and not of distinction is seen in the terms used by William: *ab omni vero possibili, et ab omni eo quod est necesse esse per aliud, est separabile suum esse, aut actu, aut intellectu,*

---

55. Roland-Gosselin, *Le De Ente et Essentia*, 163.

sive ratione.[56] The problem of the real distinction in the Thomist sense remains foreign to William of Auvergne's perspective, in so far as this text allows us to define it.

But here is a second, longer text, where some have thought they found it:

> Ego vero dico, quod ex sermonibus ejus praecedentibus et sub-
> sequentibus hunc sermonem, apparet evidenter intentio ipsius
> (namely Boethii) in eodem sermone; dicit enim in praecedenti-
> bus quia omne simplex, esse suum et id quod est, unum habet.
> Quod est dicere, quia in vera simplici, de quo ipse loquitur, non
> est aliud quod est aliquid, et quo est, sive esse; hujusmodi autem
> simplex est in ultimitate simplicitatis, sicut patefactum est tibi per
> me in prima parte istius philosophiae sapientalis, in capitulo sci-
> licet de necesse esse per se; haec igitur declaratio est necessitatis
> per se apud ipsum, quia unum per omnem modum ipsum est, et
> suum esse non est separabile ab ipso actu, vel intellectu. Ab omni
> vero possibili, et ab omni eo quod est necesse esse per aliud, est
> separabile suum esse, aut actu, aut intellectu, sive ratione. In omni
> igitur alio est aliud ipsum ens, aliud ejus esse, seu entitas. Et iste
> est intellectus sapientis illius [namely Boethii] de hoc et hoc. Et
> omne aliud ens est quodammodo compositum ex eo, quod est,
> et ex eo, quo est, sive esse suo, sive entitate sua quemadmodum
> album est album ex subjecto et albedine; haec autem conjuctio
> albi et albedinis non est veri nominis et propria compositio,
> videlicet per quam aliud novum constituatur, cum manifestum
> tibi sit ex aliis, quae alibi didicisti, impossibile esse ex substan-
> tia et accidente aliquid esse vel fieri, Accidens enim non advenit
> substantiae ad constituendum novum aliquid, sed magis ad ordi-
> nandum, decorandam et perficiendam perfectionibus forinsecis
> ipsam, cui advenit, substantiam. Non debet igitur conturbare te
> sermo este sapientis illius de hoc et hoc, tanquam per ipsum
> cogaris confiteri omnem substantiam compositam esse ex mate-
> ria et forma, sive spirtualis sit illa, sive corporalis. Sollicite autem
> attendere debes exemplum, quod posui tibi, de albo et albedine.
> Convenientissimum enim est ad id, de quo agebatur, videlicit
> de ente creato et entitate, et hoc quoniam esse, sive entitas, uni-
> cuique accidit et advenit praeter completam ejus substantiam et
> rationem, praeterquam primo principio, cui soli essentiale est, et
> unum cum eo in ultimitate unitatis.[57]

56. William of Auvergne, *De Universo*, II^a-II^{ae}, ch. 8, I:852.

57. Ibid. Text commented by Marie-Dominique Roland-Gosselin, *Le De Ente et Essentia*, 165–66, and by Pierre Duhem, *Le système*, V:300–303.

A richer and more precise text cannot be hoped for. Pierre Duhem, who already translated it and examined it closely, establish beyond dispute that it involves the mixture of Boethius's teaching on the distinction of *quod esse* and *esse* with Avicenna's doctrine on the accidentality of existence. Since Pierre Duhem showed with perfect exactness how this mixture leads William of Auvergne to translate Avicenna's thought into Boethius's language, there is no need to go over the matter.[58] On the other hand, it is important to ask whether, once Avicenna's thought is thus translated into Boethius's language, it really entailed the real distinction of essence and its existing for William of Auvergne.

The distinction taken directly from Avicenna between the being that is necessary of itself and the simply possible being, raises no difficulty. On the other hand, we must weigh with care the description of possible being that we have already recalled:[59] in everything that is possible and in everything that gets its necessity from something else, its existing is separable, either in fact, or by intellect or reason. Thus William is certainly thinking about precisely the separability of existence, not its distinction. Now the two cases are very different. It can be held that essence and existence are separable but not distinct while they are united, or inversely, that essence and existence are really distinct in their very union, and nevertheless, as St. Thomas will sustain about the immortal soul, inseparable by right. This text not only does not authorize us to bestow the real distinction upon William of Auvergne, but rather puts us on guard against this attribution.

Furthermore, the continuation of the text offers clarifications in this regard; however delicate the interpretation may be, the clarifications at least leave no doubt about the sense in which William himself understood this problem. After having recalled that according to

58. See Duhem, *Le système*, V:302. In particular, it is completely true that William gives the same sense, that of existing, to the term *esse* in Boethius's formulas as well as in those of Avicenna and Algazel. From then on Boethius's formulas receive a new meaning, since the composition of *quod est* and of *esse* (*quo est*) that they affirm becomes what it was not in Boethius himself, a composition of *quod est* and of existing. Hence Pierre Duhem draws this conclusion to which we should certainly assent: "In Boethius's expression, *id quod est* was the concrete object existing in its singularity. *Esse* was the essence understood in the sense of specific form, as in Themistius's doctrine. In the modified formula, it is *id quod est* that designates essence in the sense of Avicenna's doctrine, whereas *id quo est* designates existence as this same doctrine conceives it. It can be seen that the very role of the terms has been, so to speak, reversed" (*Le système*, 302–3). This cannot be put better.

59. See above 114.

Boethius every composite being is *hoc et hoc*, this and that, which is to say *quod est* and *quo est*, essence and existence,[60] he immediately adds that the relation of essence to existence in the existent is the same as that of whiteness to the subject in a white being. On this point, he specifies that it is thus not a question of composition in the proper sense of the term. In fact, in every composition worthy of the name, the union of components has as a result a new being, which is the composite. Now the union of accident with substance does not produce this result. The accident is not added to the substance to constitute something new with it, but rather, William specifies, to confer upon the substance that receives it (*cui advenit*) an order, a beauty, and perfections that are foreign to it (*forinsecis*). Thus it is not a question here of a composition like that of matter and of form in the substance itself. William expressly denies that Boethius's thesis (every composed substance is *hoc et hoc*) obliges us to admit Gabirol's (every substance, even spiritual, is composed of matter and form). Finally, he concludes by specifying that the example of the white being and whiteness is perfectly appropriate to express the relation of created being to its existence, since existence is added to the substance already complete in itself and in its notion. As is obvious, we always exclude the case of God in which alone existence is essential and one with it in the supreme degree of unity.

Here everything authorizes us to take the example of whiteness and the white being literally, or rather William himself obliges us to do so, since he guarantees its perfect adaptation to his point. But that very fact invites us to doubt that the problem of the distinction of essence and existence in the actually existent being is really what William of Auvergne is thinking about. What he once more affirms, thinking in terms of separability not of distinction, is that existence befalls created substance, so to speak, from the outside, as foreign to its complete notion, and consequently as an accident. But he himself specifies that a true composition does not result thereby, that is to say something constituting a new *tertium quid*. To compare this notion with that of St. Thomas is a delicate operation, full of risks, because St. Thomas himself refused to make *esse*

60. From the point of view of William's personal vocabulary, it is interesting to note here that the terms *quo est*, *esse*, and *entitas* are synonyms for him and all three can be take in the sense of existing. On the other hand, just as *entitas* can signify existence, as is the case in the text on which we are commenting, *esse* can signify essence, as can be seen in the text quoted above 89 n. 13. Thus only the context allows us to know in what sense *esse* ought to be taken.

an accident. Thus any exact correspondence between the two doctrines inevitably is lacking. Assuredly we can recur to the commentators on St. Thomas, but who will guarantee us that they faithfully express his thought? So it remains to proceed step by step, fully conscious of the risks incurred.

We can first admit that for St. Thomas as for William, the composition of substance and accident does not engender a new being, which would be the composite of the two. The union of matter and form engenders the substance, which is certainly an *unum per se*, but the union of the substance and the accident does not produce a third being, it only produces a new qualification of the same being, an *unum per accidens*. It must be admitted, moreover, that for this same reason the composition of substance and accident is not *veri nominis*, in the precise sense that William gives to this expression, and that it is so neither for William nor for St. Thomas. Perhaps we should go further still, because in a doctrine like that of St. Thomas Aquinas, where the *esse* of the accident is *inesse*, we certainly do not see how the accident would really distinguish itself from the substance while it is effectively united to it, however separable it may be from substance. As St. Thomas himself said, *homo et albus sunt idem subjecto, at differunt ratione; alia enim est ratio hominis et alia ratio albi.*[61] Whatever we make of this last point, it does not seem that William's thought and that of St. Thomas differ profoundly regarding the relation of substance to accident.

By contrast, the difficulty begins when we try to transpose the doctrine of accident into terms of existence. First, if according to St. Thomas it remains true to say with William that the union of essence and existence does not constitute an *unum tertium per se*, it must be added, since he does not hold that existence is an accident, that existence no longer constitutes an *ens per accidens* with essence. Essence is united *per se* with existence, without, however, constituting an *unum tertium per se* with it.[62] This first difference leads to a second. William does not judge that the composition of substance and accident is a *compositio veri nominis*, which does not keep him from holding that the same goes for the composition of essence and existence. Thus it is the case that for him this latter is no longer a true composition. Now everyone knows that it is different in St. Thomas, who always, without any restriction, says of

61. Aquinas, *Summa Theologiae*, I 13, 12, respondeo.

62. That is at least what Cajetan understands, rightly it seems to us, in his *In De Ente et Essentia*, ch. V, article 90, 143.

existence that it enters into composition with essence: *faciens compositionem cum essentia*,[63] even if he does not generally say that essence and existence are "really" distinct. All that can be said, with Cajetan, is that precisely because an *unum tertium* does not result from this composition, it is not exactly a composition of essence and existence, but of essence *with* existence.[64] Let us admit that; there is nonetheless a true composition. Now as the composition is, so is the distinction. If the composition of essence and of existing is not a true composition in William, the distinction of essence and existence is not so either, but as the composition of essence and existence is a true composition in St. Thomas, the distinction of essence and of existence is so equally.

Thus it is impossible to obtain any kind of coincidence here between the two doctrines for the fundamental reason that, since William never passed beyond the plane of the accidentality of existence, he was never able to distinguish it from essence except as an accident, whereas St. Thomas Aquinas distinguishes existence from essence in a completely different way. The same conclusion can be expressed in yet another form. St. Thomas acknowledge three kinds of composition: that like matter and form, from which an *unum tertium per se* resulted; that like substance and accident, from which an *unum per accidens* resulted,[65]

63. Aquinas, *De Ente et Essentia*, ch. V, 34, lines 8–9.

64. Cajetan, *In De Ente et Essentia*, 143.

65. Our interpretation supposes a definite interpretation of the relation of accident to substance in St. Thomas. We cannot establish it here, but we at least must specify it. It can be admitted that St. Thomas identifies the accident's *esse* with that of the substance (for example, Forest, *La structure métaphysique*, 89–91). It can likewise be held that St. Thomas himself did not bring this identification to completion (for example, de Finance, *Être et agir*, 241–42). Indeed certain texts work in this second sense, among others the following: "Quia enim omnia accidentia sunt formae quaedam substantiae superadditae, et a principiis substantiae causatae, oportet quod eorum esse sit superadditum supra esse substantiae, et ab ipso dependens; et tanto uniuscujusque eorum esse est prius vel posterius, quanto forma accidentalis, secundum propriam rationem, fuerit propinquior substantiae vel magis perfecta" (*Contra Gentiles* IV, 14). This indication is developed by Cajetan, *In De Ente et Essentia*, ch. VII, 227 n. 140. However, we do not think that we must refrain from completely identifying the accident's *esse* from that of the substance. First, every attentive reader will see by himself that the latter text is not opposed to the former: the accident's *esse*, which is added onto that of the substance, is only added onto it as caused by it and depending on it. Besides, another text of St. Thomas, whose importance it would be unnecessary to underline, hands us the key of all of this kind of expression: "Omnia vero quae non per se subsistunt, sed in alio et cum alio, sive sint accidentia sive formae substantiales aut quaelibet partes, non habent esse ita ut ipsa vere sint, sed attribuitur eis esse" (*Quaestio Quodlibitalis*, IX, 3, respondeo).

and that of essence with existence, from which neither an *unum tertium per se* nor an *unum per accidens* resulted. Now, if existence is assimilated to accident, as William wishes to do here, we are condemned to make the existent an *unum per accidens*, which, in good Thomistic doctrine, is absurd, since the act that confers its full actuality on a being would lower it to the level of an accident. The composition of essence and existence or their corresponding distinction cannot be the same in the two doctrines where the relations of existence to essence are so profoundly different.[66]

The historic importance of the task accomplished by William on this matter is no less than enormous, both in itself and in relation to his successors. He was one of the first Latins of the thirteenth century, and perhaps the first, to become clearly aware of the notion of existence that Alfarabi and Avicenna had clearly uncovered before him. Through what was perhaps only a happy misinterpretation in him, one that was going to have a long career, he transposed the distinction between *quod est* and *esse*, classic since Boethius, into the distinction between essence and existence. Applying this distinction to the relation of creature to creator, he concluded the separability of created essence and its existence; from this the thesis followed necessarily of their composition in what is created. This last thesis, frequently taken up after William, does not, however,

---

What else would this being attributed to them be than that of the substance itself? Indeed, for an accident, *esse est inesse*; but *inesse* is not to be nothing. It is literally true that for the accident, the substance adds to itself the very *esse* that it gives to the accident, without which this accident would not add anything to the substance.

66. In William of Auvergne, the Avicennist doctrine of the accidentality of *esse* thus first of all means the radical contingency of created being. That is why instead of leading up to positing *esse* as the very heart and proper perfection of the being like St. Thomas's doctrine, the distinction of essence and existence in William leads on to a curious depreciation of *esse*. It is literally exact to say that for him finite being is as false as a token: "Esse vero falsum quod exterius est tantum; cum vero interius consideratum fuerit, hoc est in quidditate et ratione essentiae suae, non invenietur in eo esse, sed habens ipsum velut superficie tenus, velut operiens et adumbrans quidditatem ipsius" (*De Trinitate*, ch. VI, II:6). In this sense, everything happens as if there were only one *esse*, God's: "Exemplum autem hujus est, ut quemadmodum anima est vita corporis, sic omnium esse Deus intelligatur; sicut separari ab anima mori est ipsi corpori, sic separari a Deo sit rebus destrui. Sicut etiam anima imprimis est vita spirituum, deinde nervorum, carnis et ossium, sic Deus priorum prius esse, deinde per illa aliorum. Et quemadmodum si una anima esset multorum corporum, nihilominus salva esset multitudo corporum, sic una essentia altissima quae Deus est, unum est esse omnium, scilicet quo sunt. Salva tamen est rebus sua essentialis diversitas, quoniam ut diximus, esse quo sunt non est ei essentiale, sed quasi accidit" (*De Trinitate*, ch. VII, II:9). This last expression is particularly instructive. This whole doctrine seems to have influenced Albert the Great.

seem to us to correspond to what St. Thomas will maintain about the distinction of essence and existence in the metaphysical structure of the concrete. Conceived in order to express the adventitious character of existence in regard to created essence, each time that the thesis was expressed rigorously it was satisfied with defining existence as an accident that came upon the essence from the very fact of creation. In short, it is a distinction that in William falls under cosmogony and in St. Thomas Aquinas above all under ontology, as we say since Clauberg.

In two points, however, which are his finest claims to glory, William achieved decisive progress in the very ground of ontology. Just once and as if by a happy chance that unfortunately he did not exploit, he understood that existence was of a higher order than accident and even substance. The whole ontology of St. Thomas was in that remark in germ, but William was not able to discover it.[67] By contrast he really saw and recognized, so as to never forget it afterwards, the God of Exodus's *Qui est*, whose whole essence is to exist. Here William is certainly a predecessor of St. Thomas Aquinas, perhaps even a source, and when we think of the tenacious vitality that the theologians of essence demonstrated even after him, we measure better what mental power and originality such a metaphysical decision supposed.

67. Therefore William connected the notions of active power and of operation to that of the fecundity of *esse*, as St. Thomas will do: "Iterum igitur dicamus quod potentia nominatur principium operationum, et est exuberantia vel radius ipsius esse, de qua exeunt operationes, et hoc alio nomine dicitur virtus, et nominatur potentia agens, sive activa. Per hunc modum diximus in igne esse potentiam calefaciendi, subtilizandi et disgregandi haeterogenea, eo quod de exuberantia et vehementia seu extensione sui esse vel naturae suae, exundat in has operationes super contingentem vel obviantem sibi materiam" (*De Trinitate*, ch. VIII, II:9). But in him this intuition is fused with the Dionysian and neo-Platonic theme *de fluxu entis*, which does not allow it to be developed in a Thomistic sense. William rather sees a unique *Esse*, from which a flood of participated *esse*s gush forth, with their potencies, virtues, and operations, than a radical plurality of *esse*s each one of which would itself be a source: "viae quaedam et fenestrae mediae naturae sunt, non causae, nisi aliquantulum abusive accepimus nomen causae" (*De Trinitate*, ch. XI, II:16). Again: "Nisi quis dixerit [*to himself*] naturam esse unicuique rei Imperatoris universalis imperium sive beneplacitum" (ibid., XII, 16). Or finally: "Quia igitur solus creatur solus est in seipso, solus in se copiosus, solus de se et de suo dans, manifestum est quia solus est veri nominis causa" (ibid., ch. XII, 17). Theologically speaking, the two doctrines are identical, since both are creationisms; philosophically speaking, they are not, because if William often had a premonition of what Thomist *natura* was gong to be, with the act of *esse* that perfects it, he did not succeed in completely uncovering the notion.

6

MAIMONIDES AND THE PHILOSOPHY OF EXODUS[1]

THE MOST IMPORTANT PHILOSOPHICAL event after the end of Greek philosophy is probably the introduction by St. Thomas of the distinction between the two orders of actuality—that of form, which corresponds to the specification of beings, and that of *esse*, which corresponds to their existence. The origins of this event are not well known. Still, we know that in his *Metaphysics* VIII, 4, Avicenna affirmed that God has no essence: *Primus igitur non habet quidditatem.* Alluding to this text at the beginning of *De Ente et Essentia* V, St. Thomas pronounced himself in these terms: "And this is why we find philosophers who say God has no quiddity or essence, because his essence is none other than his *esse.*"

Although the history of this doctrine has not been written, it is extremely probable that its origin goes back beyond Avicenna to Alfarabi, whom the former so often followed, and that it finally connects with the teaching of Genesis, through a series of Muslim theologians concerned with interpreting the dogma of creation. Averroes so often criticized the doctrine of the distinction of essence and existence in creatures for its religious—that is, non-philosophical—origin, that it is difficult to doubt

1. Chapter 6 of *Études Médiévales* originally appeared in the journal *Medieval Studies* 13 (1951) 223–25.

that the same origin explains the notion of God who is all existence, and consequently, without quiddity.

Whatever its origins, the doctrine presents itself fully developed in Avicenna, where it is expressed in two ways: God, or the First, is pure existence. Creatures, on the contrary, are in themselves only possible essences to which existence happens (*accidit*) in virtue of the necessity of the First. This is what the thirteenth-century Latins meant when they said that for Avicenna existence is an accident of created essence. Some, St. Thomas, for example, criticized him on this point, but others followed him, though sometimes retouching the language he had employed.

Between Thomas Aquinas and Avicenna comes Maimonides, or Rabbi Moses as he is familiarly known to the readers of the Angelic Doctor, who felt the respect toward Maimonides that any great theologian has for any other great theologian. Concerned above all to interpret the tradition of Jewish monotheism, Maimonides places the greatest emphasis on the unity of God, and to assure it better underlines the absolute simplicity of his essence to the extreme of denying any attribute to it. In the *Guide for the Perplexed*, Maimonides demonstrates that even existence is not an attribute of God.[2] To be sure, in the same text, he takes for granted that in all other beings, "existence is an accident that happens to what exists," to which his admirable translator and commentator, Salomon Munk, whose text we follow here, immediately establishes in a note that this doctrine, foreign to Aristotle, comes from Avicenna, and that the Commentator later contradicted it precisely in Aristotle's name.

If existence were an accident of essence, Maimonides could not admit it is an attribute in God without compromising the divine essence's perfect simplicity. Moreover, it suffices to read his treatment to see how he envisaged the problem. Like Avicenna, his point of departure is the consideration of created being. In so far as it is caused, the essence of a creature does not imply its existence. Anything whose existence has a cause is thereby such that its existence is added, so to speak, to its quiddity. It is not thus with God, because he is necessary existence. Assuredly he exists, but not by his existence. "His existence is his true essence, his essence is his existence." In a word, God does not have existence, he *is* it.

It is noticeable here how much closer Thomas Aquinas is to the Jewish theologian than to the Arab philosopher, because he will not say with Avicenna that God has no essence, but rather with Maimonides

---

2. Maimonides, *Guide for the Perplexed*, I, 57.

that God's essence is his very existence. It is true, and the difference is important, that Thomas Aquinas will not follow Maimonides on the path of purely negative theology. He will even criticize him expressly on this point,[3] but we nonetheless can hear a Thomistic ring when Maimonides speaks of God in the next chapter of the *Guide*: "We do not grasp of him anything other than that HE IS, that there is a being which no other being that he has produced resembles, that he has absolutely nothing in common with the latter."[4] Let us recall the text of *Contra Gentiles*: "We cannot grasp what God is, but what he is not, and what relation everything else has with him."[5]

If we can suppose that this doctrine has a biblical origin in Avicenna, it is completely certain that Maimonides himself immediately accepted it as a faithful expression of divine revelation. According to him, such is indeed the sense of the name that God gave himself in Scripture, when he called himself Yahweh, a name that ought to be pronounced only in the sanctuary and to which, in the mind of the priest who pronounces it, ought to correspond to the idea of a God completely different from his works. In the terrain of philosophical exegesis, our Jewish doctor develops remarkable prudence at the moment of imagining what might be the meaning of this name for his predecessors. However, he says, according to the way it ought to be pronounced and to what we know of the Hebrew language, he who utters it ought to understand it as signifying "necessary existence." Therefore, based on the above, this name signifies the very essence of God. In effect, existence is his essence. The divine name Yahweh then means: the necessarily existent.[6]

Such is the sense of the famous Tetragrammatom. But where does this name come from? Maimonides responds to this question, as could be expected, that it comes from God himself, and more precisely from the well known words that we read in the book of Exodus (3:13) where, in answer to Moses who asked him his name, God says: "I am WHO I AM." About this, adding his own commentary to the text, Maimonides makes us observe that this name means "existence." Then, how is this mysterious? In that it takes up the subject under the form of an attribute. But why does it do that except to affirm that God is the existence

3. *Summa Theologiae*, I, 13, 2.
4. Maimonides, *Guide for the Perplexed*, I, 58.
5. Aquinas, *Summa Contra Gentiles*, I, 30.
6. Maimonides, Guide *for the Perplexed*, I, 61.

who is existence, giving us to understand thereby that in the formula that translated his name, "the subject is identically the same thing as the attribute?" Thereby Maimonides re-encounters his own interpretation of the divine name *par excellence*: "It is therefore an explanation of this idea: that God exists, but not by existence; so that this idea is summed up and interpreted thus: the Being that is Being, that is to say the necessary Being."[7] In short, we do not know what God is, but we know that he is He Who Is.

It seems undeniable that the conjunction of a metaphysics of existence and the famous text of Exodus took place in Maimonides's thought. It can hardly be doubted that Saint Thomas, who read these texts, also grasped their importance, and we are certainly at one of the sources of the Thomistic metaphysics of being. The sublime truth—*haec sublimis veritas*—of which the *Summa Contra Gentiles* solemnly speaks,[8] bursts forth before our eyes for the first time in the fullness of metaphysical meaning that the text of Exodus will henceforth carry for Saint Thomas and his disciples. How should we determine what part of this the Muslim theologians owed to Jewish revelation, what part Maimonides owed them, and what part Thomas Aquinas owed him in turn for having conjoined the two lights of intellect and Scripture in this way? It is at least certain that here we relive one of the most solemn moments of the history of Western thought, when Judaism makes the world of Aristotelian substances burst, submitting the act of their forms to Pure Act which is not that of thought which thinks itself, but that of existence in itself. It is wonderful that the Jewish element in the metaphysics of the most profound Christian thinker let it become fully Christian; it is perhaps more wonderful that, though Judaism is little inclined to abstract metaphysical speculation, it impregnated the cosmos of Aristotle and his Greek commentators, thereby engendering a new philosophical world. Thirteenth-century Christian thought did not simply use the peripatetic universe. It metamorphosed it from within, consecrating the triumph of efficient cause over final cause. It turned each being into an existence made in the image and likeness of the Pure Act of existing.

Maimonides certainly set Thomas Aquinas on the royal road of metaphysics of *esse*, but only St. Thomas traveled it to the end. Nothing in what we know of the theologian of the *Guide* allows us to think that

7. Ibid., I, 63.
8. Aquinas, *Summa Contra Gentiles*, I, 22.

he had a premonition about the rich consequences that the existential notion of God could entail for what we now call ontology, to use a name that is dangerous at its very origin. Faithful to the teaching of Avicenna, Maimonides does not seem to have gone beyond the notion of created beings whose existence would be a sort of accidental appendage that would be added to essence to realize it. Clearly conscious of the uniqueness of the Supreme Existing designated by the Tetragrammaton, he does not seem to have seen that if the first cause of beings is such that his essence is existence, his effects necessarily must imitate him, at least in that the act of existing, by which they are beings, would not be in them as an appendage of essence, but as the act of all acts and the perfection of all perfections. In this sense, it is only in Thomas Aquinas where the theology extracted from Exodus by Maimonides has engendered philosophy properly speaking and has given birth to the new metaphysics where "the whole substance of being" is totally actuated by its own act of existing.

Boethius of Dacia
and Double Truth

FOR A LONG TIME it was held that certain masters affected by the condemnations of 1277, notably Siger of Brabant and Boethius of Dacia, had taught the so-called theory of "double truth." The text itself of the condemnation invites us to do that. According to this doctrine, certain conclusions might be "true" in philosophy, although the contrary conclusion was equally "true" from the point of view of revelation and of Christian faith. However, for some thirty years, most historians who studied the texts of these masters themselves a bit closely have coincided in concluding that no known text allows this doctrine to be attributed to them. Of course, nothing prevents that still unknown texts might someday attest to its existence. The same observation still holds today. Up to now, no known text would allow us to maintain that this doctrine has ever been expressly taught by anyone at all.

The editor of a previously unpublished work by Boethius of Dacia,[1] has seized the opportunity to reopen the debate. Very well documented

---

1. Sajó, *Un traité.* The author is a conservator of the National Library in Budapest. Regarding the important information that this unpublished texts offers us, Maurer, "Boetius of Dacia," 233–39. Our conclusions about the central problem of the notion of "double truth" match those of this historian.

about the present state of the question,[2] the scholar responsible for this valuable publication will not agree that the doctrine of double truth is a "position" imposed on Siger and Boethius by their adversaries. He does not think that it is a reduction to the absurd carried out by theologians opposed to their teaching to ensure its condemnation. According to this scholar, "The discovery of Boethius of Dacia's work *De Mundi Aeternitate* makes these recent assumptions untenable and at the same time confirms that it was precisely Boethius of Dacia who established and fixed the theory of double truth, notably, just in the spirit about which the 1277 decree of condemnation warns us."[3]

We are dealing with a question of fact here. Thus the only thing to do is to read the new document, in any case invaluable, which has just been revealed to us, and to seek the proof of this assertion in it. If we begin by reading the historical introduction that its author took the trouble to supply for the text, beyond doubt we find the sought after proof. The difficulties begin when instead of seeking this proof in the introduction, we seek it in the text. However, the problem is resolved in the simplest way in the world. It will be recalled that in the prologue to the condemnation of 1277, as we read in the *Chartularium Universitatis Parisiensis*, I, 543, a phrase denounced the general attitude of certain Masters toward theology as erroneous:

> Dicunt enim ea esse vera secundum philosophiam, sed non secundum fidem catholicam, quasi sint *due contrarie veritates*, et quasi contra veritatem sacre scripture sit veritas in dictis gentilium dampnatorum, de quibus scriptum est: "Perdam sapientiam sapientium," quia vera sapientia perdit falsam sapientiam.

So, what is necessary in order to have "established and fixed the theory of double truth, notably, totally in the spirit about which the 1277 decree of condemnation warns us"? We will not require that Boethius should have employed, even once, the expression *duplex veritas*, because as convenient as it may be, it is not found in the prologue

---

2. Sajó, *Un traité*, 34–37, especially 35: "it [this question] contains a detailed exposition of the so-called doctrine of double truth already condemned in the 1277 decree of censure, which became well known after this period." According to it, two opposed truths, which contradict each other notably one theological and one philosophical can be held at the same time (*simul stare possunt*). Long bibliographical notes are included (35 n.; 36 nn. 39, 40; 37 n. 41).

3. Sajó, *Un traité*, 37.

of the condemnation. Boethius would at least have to have said, literally or equivalently, either "certain things are true according to philosophy, which are not true according to the Catholic faith," or more simply, that there are "two contrary truths," *due contrarie veritates*.

If either of these two theses is found in the text of Boethius of Dacia, we would recognized that his new historian is right on this point. If, on the contrary, we only find the dialectical reductions of what Boethius said about the doctrine according to which there would be *due contrarie veritates*, we will regret to be unable to follow the author; not that he is necessarily wrong, but simply because such dialectical reductions do not fall under the domain of historical knowledge.

To give only one example of the impossibility of an historian discussing such positions, we will mention the following:

> However, taking this position produces a profound chasm between the dogmas of faith and the teaching of philosophers. To bridge it, the latter must find some expedient, and Boethius of Dacia believed he had found it in the thesis of the *double truth*: There is no opposition or contradiction between the teachings of faith and those of philosophy.[4]

Let us admit directly that if the doctrine of the double truth consists in saying with Boethius: *Ideo nulla est contradictio inter fidem et philosophiam* (line 962), this doctrine must be attributed to him. What remains a profound mystery for us, is in what sense a person who denies any contradiction between faith and philosophy could ever have sustained that "certain things are true according to philosophy, which are not true according to Catholic faith, as if there were two contrary truths." But precisely, where one person does not see what another takes as evidence, there any historical discussion is impossible. We will keep the investigation at the level of the text itself, just as it is, a bit literal it must be confessed, but where dialogue becomes possible.[5]

---

4. Ibid., 71

5. The author proceeds (71–74) to an analysis of the treatise in order to establish that Boethius really taught the so-called doctrine of double truth. An important contribution to history, for which we are beholden to the author, is the identification in Boethius's text of several of the propositions condemned in 1277. See Sajó, *Un traité*, 74–75, and in Maurer, "Boetius of Dacia," 234, for six propositions that seem to have been suggested by Boethius's *Question*.

POSITING THE *QUESTION*

Boethius's *Question* begins with a passage whose general sense can be rather clearly perceived, although the text is too corrupt for its translation to be certain. Boethius expresses his discomfort at being caught in a dilemma. On the one hand, it is ridiculous to try to demonstrate religious beliefs for which there are no demonstrations; he who does so looks for what it is impossible to find. On the other hand, to refuse to admit these beliefs on the pretext that they are not supported by reason is to adopt a heretical attitude. Boethius's intention is to remove this antinomy. He wants to make agreement prevail between what Christian faith teaches about the creation of the world with time and the teaching of Aristotle and other philosophers on this subject.

Let us note this conciliatory attitude at the outset There will be no question either of eliminating philosophical knowledge or of denying religious truth. There have been philosophers whom no religion seems to have convinced. In a rather curious phrase, Boethius seems to attribute Averroes's feelings about all established religious law to Aristotle himself. "We will not commit the stupidity of seeking demonstration in matters where it is not possible. We will not fall into the heresy, of refusing to believe what ought to be held by faith, under the pretext that it has no demonstration, as certain philosophers did formerly whom no established law pleased, because according to Aristotle, established laws never have demonstrations in their support" (lines 13–19).[6]

It is not at all the intention of Boethius himself to follow Aristotle on this point. On the contrary, he wants to justify the activity of philosophers in just the measure in which that can be done and in which the action reaches valid conclusions: "quantum ratio eorum concludere potest" (line 21). Indeed the conclusions of philosophers concern what is naturally possible and are based on reasons, whereas the teaching of faith often rests upon miracles, not on reasons. Besides, it must be thus, because what is held as a conclusion of reason is not a matter of faith, but rather of science. So, Boethius is going to discuss by reason the question

6. The text is defective, and the author must be praised for not having amended it. But the reader must do so to understand what he reads Here, in line 24 we substitute "innititur" for "in nullis," which we cannot understand. In line 25 we read "possibilibus" in place of "passibilibus."—A little above, in line 18 we have interpreted "placeat" as if the text contained "placebat."—It goes without saying that these chance emendations have no philological value, but we allow ourselves none with terms whose meanings involve the data of the problem and consequently would affect its solution.

of knowing whether the world is eternal, "in order to show that reason and faith do not contradict each other on the eternity of the world, and thus to show that the reasons on account of which certain heretics maintain that the world is eternal against Christian faith are not compelling."[7]

Let us observe the vocabulary that Boethius uses here. On the one hand, *ratio, demonstratio, sententia philosophorum, philosophia.* On the other hand, *fides, credere, sententia Christianae fidei.* The term *theologia* does not appear. The contrast that Boethius envisages (line 29) is between *philosophia* and *fides.* The word *veritas* does not appear in this introduction. Boethius employs it neither in regard to philosophy nor in regard to theology or faith. On the other hand, the general method that Boethius intends to follow to reconcile philosophy with faith can already be discerned. The method does not appeal to the doctrine of "double truth." If we are dealing with philosophy whose conclusions depend on rational demonstration, the believer has nothing to say, because he himself does not argue with a view to reason at all. Inversely, if we are dealing with faith, the philosopher has nothing to say, because he has no competence to appreciate miracles, which are the grounds of Christian truth. Understood in this way, the reconciliation attempted by Boethius is essentially separation. Boethius wants neither faith imposing its conclusions upon philosophy nor a philosophy, which, unable to impose its own conclusions on the doctrines of faith, is situated in heresy. No opposition could arise between the two disciplines if each is limited to the pursuit of truth by the means of which it disposes for its parts. So far, the text of Boethius says nothing of any sort of doctrine of "double truth."

PRO AND CONTRA

The body of the question consists, in the first place, of a series of arguments in favor of the eternity of the world (lines 35–106). The word *veritas* does not appear there. Next come the arguments in favor of the opposing thesis: first, the eternity of the world that implies no contradiction (lines 110–53); second, the world is truly eternal (lines 154–352):

7. "Et ut appareat quod philosophia et fides sibi non contradicant de aeternitate mundi, ut etiam pateat quod rationes quorumdam haereticorum non habent vigorem per quas contra fidem Christianam mundum tenent esse aeternum, de hoc autem inquiremus, utrum scilicet mundus sit aeternus" (lines 28–34). It ought to be apparent that where we deny that there is contradiction, double truth is not an issue. Since Géza Sajó has numbered the lines of his text continuously we limit ourselves to remit to the lines in our own text as well as in our notes.

the word *veritas* does not appear there either. But in lines 347–52, which finish this part of the work, Boethius makes the interesting remark that follows: "Likewise[8] there are reasons that certain heretics, supporters of the eternity of the world, use against the teaching of Christian faith that affirms the newness of the world. The Christian ought to behave with care against these objections in order to be able to resolve them if some heretic presents them against him."

Consequently, after declaring that he wanted to shun heresy, Boethius here affirms his intention to refute the heretics' arguments in favor of the eternity of the world. Now, let us note carefully that he will take the floor. To make him say that he considers that philosophers teach the truth on this issue or simply teach one of two possible truths on it, he must be made to affirm that he wants to be a heretic, what, on his part, would be to affirm the pro and the con regarding the same point, at the same time, and in the same respect. To tell the truth, Boethius still does not speak of truth. He seems to argue from a different approach to the question.

THE SOLUTION

The presentation of the response begins by a declaration of principle regarding the rights and duties of philosophers in everything within their domain.

All questions whose treatment only appeals to reasons fall under the jurisdiction of philosophy. There is not a single one that the philosopher ought not submit to discussion and about which he ought only to say what is true on the subject, in so far as that truth can be understood by human reason. This text is so important that it is useful to quote it verbatim:

> Primo hoc diligenter considerandum est, quod nulla quaestio potest esse, quae disputabilis est per rationem, quam philosophus non debeat disputare et determinare quomodo se habeat veritas in illa, quantum per rationem humanam comprehendi potest.
> (lines 354–58)

---

8. The text (line 347) has: "Item, sunt rationes . . ." Since no new reason turns out to be added to the previous ones, we can conjecture that the correct text would be rather: "Istae sunt rationes . . ." He would thus refer to all the reasons alleged by *quidam haeretici* against the thesis of the newness of the world.

To our knowledge, such is the only passage from this question where Boethius speaks of truth in regard to philosophy. It will be observed in the first place that, if he charges the philosopher with pursuing truth in every subject which reason can know, he does not unqualifiedly attribute to reason the power to find the truth. What the philosopher can and ought to seek and say is truth knowable by reason alone, "in so far as that truth can be understood by human reason." So, it is possible that human reason is not capable of attaining the whole truth about certain problems that it has the right and duty to treat.

In fact, that is not the object that Boethius seems to have in mind. He directly proposes to establish the philosopher's right to treat every question that can be posed by human reason and about which reason can make the best of its views, whatever their value may otherwise be. If he has adversaries here, they can only be people who deny the Christian philosopher the right to submit to the judgement of reason problems already solved by faith. Boethius responds to them that they do not know what philosophy is nor what are its methods.

> The explanation of what precedes is that all the reasons invoked in the discussion are taken from things. Without that, they would only be a fabrication of the intellect. The philosopher teaches the nature of all things. Indeed, just as philosophy teaches being, the parts of philosophy teach the parts of being. That is what is written in book IV of the *Metaphysics* (2, 1004 a 34), and it is self evident. Therefore, the philosopher has to ascertain every question that can be disputed by reason. Indeed every question disputable by way of reasons enters into some part of being. Now the philosopher speculates about all being: the natural, the mathematical, and the divine. Thus the philosopher has to ascertain every question disputable by way of reasons, and if anyone says the contrary, let him know that he does not know what he is talking about. (lines 358–72)

This general observation introduces a long development where Boethius establishes that neither the natural scientist (*naturalis*) nor the mathematician have been able to establish by reasoning that there would have been a first movement and that the world is new.

Perhaps it is useful to draw attention to the expression Boethius uses here. He does not claim that philosophers could have demonstrated by physical or mathematical reasons that the world is eternal. He undertakes to establish that philosophers have not been able to establish the novelty of the word, which places the emphasis on the negative aspect of their endeavor. No doubt, the nuance would be forced by saying that for Boethius the philosophers' undertaking was capped by failure. What he says exactly is that, *given their methods and their principles*, it would be contradictory to expect that philosophers could prove the novelty of the world or demonstrate that movement had ever had a beginning.

The reason why the natural scientist cannot so do is simple: he can only grant something in the light of his principles or those of his science. Now the principle from which all argumentation starts in natural philosophy is prime matter, which Aristotle sometimes calls nature itself. Nothing else is needed in order to establish the thesis in question, because what a nature does always presupposes the nature's existence, just as a movement always presupposes another movement that causes it. Thus there could be neither a new nature nor an absolutely first and new movement.

This fact exactly situates the natural scientist in regard to the notion of creation. Using language that is both precise and measured, Boethius says that the natural scientist cannot take it into consideration: *naturalis creationem considerare non potest* (line 449). The expression is eloquent. If we speak to the philosopher of creation, his only possible response is that such a notion can not be taken into consideration by a philosopher: "Indeed nature produces all its effects from a subject and from a matter, but to produce or to make from a subject or matter is to engender, it is not to create. That is why the natural scientist cannot take the notion of creation into consideration, because he can only take into account what falls under his principles. Now to make the world or to bring it forth into being cannot have been a generation, so it is evident it could only have been a creation. Thus it is quite right that the bringing forth of the world into being or the manner in which it was made are not taught in any part of the sciences of nature, because that bringing forth is not a natural production and the science of nature does not have to occupy itself with it (lines 450–60). We notice in this whole part of the question the frequency, which is certainly intentional, of the expressions *non potest ponere, nec potuit ponere*, and others of the same sort. The very nature of philosophy forbids in principle any consideration of this sort. Boethius does not go further.

The same argument establishes that, judging from the point of view of nature, there could not have been a first man. Indeed nature only produces in the mode of generation. A man can only engender a man, and since it is absurd to think that a man could have been at the same time first and engendered, the natural scientist can not envisage the notion of "first man." Once more, it is simply a matter of this, that his principles do not permit him to do it: *naturalis non potest illa considerare ad quae principia suae scientiae se non extendunt* (lines 468–70). With the same precision in his moderation, Boethius reduces everything to a problem of doctrinal jurisdiction: "If we attentively consider that with which the natural scientist is capable of occupying himself, it will be seen that what precedes is reasonable: indeed, not every artisan (*artifex*) is capacitated to consider every truth" (lines 470–73).

Boethius himself could only hope that this somewhat external reconciliation would be accepted without discussion. At the end of his argument, encounters and clashes between philosophers and theologians are still forbidden, but the problem of the value of their respective conclusions remains almost untouched. The long development devoted to the clarification of the problem adds nothing essential to what went before, but it is important to take it into consideration, if only in order to protect ourselves as much as possible against any serious error of interpretation. Here is what Boethius says on the subject:

> It will be objected that the truth of Christian faith or even truth pure and simple [*veritas Christianae fidei et etiam veritas simpliciter*] is that the world is new and not eternal; that creation is possible; that there was a first man; that after his death man will come back to life, without generation and numerically identical; and that this same numerically identical man, who was corruptible before, will be incorruptible henceforth, in such a way that one single and even indivisible species will contain these two differences, corruptible and incorruptible. Although the natural scientist is not capable of establishing these truths, nor of knowing them, because the principles of his science do not attain such arduous and secret works of divine wisdom, nevertheless, he must not deny these truths. Indeed, although an artisan (*artifex*) can neither produce nor know the truths of sciences known by other artisans through his own principles, nevertheless, he must not deny them. Thus, although the natural scientist cannot, starting from his principles, either know or affirm what goes before, because the principles of his science do not reach so far, he still ought not to deny them, if someone confronts him with them, even though he is not confronted by them as true in consequence

of any reasons but in the name of a revelation made by some
higher cause. (lines 474–94)

If we keep to the above, it seems difficult to find a doctrine of double truth in Boethius. St. Thomas Aquinas would have come down in agreement that philosophy cannot establish, by its methods and starting from its principles, that the world is not eternal, nor that every person will rise on the last day, numerically the same without that being the effect of a new generation. It is hard to see what theologian could not approve the attitude that the philosopher ought not to deny the teaching of revelation simply because its content escapes the grasp of philosophy. However, the formula which is so simple to write, *est duplex veritas or sunt duae veritates* is found nowhere in the text of the question. Nothing that could be regarded as an equivalent to these formulas is found there. A series of subterfuges or loopholes can be seen in its language. So we enter a long series of suppositions about the secret thoughts of people who, since they had to keep them secret, by definition rendered it impossible for historians like us to know their true thoughts. Practically speaking, there is no difference for us between what a person does not say and what he does not think. In the case of Boethius, what he says has a perfectly intelligible meaning, if it is taken literally. Let us suppose that we ask a biologist what he thinks about the resurrection of the dead. His response will be that, judging as a biologist, such a thing is impossible; *ista debet negare naturalis, quia naturalis nihil concedit, nisi quod videt esse possibile per causas naturales* (lines 511–13). What did we expect him to say? That natural science, precisely as such, can admit the possibility of miracles? But, if miracles are naturally possible, they do not exceed the forces of nature, they are not at all miraculous. Boethius is not mistaken; in any case he says only what is perfectly intelligible in maintaining that what a natural scientist holds to be impossible from the point of view of science, he holds to be possible in virtue of a higher cause, which is the Cause of all nature: *ideo sibi non contradicit in hoc, sicut nec in aliis* (lines 513–16).

What bothers his interpreters is precisely the skill that he demonstrates in only speaking about "consideration" or "affirmation" without ever saying whether what the philosopher affirms is affirmed by him as true. Let us admit that the biologist declares that the resurrection of the dead is a natural impossibility and that he limits his affirmation to what it is possible to know from the viewpoint of reason alone, how is it not obvious that the theologian himself will not be satisfied by that answer? He will object, if the Christian teaching about the resurrection of the dead is true, does it not follow thereby that the philosopher who denies it says something false?[9]

That is precisely what Boethius himself said. In an expression that seems definitive to us, Boethius declares:

> It is simultaneously possible (*simul stant*) to maintain that there was a first movement and that the world is new, but that the novelty of the world does not stem from natural causes or natural principles. Indeed, it is simultaneously possible, if we are attentive, that the world and a first movement be new, but that the natural scientist should deny the novelty of a first movement and of the world, because that he denies the novelty of the world on the basis of the principles of nature, is natural itself. Indeed, all that the natural scientist denies or admits, in so far as he is a natural scientist, he denies or admits from the viewpoint of the causes and principles of nature. Thus, the conclusion in which the natural scientist says that the world and the first movement are not new, is false taken absolutely, but if it is related to the reasons and principles from which he draws the conclusion, it follows from them. (lines 522–35)

These words ought not be either overestimated or given less than their full significance: *Unde conclusio in qua naturalis dicit mundum et primum motum non esse novum, accepta absolute, falsa est* (lines 531–34). Boethius does not say that this conclusion is absolutely false. He does not even say that it is false absolutely speaking. He simply says that, taken absolutely, it is false. Indeed, it is false to say that the novelty of the world and the beginning of movement are false conclusions from the viewpoint of faith. But then, won't we say that these negations are true from the point of view of the natural scientist and the philosopher? Boethius does not say so. Connected back to the principles to which the philosopher, the natural scientist, or the scholar appeal, all the negations of this sort follow: *ex illis sequitur* (line 535). Once again, Boethius refuses the chance that he offers to himself to declare true a philosophical conclusion that is irreconcilable with the teaching of revelation.

---

9. "Si autem ulterius opponas, cum haec sit veritas, quod homo mortuus immediate redit vivus et idem numero, sicut ponit fides Christiana quae in suis articulis verissima est, nonne naturalis hoc negans dicit falsum?" (lines 517–21).

Only one question remains: how could Boethius's editor, who, we can be sure, did not fail to read a single word of the invaluable text we owe to him, write that his author taught the doctrine of double truth? Pursuing this question will offer us the solution to the problem.

Let us recall the conclusion reached above. Boethius could have concluded that the natural scientist's conclusion is true on the basis of the principles that guide him. He did not say so. He merely gave us to understand that it is perfectly true that it follows from them. He did not say that the conclusion is true. From these positions, his historian deduces nothing less than that Boethius taught the doctrine of double truth. He even quotes Boethius's own words: *uterque dicit verum* (p. 72). And it certainly must be recognized that if he said that, Boethius certainly held the thesis in question. But did he truly say it? Let us first hear his editor and historian:

> Therefore the two theses, apparently opposed, each state a truth (*uterque dicit verum*). But let us hear Boethius himself: "Indeed we know that he who says Socrates is white and he who denies that Socrates is white, both say what is true under a certain viewpoint."[10] Likewise the Christian speaks the truth when he affirms that the world and the first movement are new, that there was a first man, that each man will come back to life numerically the same, and that an engenderable being can come to existence without having been engendered, provided only that we admit that it is possible by a cause whose power is greater than that of a natural cause. But the person who says that that is not possible by natural causes and principles also tells the truth (*veritatem etiam dicit qui dicit hoc non esse possibile ex causis et principiis naturalibus*). Indeed the natural scientist (*naturalis*) only concedes or denies anything on the basis of natural principles and natural causes in the same way that the grammarian, speaking as such, denies nothing, and concedes nothing except based on grammatical principles and grammatical causes. As he only considers truths of causes, the natural scientist (*naturalis*) says that neither the world nor movement are new, whereas, taking into account a higher cause than nature, Christian faith says that the

---

10. "Scimus enim quod qui dicit Socratem esse album, et qui negat Socratem esse album, secundum quod, uterque dicit verum" (lines 535–38). We would expect "album secundum quid." Examining the text as it is, we hesitate between referring *secundum quod* to *esse album* or to *dicit verum*. In any case, the sense remains the same: from certain points of view, it is true that Socrates is white (skin color); from certain others, it is true that Socrates is not white (hair color).

world can be new in virtue of this cause. They do not contradict
each other in any way. Thus two things are evident: one is that the
natural scientist does not contradict Christian faith regarding the
eternity of the world; the other is that the newness of the world
and of the first movement cannot be demonstrated by natural
reasons. (lines 535–38)

It thereby becomes possible to specify the sense of the doctrine.
Since Socrates is white, but not totally white, someone who affirms
that Socrates is white and someone who denies it are each right from
a certain point of view. Thus both speak the truth in a certain sense.
Similarly, the Christian speaks the truth when he affirms, in the name
of faith, that the world had a beginning. As for the philosopher, scholar,
or natural scientist, Boethius does not say that he is right to deny the
eternity of the world, but that he is right to deny that such a thing would
be possible based on natural causes and natural principles. Once again,
at the moment when he speaks of a rational thesis that contradicts revelation, Boethius hedges. His *uterque dicit verum* is certainly applied to
the truth of faith, but it is not applied to the conclusion of philosophy.
The thesis that it seemed this expression ought to demonstrate still slips
through our fingers.

The same attitude is found in subsequent developments where
Boethius establishes that the teaching of Christian faith on these several
points does not admit mathematical demonstration. Perhaps Boethius
even goes further here in the direction of what is labeled his reserve,
his reticence, his prudence, in short what one pleases, in regard to the
possible truth of such philosophical conclusions. Still speaking about
the possibility of eternity of movement and of the world, Boethius declares that we are dealing with a false supposition here: *Dato hoc etiam
falso quod motus primus et mundus sit aeternus* (lines 591–92). Thus he
speaks as if he held the conclusion of faith to be a truth, and that of
philosophy that contradicts the first truth as an error.

The same applies in the course of the developments where Boethius
establishes that the metaphysician can demonstrate nothing about this
subject. Completely in agreement with St. Thomas Aquinas on this
particular issue, Boethius asks how a point could be demonstrated that
depends solely on the divine will. That would be madness.[11] It is in fact

11. "Dicere enim quod metaphysicus possit hoc demonstrare, non solum figmento,
sed etiam credo, dementiae simile est: unde enim demonstratio, per quam voluntatem
divinam perfecte investiget?" (lines 622–26).

completely clear that if the world is created, it only depends on the divine will that it should be in time or from all eternity. Boethius thus continues to harmonize the two disciplines by assuring philosophy its complete autonomy precisely because, on the points where his conclusions contradict those of revelation, it is not a matter of regarding them as true. Provided that Christian faith does not claim to justify itself by philosophical demonstrations, no conflict is to be feared.[12] Meanwhile, let us not doubt for an instant what is the pure truth in these matters: *Dicimus autem quod mundus non est aeternus, sed de novo causatus, quamvis hoc per rationes demonstrari non possit* (lines 671–73); and again, the passage where Boethius announces that he is going to refute *rationes quae nituntur probare contrarium veritati, scilicet mundo Deo esse coaeternum* (lines 682–85). Of course, the reasons that claimed to demonstrate the creation of the world in time, or as Boethius says, the newness of the world, are sophistical (lines 934–35), but precisely if he cannot approve them, he grants them, because at least their conclusion is true: *rationes ad partem oppositam [scilicet novitatem mundi] concedantur, licet solvi possint, cum sint sophisticae.*

It would be a mistake to imagine Boethius as a timid individual constantly held back by fear of theologians. There is no such thing in his character. Boethius is a philosopher. None of his words permits us to doubt the sincerity of his faith or the absolute respect he has for the teaching of revelation, but he cannot bear the tribe of theologians who, in meddling in philosophy without having truly studied it deeply, attempt to impose conclusions in the name of reason that they really hold only on faith. "Do not believe," he says to these theologians, "that the philosopher who has spent his life in the study of wisdom,[13] has contradicted the Christian religion in any way whatsoever, but rather, since you are a small mind in comparison to the philosophers who were and still are the wise men of this world, study therefore in order to be able to understand their words" (lines 964–69). Perhaps it would not misrepresent his true thought if we attributed this fairly simple sentiment to him: philosophy is not faith, but it is a beautiful thing in itself; if you are ignorant of it, study it; in any case, respect it.

12. Lines 627–70.

13. We retain the manuscript's lower case *p*, with almost inner certainty that there ought to be a capital *P* here, and that we are dealing with Philosophy here. But this is not completely certain.

Indeed the feeling that is perceptible underneath his words reveals the deep concerns of Boethius. At the same time as he forbids his philosopher to oppose faith, Boethius means to guarantee the rights of the Christian to practice philosophy: "Indeed they say that the Christian as such cannot be a philosopher, because his religious law obliges him to ruin the principles of his philosophy." If the separation proposed by Boethius is admitted, the principles of philosophy remain intact in the mind of the believer, without the object of his faith thereby suffering in the slightest. Indeed the Christian thus grants that the conclusion that is deduced from philosophical reasons could not be different from what it is, if we start from these principles and from the examination of natural causes from which it is concluded, but he maintains that the conclusion must be different, if we argue, as the Christian does, from a higher cause, which is the cause of nature itself and of every caused being.

That is what seems to stand out in Boethius own words:

> So if the Christian's intellect is free enough, his religious law does not oblige the Christian to ruin the principles of his philosophy, but he safeguards the faith and philosophy as one whole without picking one or the other. As for those for whom philosophy is too difficult to understand, even if someone among them is established in a position of dignity [the Bishop of Paris?], let him obey one wiser than he and let him believe the Christian law, not on account of a sophistical reason, which would always be deceitful, or for a dialectical reason, which could not produce a habit as solid as faith since the conclusion of dialectical reasoning always involves the danger that the alternative might be true; nor finally by demonstrative reason, which is not always possible in matters of faith, and which, moreover, would cause knowledge in us. Indeed, a demonstration is a syllogism that makes us know,[14] while to believe is not to know. As to what comes from Christian law, to which every Christian must adhere, may He deign to make him believe it, as befits Him who is the glorious author of this very Law of Christ, God, blessed for world without end. Amen. (lines 986–1002)

Assuredly, Boethius's position was not of the sort that could satisfied those who insisted on demonstrating by philosophical reasoning that the world began in or with time. But good minds like St. Thomas Aquinas did not believe that demonstration possible either. If his overall attitude

14. *Posterior Analytics*, 1, 2, 71 b 17–18.

can be judged by this text, Boethius seems to have used a remarkably moderate language, and nothing lets us suppose that this moderation in tone was not also moderation in thought. In any case, after, just as before, the publication of this question *De Mundi Aeternitate*, we still await for the first text to be discovered in which the thesis condemned in 1277 is expressly maintained, and whose statement is so clear: *dicunt enim eas esse vera secundum philosophiam, sed non secundum fidem Catholicam, quasi sint due contrarie veritates.* Nobody claims that such a text does not exist. The monstrous absurdity of a thesis like this unhappily does not prove it was never held. It only invites us to show a little diffidence about the proof of its existence. After having read this text by a mind, certainly divided and muddled, but noble, lofty, in love with the wisdom of this world, and, at the end of the day, worthy of having conceived the touching little work *De Summo Bono*, we feel a kind of relief seeing that nothing forces us to make him bear the responsibility for such a mediocre attitude. If history one day discovers the guilty party, he will doubtless not be a man of the same rank as Boethius. Above all, we would like to hope that it will not be he.

PERSPECTIVES

Boethius of Dacia was badly known. From now on he will be a little less so thanks to the discovery and publication of this remarkable *Question*. We are beholden to Mr. Géza Sajó for new information on Boethius of Dacia's particular attitude in regard to the problem of the relations between philosophy and faith. This *Question* is perhaps the most explicit text we might consult on this problem, and the information that it offers contributes to the clarification of an important area of doctrinal history of the thirteenth century.

There is much more real agreement among historians than so many sterile controversies about names would allow us to think. Historical labels are only symbols of facts or groups of facts, whose description they can in no case replace. Doctrinal labels are not chemical formulas. The doctrines themselves are not chemical bodies. No label designates any doctrine correctly, because no doctrine is exhaustively analyzable. A doctrine properly bears only one name, its author's, and this of all cases is the one where the mere label shows us the least about the doctrine's content. The label then becomes a proper name. It designates an individual doctrine and only one.

Boethius of Dacia seems to have been one of those masters of arts in charge of teaching Aristotle's philosophy at the University of Paris, who not only did not have to teach theology, but to whom it was positively forbidden to meddle with it. That alone put them in a state of separation laden with all kinds of misunderstandings. For, in the last analysis, they were only authorized to meddle with theology in order not to contradict it, and that alone would have obliged them to occupy themselves with it.

From the outset, this type of teaching collided with a particular difficulty, which was the absence of tradition. There was a long tradition for the teaching of logic. There were even several. For the teaching of Aristotle's books on nature, metaphysics, ethics, and politics, there was none. However, there was the Commentator, Averroes. For every professor of Aristotelianism, Averroes was indispensable. Everyone made use of him. St. Bonaventure himself quotes him verbatim in his commentary on the *Sentences*. St. Thomas always keeps him at hand in difficult passages, and if he does not always agree with him, he never neglects him. The masters of arts could not do otherwise. For them, taken as a whole, the teaching of Aristotle and the commentary on it by Averroes were one thing. Nothing forced them to deposit such confidence in the Commentator. Avicenna might have been given preference, and some occasionally did so. The exactness of certain interpretations of Aristotle proposed by Averroes could have been challenged, with texts in hand, and Thomas Aquinas did so. It is very bold for an historian of our times to take part in this controversy and declare that the Aristotle of Averroes was the real Aristotle. Who is the real Aristotle? That of Eduard Zeller or that of Franz Brentano? Historically speaking, it is sufficient for us to know that certain masters of Paris accepted, overall, the Averroist interpretation of Aristotle's doctrine That is what made them be called Averroist, a sort of label that never meant anything else, and which like all labels turns out to be inadequate as soon as we want to make it a description.

However, Averroes's influence extended beyond the mere interpretation of Aristotle. It touched on the delicate point of the relations between philosophy and religious faith.

The interpretation of Averroes's own thought on this problem is an exhaustible source of controversies. Thus, it is not a matter here of starting from it to situate the Christian masters who underwent its influence. There is even a point where neither Siger nor Boethius, as far as we understand their respective attitudes, ever spoke like Averroes. Whatever interpretation of his doctrine is adopted, it is absolutely certain that in Averroes's mind, philosophical knowledge is the highest type of knowledge and of truth available to man. Apart from the unique case of the Prophet, in whom the perfection of philosophical knowledge and religious knowledge coincide,[15] the revelation offered to the faith of the believers only proposes to them under a form that is efficacious as a practical matter, but imaginative and crude, a substitute for philosophical truth to which it is impossible for them to accede. The philosopher after the heart of Averroes is most careful to avoid touching on popular faith. He is no less careful to keep from popularizing his philosophy before a public unable to understand it. But that knowledge by simple faith, founded on revelation alone, might be superior in certainty and truth to philosophical knowledge, is something that Averroes never granted.[16] It is even what he expressly denied. By contrast, Boethius proclaims loudly that in case of disagreement between philosophy and faith, truth pure and simple is found on the side of revelation and faith. The disagreement is important, and it must be noted.

However, on this very point a secret thread links the head of the school to those whom we name after him. The preferred adversaries of Averroes are not simple believers, who certainly are right to believe what they have been told to believe for the tranquility of public order and peace of the State. Likewise they are not the public preachers who, quite rightly using the resources of rhetoric, energetically strive to implant faith in the hearts of the masses by promising them a paradise on the level of their mediocrity or by threatening them with punishments calculated to inspire fear in them. The adversaries whom Averroes attacks are the theologians. He does not excuse them for putting at the service of revelation a bastard dialectic that tries to pass for philosophy. In his eyes, theology is neither the healthy and kindly faith of simple people nor the noble truth known by a small number of philosophers only. It is a simply probable doctrine, incapable of keeping the masses in order as revelation does, nor of satisfying the intellectual desire for certain knowledge

15. The observation holds for all prophets. Furthermore, let us note that the doctrine of the separate agent intellect, taught by Averroes, situates the philosopher and the prophet, certainly not at the same level, but in the same line of intellectual illumination. The distinction remains no less clear: "Every prophet is a philosopher, but not every philosopher is a prophet." See Gardet, *La pensée religieuse*, 119 n. 4.

16. Gauthier, *La théorie d'Ibn Rochd*. By the same author, "Accord de la religion."

as philosophy does. Since transforming faith into science in an impossible undertaking, theology is sophistry. His vigorous denunciations of those positions of Avicenna that, under color of philosophy, teach badly disguised theology are particularly useful to consider for someone who wishes to understand Averroes's attitude on this point.

Here again, Averroes's influence was very extensive in the sense that, even when they opposed him, Catholic theologians including St. Thomas Aquinas himself, owe him, at least in part, their having understood what philosophy is and the need to take it seriously. That was not a small thing. Philosophical knowledge is what it is. It cannot be made to say what one pleases. St. Thomas maintained it *contra murmurantes*, and furthermore, that is why those who did not wish him well took pleasure in confusing him with the crowd of followers of Averroes. They were mistaken, but their instinct did not mislead them entirely. Averroes's example certainly enters in part into St. Thomas Aquinas's philosophical formation.

However, the fact remains that if Averroes had been followed on this particular point, he would have prevented the flowering of all the great theologies that are the honor of the Christian thirteenth century. The fundamentally anti-Averroist challenge sustained by St. Thomas was precisely to show that far from perishing by integrating itself into Christian theology, philosophy achieved the fulfillment of a confused desire of natural reason in the climate of revelation and grace. Just as nature becomes a better nature under the fertilization of grace, philosophy ought to become better philosophy in order to become usable by the theologian. It is true that theologies differ by their philosophy, but it is no less true that theologies make themselves the philosophies by which they differ. If Averroes's influence had triumphed in the thirteenth century, the history of medieval philosophy would be reduced to the history of Aristotelianism in the Middle Ages. Its historians then would have no other resource than to attack one another, because they would have nothing to tell.

This is why the thirteenth-century theologians showed themselves so harsh toward the "Averroists." They were not completely wrong: the existence of theology itself was at stake. If triumphant, Averroism would have authorized the coexistence in separation of a philosophy alien to any religious concern and religious predication without contact with philosophical speculation. The great theologies of St. Bonaventure, St. Thomas Aquinas, Henry of Ghent, John Duns Scotus, and even Ockham, who all speak the language of Aristotle, though none of them teach his doctrine even in the area of philosophy, would never have been able to reach birth. The Christianized metaphysics of the seventeenth century would probably have become impossible. We no more would have had Descartes than St. Thomas Aquinas. It is not even totally certain that we would have had the infinite substance composed of an infinity of infinite attributes that Spinoza bequeathed to us.

The thirteenth-century theologians did not see so far ahead. They certainly did not concern themselves with preparing the way for Descartes and still less for Spinoza. But they had a lively interest in the theology as they conceived it themselves, and they saw clearly that the effect of an attitude like that of Boethius of Dacia would have rendered all theology impossible.

The crucial point at issue is that, following Averroes, Boethius holds the use of any philosophical argumentation in theology to be purely dialectical. Contenting himself with what is probable, the theologians commits the absurdity of re-enforcing the habit of faith, unshakeable in itself, with simple rational probabilities, always accepted *cum formidine alterius partis* (lines 990–93). Even more, since an effort is demanded of philosophy that it cannot supply, the probability that is expected of her in theology is inevitably sophistical. This denunciation of the theologians' dialectic strikes at the heart of theology: *Unde pro fide non debet adduci ratio sophistica, sicut per se patet, nec ratio dialectica, quia ipsa non facit firmum habitum, sed solum opinionem, et firmior debet esse fides quam opinio* (lines 676–79). "Sophistical" is the expression applied by Boethius of Dacia to the arguments invoked by some theologians in favor of the newness of the world, and since they pretend to demonstrate the indemonstrable, all these dialectical arguments are indeed sophisms.

Boethius's attitude toward the theological method of the scholastics comes to him in a direct line from Averroes. We ourselves see it at work, more clearly perhaps than Boethius saw it in the Commentator's treatise against Algazel, *The Destruction of the Destructions*. In the "First Discussion," which Averroes devotes to the problem of the eternity of the world, the first response to the first proof offered by the theologians in favor of the newness of the world begins with these words: "This argument is dialectical in the highest degree, and does not rise to the level of a demonstrative proof."[17] From that point, we do not go long without

17. Van Den Bergh, *Averroes' Tahafut*, I:1.

meeting more summary judgements of the same sort: "The argument is sophistical . . ." "The argument is extremely feeble . . ."; but above all, "He who tries to prove the existence of an agent in this way, only provides persuasive arguments, dialectical arguments, not an apodictic proof. Alfarabi and Avicenna are thought to have followed this path to prove that every act must have an agent, but it is not a good proof that comes from the ancient philosophers, and both simply borrowed it from the theologians of our religion." In short, as Averroes says, "All these arguments, whatever they may be, are purely dialectical arguments."[18]

When the term "Averroist" was first applied to certain Latins, it referred less to the content of their doctrines, about which almost nothing was known in what concerns the thirteenth century, than to the separation between religion and philosophy, paralleled by a natural opposition to the dialectical methods that the scholastic theologians used. These masters pretended to reserve exclusively to themselves the employment of philosophy, the right to scientific demonstration, in short, the capacity to go beyond the level of the probable to achieve that of demonstration. The issue was to know whether theology was going to abdicate every right to make use of reason. What was directly at stake in the Averroist crisis was not the interpretation of Aristotle it was the very possibility of *fides quaerens intellectum.*

Thomas Aquinas saw perfectly the point at which, in their critique of theological method, the philosophers made things easy for themselves by reserving to themselves the privilege of necessary demonstration and of the correct use of reason. One of his first concerns in the *Summa Theologiae*[19] is precisely to reclaim the right for the theologian to philosophical argumentation whose monopoly Boethius of Dacia reserved for philosophers. Far from bowing to this demand, Thomas makes clear that since the truth of faith is unshakable, the theologian can and must argue against all those who deny it, with the certainty that any reason directed against it is an refutable argument. In the same article's response to the second objection, Thomas goes further. He expressly reclaims the right for the theologian to use human reason, not to demonstrate faith, which would destroy its merit, but to clarify what theology teaches in some measure: *Cum enim gratia non tollat naturam, sed perficiat, oportet quod naturalis ratio subserviat fidei, sicut et naturalis inclinatio voluntatis*

18. Ibid., I:31–32.

19. Aquinas, *Summa Theologiae*, I, 1, 8.

subsequitur caritati. That is not all; even philosophical authorities can be presented by the theologian in favor of faith, although sacred doctrine uses these authorities only as arguments that are alien to its essence and merely probable: *quasi extraneis argumentis et probabilibus.* What would have remained of this theological method and of scholastic theology in general, if views like those of Boethius of Dacia had prevailed in the thirteenth century? No doubt, not much. Perhaps absolutely nothing. It is not at all certain that in the last analysis Averroes and Averroism in all its forms, even in its latent forms, did not finally achieve victory. But when that event occurred, scholasticism existed and the great theologies of the Middle Ages had already accomplished their task. They are what saved Western philosophical speculation from sliding into Aristotelian commentary, with the option to choose between Avicenna, Averroes, and Alexander of Aphrodisias. But it would be necessary to wander much too far from Boethius to enter once more into that view of history which could not obtain the favor of today's historical Averroism.

8

$$\mathcal{\approx}$$

NOTES FOR THE HISTORY OF
EFFICIENT CAUSALITY

AMONG PHILOSOPHERS, THE NOTION of efficient causality is no-
torious because of the obscurities that it conceals. Perhaps these
obscurities might be clarified a little if history would take more pains to
study the origins of the concept. Of course, a strictly philosophical answer to the difficulties that this concept presents would not be obtained
from history, but the problem's data will be much more definite. Perhaps
several of them will be seen, whose importance or sometimes even existence has not yet been observed. The only object of the notes that follow
is to draw attention to certain of them.

ON THE FIFTH KIND OF CAUSE

We recently devoted a short study to "Avicenna and the Concept of Efficient Cause." It can be found in the *Atti del XII Congresso Internazionale
di filosofia*, 1961. Part of that essay deals with a text of St. Albert the
Great, where the concept of efficient cause is discussed on its own, as
distinct from those of agent cause and motor cause. The problem is of
great importance because it involves that of knowing whether Aristotle's philosophy had room for the concept of *causa efficiens* or simply of
causa agens over and above that of motor cause and distinct from it. All

these concepts became so inseparable, especially after St. Thomas Aquinas, that we run the risk of encountering only incredulity when we pose the question. However, it has its importance, because only the correct answer lets us distinguish the first way from the second in St. Thomas's famous *quinque viae*. Let us first recall St. Albert's text:

> Scitur etiam ex hiis quae dicta sunt, qualiter quidam dixerunt quinque esse causas, eo quod efficientem quam sequitur esse in quantum est esse, diviserunt a causa movente in quantum est movens. Quidam autem quatuor esse dixerunt, eo quod una est in communi ratio efficientis et moventis; et hujus est facere esse quod non est. Patet autem quod efficiens secundum istam rationem est ante omnes alias substantia et ratione et ordine naturae. Sed non oportet quod movens in eo quod movens sit ante alias omnes substantias, nisi in quodam quod videlicet movetur, sed simpliciter et universaliter accipiendo non est verum, quin potius finis ante erit, et etiam forma quaedam si qua est forma prima: sed in sequentibus erit de talibus tempus loquendi.[1]

Who were those *quidam* who admitted five kinds of causes and not four, against the commonly accepted thesis? We did not and still do not know, but we wish to recall the existence of a text of Seneca, moreover, one well known by historians of medieval philosophy, although it is ordinarily read in relation to the problem of the Platonic doctrine of ideas rather than of the division of causes. Hence the scant attention it receives in this regard. By contrast, it becomes impossible to not take note of what it says when we find it quoted in a question of Henry of Harclay on the divine ideas, recently edited by Fr. Armand Maurer, CSB. Harclay himself, we see, approaches the question from the Platonic doctrine of Ideas. This whole part of his question even offers the example of a theologian, rather unusual before him, whom the desire of better understanding Augustine engages in a detailed examination of the texts of Seneca's letters to Lucilius, where we find the Platonic doctrine of Ideas summarized and interpreted. The precise point that holds Harclay's attention is the relation of the notion of idea to that of production. The idea, he correctly observes, is not required with a view to production as such, but with a view to rational production. Without the Ideas, it could still be held that God produced things, but not that he produced them rationally: *solummodo ad productionem rationalem requiritur*

1. Albert the Great, In V *Metaphysicorum*, tract. 1, ch. 3, 270.

[*idea*]; *ergo non propter productionem simpliciter.*[2] This relation between the concept of Idea and that of production explains the relation that we would like to establish between the doctrine of Ideas and that of causes.

In letter 58 to Lucilius, where he complains about lacking a Latin word to translate the Greek τό ὄν. Seneca recalls that a scholar friend had just told him precisely that Plato understands it in six different senses. In its most general sense, it can be rendered into Latin by *quod est*. According to the classification reported by Seneca, *quod est* thus taken in its universality and absolute abstraction would be the first sense of the Greek term that the Latins lack. It is an intelligible that can be conceived but not seen or touched. Using a comparison, Seneca establishes the same relation between the notion of *quod est* and that of particular beings as between the notion of man and those of Cicero or Cato, or between the notion of animal and those of horse or dog. Cicero can be seen, man cannot be seen; he can only be conceived. The same holds for other concepts of the same type: *Animal non videtur, sed cogitatur; videtur autem species ejus, equus et canis.* The other five senses of the same word are the following: That which is *par excellence* and which deserves the name because it possesses it in the highest degree. Thus conceived, being is to other beings roughly like Homer to other poets. Homer is the poet *par excellence*; he who is being par excellence is the god: *Quid ergo hoc est? Deus, scilicet maior ac potentior cunctis.* In the third place come beings properly speaking, that is to say the genus of things of which it can be said that they are, in the strict sense of the term They are innumerable, but invisible: *tertium genus est eorum, quae proprie sunt; innumerabilia haec sunt, sed extra nostrum posita conspectum.* These are Plato's Ideas: immortal, unmovable, inviolable; they are the eternal models of natural beings. The form of natural being can be distinguished: *idos,* from the previous form that is that of the model: *idea.* In this sense: *Idos in opere est, Idea extra opus; nec tantum extra opus, sed ante opus.* The *idos* (which corresponds roughly to the Aristotelian form) is the fourth kind of being, or the fourth meaning of the word. The fifth meaning designates what we usually call beings, animals, men, etc. The sixth meaning designates what is being by approximation, like the void or time. It is the purely Platonic aspect of being that characterizes the Idea: Immutability. But it is remarkable that here the god is placed

---

2. Maurer, "Henry of Harclay's Questions." The passage quoted is found on 191.

above the idea, something not found in Plato himself. Seneca's Platonism is very seductive in the eyes of Christian theologians.

The passage from being to cause takes place in Letter 65, *Hesternum Diem*. There, Seneca starts from the Stoic division of beings in two parts: matter and cause. Matter is that of which a thing is made, cause is that which makes it: *esse debet ergo unde aliquid fiat, deinde a quo fiat: hoc causa, illud materia*. Thus there is only one cause properly speaking, efficient cause: *Stoicis placet unam casam esse, id quod facit*. Stoicism thus represents an entirely different tradition from Aristotelianism in what concerns the doctrine of causality. However, it must be observed that Seneca himself does not employ the denomination *causa efficiens* that we almost irresistibly attribute to him, so familiar has it become to us. Here as elsewhere, the Latin lacks abstract words. Seneca simply says *quod facit*. Matter is that of which a thing is made (*unde aliquid fit*), cause is that which makes it (*a quo fit*). To say *cause* or to say *productive cause*, is the same thing.

The four-part division of causes in Aristotle is so well known that it will suffice here to recall it: material, formal, motor, and final. But it is worth noting the important modification or, at the very least, specification, that this division receives in Seneca. Even today, most all the interpreters of Aristotle who read him, consciously or not, in the light of Thomas Aquinas, identify what Aristotle called "the origin of movement," or motor cause, with what we call today the efficient cause. The issue here is not to settle a debate where the whole interpretation of Aristotle's teaching is at stake. In Aristotle, we can either identify the origin of movement with the form acting as final cause, or, on the contrary, endow the form with an efficacy that makes it an efficient cause properly speaking. What is certain in any case is that Seneca himself interprets the doctrine in the second sense. He makes "that from which the movement comes" into a Stoic efficient cause. The second Aristotelian cause then becomes the artisan: *Secunda opifex*. Assuredly, Aristotle himself teaches that the artisan is a typical example of causality in the mode of origin of a moment, but it can always be asked how the artisan produces the movement from which the work was born. Or how the doctor produces the movement in the body from which the recovered health in the patient will be born. Aristotle says nothing specific about it, and that is one of the principle reasons to doubt that he ever conceived the notion of productive efficacy, that very same thing that Hume would later doubt that any one can truly conceive. Seneca, on the contrary, interprets Aristotle's motor cause as the efficient cause of Stoicism: *Secunda causa artifex est: non potuisset enim aes illud in habitum statuae figurari, nisi accedissent peritae manus.* The two following causes do not occasion difficulties. They are the form and the end. The formal cause is thus here completely different from the efficient cause and the final cause. The efficient cause itself is easy to imagine if not to understand, because it exercises a causality analogous to that of the worker or the artist. Whatever the thought of Aristotle himself may be, Seneca gives the example here that all will follow for whom the cause *a quo* will be a *causa efficiens.* Others preceded him with a similar move, but the text of the *Letters* to Lucilius was one of the few sources of Platonic teachings available to the Latins of the Middle Ages.

Passing on to Plato, Seneca calmly adds, as if Plato had come after Aristotle: *His* [*causis*] *quintam Plato adjicit exemplar, quam ipse Ideam vocat: hoc est enim ad quod respiciens artifex, id quod destinabat, efficit.* Interpreting the relation of the Idea to the efficient cause as St. Augustine, St. Anselm, St. Bonaventure, St. Thomas, and all the *sancti* will do after him, Seneca makes God the place of the Ideas, something it would be hard to find in Plato unless one inserts it.[3] We would think we were reading St. Augustine: *Haec exemplaria rerum omnium Deus intra se habet, numerosque universorum quae agenda sunt, et modos mente complexus est, plenus his figuris est, quas Plato Ideas appellat, immortales, immutabiles, infatigabiles.* We thus arrive at the conclusion formulated by Seneca himself: *Quinque ergo causae sunt, ut Plato dicit: Id ex quo, id a quo, id quo, id ad quod, id propter quod, novissime id quod ex his est.* Let us return to the example of the statue: *ex quo* is bronze; *a quo* is the artist; *id quo* [Gilson has *id quod* here, trans.] is the model that the artist imitates; *id propter quod* is the end, lucrative, religious, or other, in view of which the statue was made; *id quod* is the statue itself. The world itself has all these

---

3. The complexity of this historical imbroglio can be seen in a note by Justus Lipsius in his edition of the letters: *L. Annaei Senecae Philosophi Opera,* 493 n. 8: Justus Lipsius cites a text from Plutarch attributing a tripartite classification of causes to Plato: "A quo, Ex quo, Ad quod. Proprie vero dici maxime censet eam A quo: quae est efficiens, id est Mens; Cum sic dividit intelligt Efficientem, Materialem, Finalem. Tum autem Exemplaris et Formalis in Efficiente intelliguntur inclusae." With appropriate glosses and if we are not to concerned with what belongs to each philosopher, any classification of causes can include any other. So it is always possible to "reconcile" Plato, Aristotle, and Zeno.

causes including its efficient cause: *Faciens, hic Deus est.* Further on still in Letter 65: *Quaerimus quid sit causa? Ratio faciens, id est, Deus.*

We cannot refrain from dreaming about this accumulation of philosophical materials so long left unused by the masters of the Middle Ages. Nothing shows better the degree to which the peripatetic approach overshadowed all the others. However, St. Augustine must have often reread the letter whose language so frequently announces his own: *Nam corpus hoc, animi pondus et poena est.* It is especially at the point when certain theologians, following Bonaventure's examples, looking to Augustine as a guide in philosophical questions, that Seneca becomes a source of metaphysical information in his turn. He had played this role on ethical questions since the twelfth century, and even before, but the question by Harclay shows him quoted in competition with Aristotle and Avicenna in the first third of the fourteenth century.[4] Furthermore, Plato is not represented there exclusively or even principally, but rather the Stoic tradition that identifies the two notions of cause and of efficient cause. But finally, to return to our problem, it is necessary to recognize clearly that neither Harclay nor Seneca explain the difficulty created by Albert the Great's text. They even add a new one. By writing in Letter 65: *Quinque ergo causae sunt, ut Plato dicit,* Seneca seems to quote a passage from Plato which, for our part, we do not find in the philosopher's writings. Thus this passage must, no doubt, be understood as a summary by Seneca himself of the Platonic doctrine of causes rather than as a reference to some particular text. And it allows the first question to stand, because the doctrine of five causes is presented here by the addition of Plato's exemplary cause (the Idea) to Aristotle's four causes, and not as Albert the Great said, by the division of the productive cause into motor cause and efficient cause. We are thus remitted once more to a different source, both historically and philosophically. Seneca must no doubt be considered simply as a possible secondary influence in favor of the emphasis on the notion of efficient cause, so difficult to explain by the influence of Aristotelianism alone, where it is hard to find.

To re-encounter a philosopher who adds a fifth kind of causes to the four Aristotelian causes and who had gotten this fifth cause by unpacking

4. Maurer, "Henry of Harclay's Questions," 191–93, where Seneca's testimony about the Platonic doctrine of ideas is presented and discussed according to the two letters to Lucilius, 58 and 65. Harclay follows a different enumeration from the one that was subsequently adopted. Fr. Maurer naturally reestablishes the latter in the notes to his edition of Harclay's text.

Aristotle's motor cause, we must return to Avicenna or to that Algazel whom the Latins took, against his intention, to be a faithful follower of Avicenna. We will not return to this point, which we have developed elsewhere.[5] It is certain that, unlike St. Thomas Aquinas in whom the problem is intentionally buried in favor of a quite general notion of efficient cause, that after which any change *whatever* is produced—Albert the Great emphatically stressed the distinction of two types of causality corresponding to two different types of effects produced. The first is a change properly speaking, that is to say, a change of state. Every change of this kind is the effect of a movement, whether we are dealing with the production of a new quality in an already existing substance, or of that of a new substance starting from already existing matter, the instrument of production is a moment, and the cause is the point of departure or the point of origin of this movement. That kind of production must be distinguished from the one whose result is the very being of the effect produced. Since the terminology of all the authors who speak of this question is quite variable (*causa movens, agens, efficiens*), it is practically inevitable to simply and unify it when reporting their opinions. Again the reader must be warned that we are doing this and above all that in doing so, we tend to apply the expression *causa efficiens* everywhere to distinguish it from *causa movens*, whereas the authors themselves made a more restricted usage of it. No doubt the expression especially evoked in their minds the particular cause of efficiency that is production by an artist or an artisan of an object whose idea pre-existed in his spirit. Whatever we do, we do not avoid the confusion of language that prevails in all the discussions of the notion of cause in this period. Indeed we really gain nothing by calling efficient the cause that produces beings, because it produces everything except precisely *esse*. The problem of terminology is lost here in a problem of pure metaphysics, the most difficult of all, for it puts into play that first notion of being on which metaphysicians are in disagreement.

The problem has gained in complexity through a new piece of evidence thanks to a study by William B. Dunphy on *The Doctrine of Causality in the* Quaestiones in Metaphysicam *of Peter of Auvergne.*[6] The principal interest of this study is that it establishes beyond possible

---

5. "Avicenne et les origines," 125–26.

6. Dunphy, *Doctrine of Causality*. Publication of this work, long delayed, would be highly desirable; it opens new perspectives on the history of the efficient cause.

doubt the decisive role played by Avicenna in subdividing the notion of productive cause. What would otherwise be no more than a highly probable hypothesis becomes an indisputable historical certainty here. Peter of Auvergne is a personality whose biography remains unclear. Trusting in plausibility, which is sometimes the historical truth, his biographers meld into one the master of arts to whom we owe numerous questions on the books of Aristotle[7] and the personage of the same name who later becomes bishop of Clermont. The Peter of Auvergne named Rector of the University of Paris May 7, 1275, is the one who interests us, and he does so for more than one reason, because he was a master in charge of teaching Aristotle's philosophy who was not an Averroist in any sense of the word and whose reflections bear directly on the meaning that certain notions of Aristotelian origin assumed after their integration into theology, especially that of St. Thomas Aquinas. Nothing is more interesting for doctrinal history than a witness of this caliber, when, on his own initiative, he poses problems that we see from too far away to resolve them. In our case, St. Thomas leaves us to grapple with a supposedly solved philosophical problem. He himself calls every

7. Hocedez, "La vie et les oeuvres," 3–36. The diligence of the late Fr. Hocedez, to whom medieval studies owe so much, is at the origin of this whole investigation. The care with which he published the table of contents of Peter of Auvergne's unedited questions suffices to reveal the existence of texts where the problem of the exact nature of divine causality was evoked by the master of arts of the University of Paris. It would not be necessary to say more to suggest to the reader aware of the existence of the problem of the efficient cause the hope of finding the trace of Avicenna's influence there. That influence is what William B. Duphy's thoroughness has completely demonstrated. I limit myself to indicating an ancillary problem about which, unfortunately, only a completely personal reflection can be made. Peter of Auvergne passes for being "Thomist," and not without reason, because St. Thomas's influence is everywhere visible in his work, to the degree that it has been believed that we can draw from it in order to complete certain unfinished writings of the master. However, St. Thomas was essentially a theologian. Peter of Auvergne was essentially a member of the Faculty of Liberal arts. We must therefore ask ourselves about the exact relation of St. Thomas's teaching to Aristotle in cases where, using philosophy with the authority of a theologian, which he did even in his commentaries on the Philosopher, the Saint merges ideas in a way whose legitimacy, certain in his mind, was not evident to his readers. Peter of Auvergne wrote *quaestiones*, not a commentary. He taught philosophy for its own sake, not theology. Thus he was free to chose for discussion certain problems posed by the use St. Thomas had made of Aristotle's philosophy, or at the very least, the meaning of certain notions that this use implied. Thus we can see Peter of Auvergne's work as a particular illustration of the difference between the point of view of the philosopher and of the theologian. Peter submitted to detailed and rigorous critique certain philosophical notions whose integration into a theological synthesis gave difficulty.

cause "efficient" whose effect is any change whatever. As we have said, he does not essentially distinguish between *causa agens, causa efficiens,* and *causa movens,* to the point that we would not be false to his personal line of thought to interpret *causa movens* as the efficient cause of movement. It is even a source of confusion for commentators on the *quinque viae,* because, according to this perspective, the proof by the motor cause is hard to distinguish from the proof by the efficient cause. To distinguish them, we must admit, as St. Thomas probably does in the event, that the efficient cause properly so-called is that whose effect is no longer simply a movement (*prima via*), but the very being that the movement produces. As often happens, the theologian compresses philosophical stages here, and leaves us the difficulty of reconstructing hypothetically the reasoning whose conclusion alone has been handed down to us. Here Peter of Auvergne reconstructs the operation's mechanism for us.

Like Albert the Great, he refers directly to Avicenna to such an extent that, as it happens, his *Questions on Metaphysics* deal as much with that of Avicenna as that of Aristotle. In his *Metaphysics,* part VI, chapter 1, folio 91 recto a–b, Avicenna defines separately the efficient cause as that by which the effect acquires a being different from that of its cause. In so far as the efficient cause is that by which another thing receives being, it agrees with the form, to which it belongs to give the being: "but in so far as the efficient [cause] is other than that whose being it cause, it differs from the form." Let us note this clear distinction between efficient cause and formal cause that remains so indistinct for the reader of Aristotle. The efficient cause differs from the form in that it is other than the effect to which it gives being. Indeed the form is not essentially distinguished from that whose form it is. These remarks lead Peter of Auvergne to distinguish clearly two different kinds of productive causality: "One is a principle that makes another thing acquire being by means of movement, as is the case in nature, and generally speaking, in all transmutations. But there is also a principle that makes another thing acquire being by simple eduction and emanation, as happens for immaterial and immobile beings. Understood in the first sense, the efficient cause is that which only acts by means of movement, and it is called *unde principium motus.* Understood in the second sense, it is called *unde principium esse.* The first efficient cause is used for natural things, the second for mathematical things and the divine."

This text would call for long reflections, but they are found in William B. Dunphy's work. Accordingly, we will take from it only what directly involves the problem of terminology that we have posed ourselves. The testimony of Peter of Auvergne explains one part of that of Albert the Great, namely the distinction introduced by certain authors between the "motor cause" and the "efficient cause" properly speaking. Moreover, he confirms the Avicennist origin of the operation that from a hypothesis becomes a demonstrated historical truth. On the other hand, Peter of Auvergne does not speak of five causes. On the contrary, far from adding the efficient cause to the motor cause and of thus bringing the number of causes from four to five, he expressly includes the origin of being (*unde princium esse*) and the origin of movement (*unde principium motus*) in the common notion of efficient cause. The *primum efficiens* and the *secundum efficiens* seem to be two varieties for him of one same species, which is that of the efficient.

To start with, we see from this that, far from speaking of five kinds of causes, Peter rather refuses to do so, because he refers the two varieties of motor and efficient back to the unity of one single cause. Thus, since Harclay and Seneca's five causes are not obtained by dividing the motor cause, but by the addition of the exemplar cause, the dividing of the motor cause in Peter of Auvergne does not give rise to the addition of a fifth cause, because he includes its two varieties in the unity of one single cause, the *efficiens*.

Besides, it is striking that Peter should have chosen *efficiens* rather than *movens* to unify the two notions of origin of being and origin of movement. In this he remains faithful to Avicenna's spirit and to the indication St. Thomas gives in passing, by including under the notion of efficient cause all those notions that signify the origin of any change whatsoever. Nevertheless, this very choice itself reveals the *aporia* that is hidden at the heart of the notion of causality. It can be maintained that the principle of movement from which a being results is itself a principle of being, and, in this sense, it is natural to include *unde principium motus* under *unde principium esse*, but that can only be done if the principle of movement is understood as a principle of the very being of the movement it causes. In other words, we understand that the principle of being should also be that of moment, but it is hard to see or we do not see at all why the origin of movement would be at the same time that of being, especially if we posit the notion of being beyond the level of the generable substance to attain that of its very existence. Without doubt, that is why, having to choose the name of the species common to the two sorts of causality, Peter of Auvergne preferred to include both under the notion of efficiency, rather than under that of motoricity. Thus he only keeps four causes, which puts him in agreement with Aristotle and the tradition of the schools: material, formal, final, and efficient, the latter being separated in turn into cause of being and cause of movement.

Peter follows the suggestions of Avicenna in this also but makes them notably more specific, and, perhaps even more than Avicenna himself, who only suggests they be made more specific. Indeed the question is to know whether the *unde principium motus* belongs to the same kind as *unde principium esse*. Avicenna had already observed that the motor cause belongs to the order of the physical, which is that of natural transmutations through induction of forms in suitably prepared matter, while the cause productive of being belongs to metaphysics and perhaps even to theology. Indeed, to give being, to make exist, is properly to create, and the Muslim theologians were not mistaken in this. To cause the very being of the effect is not becoming, it is to exercise an activity for which philosophy has not even a name, because its act consists in making something that was nothing be, starting from the cause alone and without requiring any matter. In short, the efficiency properly speaking is characterized by production of being without any becoming. There we have the simple emergence from the cause, *eductio*, or again, to employ a term that modern theologians mistrust as establishing pantheism, but that Thomas Aquinas freely used, an *emanatio*. The term is exact, because between the creative cause and the effect there is nothing. The being of the world is not manufactured or engendered. It flows from the source: *Dixit et facta sunt*. Perhaps two radically different types of causality are forced into one and the same species.

Reading Avicenna is not part of the education of a modern philosopher. Furthermore, we still await a careful edition of his metaphysics in the Latin translation, which we have needed for so long. Such as it is, the text of the 1520 Venice edition, despite its defects, suffices to give an exact notion of his way of understanding causality. The translator regularly employs the expression *causa agens* (not *causa efficiens*): "Agens vero est causa quae acquirit rei esse discretum a seipso." (*In Philosophia Prima*, tractate VI, chapter 1). By this we understand that the agent cause produces an effect whose essence is distinct from its own and whose form is not that of the being that causes it. The paradigm of this kind of causality is what the theologians call creation: "Divini philosophi non intelligunt per *agentem* principium motionis tantum, sicut intelligunt naturales, sed principium essendi et datorum ejus, scilicet creator mundi." This distinction between the agent cause that produces the effect's being and that which is only the origin of a movement, marks a decisive point in the history of the notion of efficient cause. The evolution of this notion has been so extensive that today the motor cause has been absorbed, as it were, by the efficient cause. In his *Lexicon Perpateticum Philosophico-Theologicum*, Signoriello distinguishes three kinds of causes external to the effect produced, the final cause, the efficient cause, and the exemplar cause.[8] Absorbed by the efficient cause, the motor cause is no longer designated by a separate name. Avicenna is satisfied to maintain the division in four causes, but not without indicating the possible subdivision of the agent cause in cause of being and cause of movement. The agent cause of being gives it without movement.

Peter of Auvergne refers to this decisive chapter in Avicenna, but he interprets it in a way that is especially interesting to us, because, as was natural, he tries to clarify the problem from the point of view of a reader of St. Thomas Aquinas. In other words, he discusses all the problems whose solutions St. Thomas had given without demonstrations. Following the terminology of Algazel's translator, he normally employs *efficiens* rather than *agens*. Next, he very clearly distinguishes the two kinds of efficient cause. According to him both have producing *esse* as their effect, but one produces it by means of movement, the other by simple emanation; the first is applied to physics, the second is applied to immaterial and divine beings:

> Item efficiens acquirit esse non cuicumque, sed discreto ab ipso, nam idem sibi non est causa in aliquo genere causalitatis. Aliquid autem est principium acquirendi esse alii per motum, sicut contingit in naturalibus et universaliter in transmutationibus. Aliquid etiam principium est acquirendi esse alii per simplicem eductionem et emanationem, sicut contigit in immobilibus et immaterialibus. Efficiens vero primo modo dictum, quod non agit nisi mediante motu, dicitur unde principium motus, sed secundo modo dicitur unde principium esse. Primum efficiens usitatur in naturalibus, secundum autem in mathematicis et divinis.[9]

8. Signoriello, *Lexicon Perpateticum Philosophico-Theologicum*, 59–60.

9. The quote follows the text established by William B. Dunphy in the as-yet unpublished work, whose publication we recommend.

So far as can be judged by the passage taken literally, Peter of Auvergne does not have the desire to innovate in terminology. The words *dicitur* and *usitatur* give the impression rather that he follows received usage. Besides, he nowhere (in what we have read by him) speaks of five causes or five kinds of causes. He is satisfied to divide Aristotle's motor cause in *causa efficiens unde principium esse* and in the cause *unde principium motus*, or again, as he says at the end of his Question III, 3: "Philosophus ergo intendit quod in immobilibus non est motus, quia non est ibi *causa activa ut principium motus, sed solum ut principium esse*."[10] Nonetheless, in the present state of our knowledge we are in a paradoxical situation. Albert the Great speaks of authors who admit five causes and not four, because they have distinguished the efficient cause properly speaking from the motor cause; we find in Harclay a reference to Seneca, who in fact attributes five causes to Plato, but for the completely different reason that he added the exemplar cause or Idea to the four causes habitually recognized since Aristotle. Finally, with reference to Avicenna, we find in Peter of Auvergne the division of *causa agens* into the cause of being and the cause of movement, but Peter of Auvergne includes both causes under the general concept of *causa efficiens*, one being the immediate cause of being, the other the cause of movement and of the kind of being that can result from it. We thus remain ignorant regarding the identity of those whom master Albert designates anonymously "Quidem dixerunt quinque esse causas, eo quod efficientem quam sequitur esse in quantum est esse, diviserunt a causa movente in quantum est movens," because those who carry out this division continue to speak of four kinds of causes and those who speak of five causes do not derive that number on the basis of this division.

---

10. The unpublished question on the *Metaphysics*, book III, question 3, was likewise transcribed by Dunphy following the Mazarine Library manuscript 3481. The following passage is especially interesting for the history of causal terminology: "Intelligendum secundum Avicennam quod efficiens est illud per quod acquiritur esse alii discretum ab ipso, ita ut agens secundum intentionem non sit ipsius esse receptivum, quia idem non est receptivum sui ipsius, ut superius visum est. Dicitur autem aliquid esse causa activa quia est causa motus et esse per transmutationem. Motus ipsius enim est causa per transmutationem, esse autem per simplicem productionem. Prima autem activa causa dicitur unde principium motus, secunda unde principium esse. Prima reperitur in naturalibus, secunda in divinis, quae sunt immobilia. In naturalibus autem, non tantum est principium motus, sed etiam principium esse." This text is quoted according to Dunphy's transcription.

For the moment, it thus only remains to await for the chance that a reader, now informed about the problem's existence, should encounter in some writing one of the *quidam* mentioned by Albert the Great. In the meantime, we can at least question him about his own way of conceiving the efficient cause. The *digressio* from which we have taken the passage quoted at the beginning of these remarks is in fact wholly devoted to the problem of the number of causes, and what it says about the efficient cause especially deserves our attention.

First it will be observed that we now know some representatives of the second position defined in this passage: *quidam autem quatuor [causas] esse dixerunt, eo quod una est in communi ratio efficientis et moventis; et hujus est facere esse quod non est.*[11] Although Avicenna expressed himself less clearly, he seems to have favored this posture. At least justification for this way of talking can be found in him. This is even why, at least to our knowledge, he never said that there are five causes. Peter of Auvergne hardly did more than to explicate Avicenna's position on this point and make his language exact, but we can wonder whether in doing so he did not take advantage of the reflections contained in Albert the Great's *Metaphysics*.

The latter begins by announcing that in first philosophy he will follow the path already laid down in physics, except that instead of considering the causes of the movable body, as physics does, he will consider the causes of being that is the proper object of the metaphysician: "Videtur autem a nobis tenendus esse idem modus quem tenuimus in secundo *Physicorum*, nisi quod hic dicemus causas secundum quod sunt entis; ibi autem diximus eas secundum quod corporis mobilis."[12] From this point one can foresee that Aristotle's structures are going to undergo a strain for which they were not calculated, because, since the concept of being is not the same in him as in his Christian disciples, the notion of a possible cause of being in them will necessarily have to be posed from problems that are not posed by him. Albert nonetheless seems to follow Aristotle as far as he can, which is to say, precisely up to the point where physics borders on metaphysics. Thus, he in his turn admits the four classical causes: matter, form (a bit expanded: *forma, species et exemplar seu paradigma*), the origin of movement, and the end. Regarding the origin of movement (*id unde est principium motus et quietis*), Albert is

11. Albert the Great, *In V Metaphysicorum*, tractate 1, chapter 3, 270.

12. Ibid., tractate 1, chapter 2, 264.

very inclusive: an adviser is a cause of this sort, the father causes the child in this way. In this sense, all that makes something is the cause of what it makes, and even, still more broadly, every cause of change (*mutans*) or of movement (*movens*) is the cause of the changing thing that has moved: "et generaliter omne faciens hoc modo est causa facti, et hoc modo mutans sive movens est causa mutabilis quod movetur." Setting aside the numerous accidental modalities of causes, several of which Avicenna had noted, we can thus say that the causes are four in number: *divisio essentialis causarum est in quatuor dictos modos*: and further on: *Omnes vero cause dictae in quatuor modos cadunt manifestissimos et essentialis.*[13] Albert has done nothing to enlarge the classical scheme of Aristotelian etiology, but he has modified its content.

It will be immediately observed that in dealing with the division of causes in his metaphysics, Albert only quotes examples of causality taken from the physical order. There is not one that fails to involve directly or otherwise bodies in movement: "sperma vero et medicus et consiliator et universaliter omne efficiens, omnia haec sunt causa quam vocamus causam unde est principium motus et permutationes, aut status et quietis."[14] We see none of these causes that involves the production of being as such; all concern the production of some change of state in an already given being; the completely formed body in the case of semen, the healthy body in the case of the physician, acts, the operations, and works in the case of the adviser. Everything goes on as if after having distinguished the physics of causes from the metaphysics of causes, the metaphysician was preparing to speak about them only as a naturalist.

Of course, St. Albert realized this, and no doubt that is what got us the *digressio* in chapter II where the same question is taken up again and studied more closely: "Subtilius autem ista speculando, eo quod in his consistit magna pars hujus sapientiae . . ." There he divides the completely general notion of the causality that includes all that contributes to make something be: "Cum autem causa sit quam sequitur esse, causa est quae facit habere esse." In this sense, the four Aristotelian causes deserve their title, because they all have as their effect that something is. Intrinsic causes (matter and form) or extrinsic causes (efficient or final)—the being of their effect can be said to depend on them. But we cannot say without further explanation that what depends on them is the being of

13. Ibid., 265.
14. Ibid., 266.

their effect in so far as being. To the contrary, as long as we remain in the order of movement and the movable, we are still in the order of the material and physical, to the point that every effort to transcend the motor cause requires us to go beyond the level of nature and of such and such a being to attain that of being as such. In short, it seems that the notion of the efficient cause of being refuses to let itself be included in the physics of causes as Aristotle conceived it.

It is easy to observe the crucial point in the bold reflection to which Albert submits the strictly metaphysical notion of efficient cause. Speaking of Aristotle's physics, he first recalls that the general consideration of movers and moved things necessarily leads to positing a first motor, because all multiplicity supposes unity. But Albert goes further by adding that once assured about the first unmovable mover, it still remains as to whether the cause of the movement of beings is the same as that of their being. In short, it remains to ask whether the cause that makes them move is the same as that which makes them exist. The reply is inevitable. Indeed, it cannot reasonably be doubted that before moving or being moved, it is necessary that the movable or the moved should be, that is to say, that there should be being. That leads necessarily to posit a first cause of being in the sense of actual existence, beyond the cause of movement and prior to it in the order of reflection.

St. Albert here recalls a truth on which he frequently insists speaking about causes, that is that in the order of *esse*, the first of the causes is the efficient cause. He is led from that not only to clearly distinguish the efficient cause from the motor cause, but also to put the efficient cause before the motor cause and as cause of that cause. With his usual penetration, he immediately sees that his doctrine entails the affirmation of a first cause of being, higher than and prior to that of movement, and which is efficient by its very essence. There is, accordingly, a separated essence, which causes the very being of everything.[15]

15. "Simpliciter autem movens est id quod est regens et ordinans omne particulare movens [*note that it is not a question of the first mover producing the being even of movement*], sicut est coelestium. Ad hoc autem in simpliciter et universaliter moventibus, omnis multitudo necesse est quod reducatur ad unum primum movens; et de ipso est adhuc considerandum utrum ejusdem est facere et movere id quod est et mobile est vel non; cum enim omne esse sit necessario ab ente primo, eo quod principium universi esse sit necessario unum, non puto quemquam sapientium dubitare, quin ante movens hoc motum et hoc mobile sit esse hujus moventis et hujus mobilis: hoc autem esse cum jam sit in pluribus et de pluribus praedicatum, et non aequivoce omnino, oportet ad unum reduci principium, quod sit ipsius causa et a quo ipsum fluit in multa; erit igitur

This position's consequences are endless, since they put into question the philosophical status of the notion of creation itself. Each theologian has his personal way of talking, because creating is an act of divine omnipotence; and since the latter is an article of faith, it is difficult to decide *a priori* if the notion of creation falls under philosophy or under theology properly speaking, which is theology of the *revelatum* and not that of simple *revelabilia*. As time will pass, the impact of the dogma of divine omnipotence in the sense that Christian faith professes will stamp theology more and more deeply and will reduce the share of what is rationally demonstrable. From Thomas to Duns Scotus and from Scotus to Ockham, in whom the argument *de potentia Dei absoluta* produces devastating effects, that rationally demonstrable part can be seen to diminish progressively. In St. Thomas himself it is difficult to decide, because it seems that for him this is one of the articles of faith (like divine unity) that satisfy the aspirations of reason so deeply that reason accepts them with the sensation of seeing one of its own evidences revealed. Finally, the answer to the discussion inevitably varies according to the manner in which we understand the being or *esse* that the efficient cause in question produces. Are we dealing with an eternal and necessary emanation of forms uniting themselves successively to matter that is itself eternal as in Avicenna? Are we dealing with the simple production of a substantial being as Aristotle and Averroes expressly admit? Or rather are we dealing with the free production of the total being of each being, form and matter, substance and existence, as the Christian faith has it and as St.

---

causa esse ante movens primum secundum ordinem naturae et rationem. Cum autem causa esse sit, non est causa formalis, quia forma est in omnibus his quorum est forma [*therefore it is an intrinsic cause, not extrinsic like the efficient cause*], et hoc non potest esse primum, nec potest esse finis, quia ille est ultimus secundum esse: oportet igitur quod sit causa efficiens; ergo causa efficiens est ante causam moventem secundum naturae et intellectus ordinem: esse autem sibi secundum intellectum nihil ante ponit a quo fit. Cum igitur sit a causa efficiente, necessario fit ex nihilo; jam autem ostensum est quod ipsum est a causa efficiente. Amplius efficiens illud non est nisi efficiens: igitur per essentiam suam est efficiens. Oportet igitur quod sit essentia separata omnia efficiens secundum esse. Si enim detur quod est composita substantia sicut ignis, tunc sequitur quod agit per virtutem aliquam quae in ipso est, et non per essentiam, sed per aliquid additum essentiae, et sic non est primum nec per se et essentialiter agens: quae omnia sunt impossibilia" (Albert the Great, *In V Metaphysicorum*, tractate I, chapter 3, 269). It would be impossible to trace more strongly the connection of the concept of efficient cause, of existential being, and of creation *ex nihilo*. Note the completely unambiguous expression: "causa efficiens est ante causam moventem secundum naturae et intellectus ordinem."

Thomas Aquinas understands along with faith? We run the risk of confusing these different positions, and each of them sometimes hesitates to
define itself with complete rigor. There is a frontier between metaphysics
and theology based on revelation where certain theologians, above all
St. Thomas, without in any way confusing the two domains, especially
dedicate themselves to pushing the *intellectus fidei* to the point where intelligibility of faith takes on the appearance of an almost complete philosophical evidence. St. Albert the Great is no less intrepid than his pupil,
on whom perhaps he stamped his influence in this regard. For Albert,
the motor cause comes under the natural philosopher's consideration,
the efficient cause comes under that of the metaphysician.[16] It is on the
very occasion when he mentions the anonymous *quidam* according to
whom the causes are five in number, "because they have divided the efficient cause from which being in so far as being results, from the motor
cause as such." We hesitate to attribute to Master Albert more precision
than he gives in this passage, but since he mentions Algazel in it, it can
be admitted as highly likely that he held creation to be philosophically
demonstrable, at least to the same degree in which a philosopher like
Avicenna judged he had demonstrated it.

Thus, it seems first that the union of the notions of cause and of creation invited thirteenth-century Christian philosophers and theologians
to reflection. Aristotle's authority hardly permitted them to change the
doctrine of the four kinds of causes. Moreover, if creation responded to a
certain type of causality, it could be assimilated to no other known cause
than the motor cause, which thanks to the movement of matter worked
upon by form explained the generation of sublunary beings, and thus
also their production and their existence. Besides, the notion of factivity
has been largely suppressed in Aristotle to the point that he tended to
reduce the artisan's making to the motion of a nature rather than to conceive the motor cause as carrying out a doing analogous to the artisan's
factivity. In his philosophy, the highest point of being is occupied by
the First Unmoved Mover, therefore by a motor cause whose operation

16. "Haec ergo est vera consideratio causae agentis secundum hujus sapientiae [i.e.
metaphysicae] propriam considerationem: et ex ista consideratione scitur, quod causa
movens est intendens, et quod illa est de consideratione physici. Causa autem agens
prima est per essentiam separatum agens, et hoc est proprie de consideratione primi
philosophi. Scitur etiam qualiter esse pendet ex causa ista, qualiter ipsa est una de causis
quatuor et prima inter eas. Scitur etiam ex his quae dicta sunt, qualiter quidam dixerunt
quinque esse causae . . . etc." (*In V Metaphysicorum*, tractate I, chapter 3, 270).

presupposes its own being at the same time as that of its effects. We intentionally set aside the further question of knowing whether, in the order of movement itself, the First Mover acts as its efficient cause or only as its formal and final cause. The discussion of the efficient cause changed by the mere fact that the notion of the order of substantial production was extended to that of existential creation. There Aristotle left without resources the Christian who asked for assistance in giving his faith intelligible formulation.

We said that endless consequences resulted from this change in posing the problem of causality. We openly confess that their analysis is a task that is beyond us. Besides it would lead to calling into question doctrinal positions that have been received as evident for so long that it would be unwarranted to put them in doubt. The supreme skill with which St. Thomas was able to transcend the metaphysics he employed to the benefit of theology contributed in no small measure from that time on, and still today, to erasing the sensation of philosophical difficulties submerged in his peculiar doctrinal synthesis. By contrast, they appear fully in Peter of Auvergne and Albert the Great.

If the efficient cause falls under the metaphysician's jurisdiction and if the motor cause belongs to that of the natural philosopher, the proof of the existence of a First Mover is a physical proof. It does not lead directly to the knowledge of a first being that would itself be cause of being. Thus, we understand the difference in viewpoints that distinguishes the *prima via* from the *secunda via*. Consequently, the proof by the first mover, the more manifest of the two ways, precisely because it is developed in the physical order, as is apparent, moreover, in the example of Aristotle himself, *Physics*, books VII and VIII, does not reach as far as that by efficient causality, whose metaphysical nature Thomas himself notes.[17] The plurality of philosophical levels that St. Thomas combines in his theological synthesis becomes evident when we take the trouble to rediscover them in their respective sources. A pure philosopher like Averroes knew very well that he had to choose between proving God's existence *either* as First Mover, *or else* as First Efficient Cause. He also knew that Avicenna had only gone beyond Aristotle in this by following the example of theologians anxious to find agreement between the two notions of motor cause. Besides, he himself invoked Avicenna's example as proof of the fact that philosophical reason is capable of justifying the notion

17. Aquinas, *Summa Contra Gentes*, I, 13, paragraph 33.

of creation *ex nihilo*,[18] but how Avicenna himself had accomplished this advance, St. Thomas never said anything. The bitter criticisms Averroes directed against Avicenna on this exact point do not seem to have moved him.[19] This is just one more point on which we know what St. Thomas thought without managing to know how he came to think it. He is no longer there, and we can no longer pose our questions to him about his thought. That is unfortunate, but an historian must resign himself to being ignorant of many things.

EFFICIENCY AND CREATION

St. Thomas explicitly pronounced himself regarding the nature of the creative act, about the knowledge that we have of it, and even about what might be called the sources of his thought on this point. The nature of creation *ex nihilo* is not the issue here; we desire only to recall some important points regarding the other two questions.

Creation is one of those truths that are at the same time revealed and accessible to the natural knowledge of reason: "creationem esse, non tantum fides tenet, sed etiam ratio demonstrat."[20]

The rational demonstration of creation presupposes that philosophy has distinguished between two kinds of efficient cause, that which produces movement and, through movement, generable and corruptible substances, and that which produces the being itself of the effect. St. Thomas, whose terminology is always free, most frequently calls the common genus that includes these two varieties *causa agens*. In this he follows the language of the Latin translation of Avicenna.

To demonstrate creation in the sense of the cause of being itself, two points must be established: The first is that nothing in the created thing should be presupposed for the creative act to be possible. Creation is thereby distinguished from simple generation and alteration. Alteration presupposes the existence of the subject that undergoes it; generation presupposes the existence of matter that movement makes pass from potency to act. The creation of being supposes nothing that belongs to created being. The second point is that, in the created thing itself, non-being precedes being, not by priority of duration, but by priority

18. See below 170.
19. See below 170 n. 23.
20. Aquinas, *In II Sententiarum*, distinction 1, question 1, article 2, solution, I.17.

of nature. That means that, left to itself, the creature would not have a way to exist. It only exists in virtue of the influence of a higher cause, to tell the truth, a divine cause, because the order of nature and of physical movement must be transcended to attain that of creation.[21] Let us call to mind that the notion of creation *ex nihilo* does not imply that nothing-ness precedes the existence of the creature in time; creation could be at the same time *ex nihilo* and *eternal*.[22]

Thus the distinction between generation and creation presupposes or implies the distinction between the cause of movement and the cause of being, the first natural, the second divine. St. Thomas always refers this fundamental distinction to Avicenna.[23] If his own language is observed closely, we observe the tendency in St. Thomas to use the word *agens* to designate the movement of the natural agent and the word *actum* to designate its effect, while the word *factum* sometimes comes spontane-ously to his pen to signify the product of the creative act: *duplex actum vel factum*. The two words are acceptable and St. Thomas uses them freely, but *factum* comes naturally to his pen to designate the production of be-ing. The influence of Avicenna favors the usage of *agere*, but *facere* has Scripture for it (*Genesis* I, 1), and also the influence of Augustine, who preferred *facere* even to *creare*. St. Thomas discussed this Augustinian usage of the term "create" in *Summa Theologiae* I, 45, 1 ad 1.

Just as he refers this distinction to Avicenna, St. Thomas expressly attributes the notion of creation *ex nihilo* to him.[24] He speaks of *aliqui,*

21. Ibid., distinction 1, question 1, article 2, solution, I:18. Note: "Tum ita quod remaneat ordo creationis ad nihil praeexistens, ut affirmatus: ut dicatur creatio esse ex nihilo, quia res creata naturaliter prius habet non esse quam esse; et si haec duo sufficient ad rationem creationis, sic creatio potest demonstrari, et sic philosophi cre-ationem posuerunt."

22. Ibid., distinction 1, question 1, article 2, solution, I:18. "Si autem accipiamus tertium oportere ad rationem creationis, ut scilicet etiam duratione res creata prius non esse quam esse habeat, ut dicatur esse ex nihilo, quia est tempore post nihil, sic creatio demonstrari non potest, nec a philosophis conceditur, sed per fidem supponitur."

23. Ibid., distinction 1, question 1 article 2, ad 1, I:18–19. "Ad primum ergo dicen-dum, quod secundum Avicennam ... duplex est agens: quoddam naturale quod est agens per motum, et quoddam divinum quod est dans esse, ut dictum est. Et similiter oportet accipere duplex actum vel factum: quoddam per motum agentis naturalis. Quoddam vero est factum, inquantum recipit esse ab agente divino sine motu."

24. "Dicendum quod illi qui posuerunt mundum aeternum, dixerunt mundum fac-tum a Deo ex nihilo; non quod factus sit post nihilum, secundum quod nos intelligimus per nomen creationis; sed quia non est factus de aliquo. Et sic etiam non recusant aliqui eorum creationis nomen; ut patet ex Avicenna in sua Metaphysica (libro IX, capitulo 4)" (*Summa Theologiae*, I, 46, 2 ad 2).

no doubt in order to include Algazel with Avicenna. Moreover, he uses the indirect formula *non recusant*, suggesting thereby that their use of the word "creation" is a kind of concession made by them to a terminology that is not habitually theirs.

This reference to Avicenna can be verified. In *Sufficientia*, book I, chapter 10, the Aristotelian classification of the four causes is revisited, with the characteristic difference of the substitution of the formula "efficient cause" for the cause of the origin of movement: "Iam praemisimus in praedictis intentiones significantes esse causam materialem, et causam efficientem, et causam formalem et causam finalem." In the same passage, Avicenna clearly distinguishes the physical cause of the substance from the metaphysical cause of being. After describing the *principium modus* as either *praeparans* or *perficiens*, he adds: "Hoc ergo est principium efficiens respectu rerum naturalium. Sed quum accipitur principium efficiens non in respectu rerum naturalium tantum, sed respectu ipsius esse, erit communioris intentionis quam sit hoc; et erit hoc quicquid est causa essendi, sed remotum a sua essentia. Unde autem est remotum, et unde non est illud esse propter ipsum, causa est efficiens." As for the word "creation," or others of the same family, they are encountered again in the Latin translations of Avicenna's *Metaphysics*, for example tractate IX, chapter 4: "igitur ea quae primo sunt ab eo, et haec sunt creata, non possunt esse multa . . ." Disregarding the presence in this text of the famous proposition "ex uno secundum quod est unum non est nisi unum" (*ibidem*), and only by attending to its creationist language, St. Thomas's remark will be admitted to have some justification. Likewise: "ut possibilitas essendi haec tria sit ab intelligentia prima in creatione . . ." (*ibidem*). Avicenna really taught the eternity of the world, but at the same time he endowed the First (that is to say God) with productive quality (*proprietas activa*). This active universal cause is necessary and one: "necesse esse per se unum est."[25] Its efficacious action does not presuppose anything else, and that is even why creation is eternal; it cannot be said that before creation "jam fit aliqua factura quae praeteriit antequam crearet creaturas et illa factura est creata ab eo" (*ibidem*). In short, Avicenna knows very well that certain authors attribute creation in time to the First, and he cannot recall their position without using their language ("Necesse est autem ut concedant quod Deus antequam creasset hunc mundum . . ." *ibidem*). The refutation of creation in time obliges him to speak of it, which he

---

25. Avicenna, *Metaphysicorum*, IX, 1.

does at length, but it also offers him the occasion to affirm that the First, if it is not principle or origin of movement in time, is so nevertheless as creator: "modus est qui non habet initium in tempore et . . . non est ei initium nisi ex parte creatoris" (ibidem). Thus St. Thomas could fairly say on the authority of these Latin translations that Avicenna had not refrained from speaking about creation, and had done so in the very texts in which he had affirmed its eternity.

St. Thomas does not seem to have ever hesitated on this point, although, whether from prudence, or for a completely different motive, what he said about it is not always ultimately precise, at least for us who come so long after him. This is a strange thing, since we ordinarily find him concerned to maintain that reason by itself can demonstrate the existence of God; it suffices for him to be reminded that Avicenna in fact demonstrated it and with it creation, for him to immediately limit the scope of the assertion. First, he makes us observe that God's existence is not an article of faith, but rather "that God is in the sense in which faith says." That is to say a God who is providential, rewarding the good and punishing the wicked, as the Apostle says, Hebrews XI, 6: "And without faith it is impossible to please God. For he who comes to God must believe that God exists and rewards those who seek him." God's existence thus becomes an article of faith in so far as it is lumped with faith in divine providence and the rewards or punishments of the hereafter, the latter being inseparable from the notion of salvation. The response, we see, is elliptical. The formula, Deum esse simpliciter non est articulus, sed Deum esse sicut fides supponit, forces the reader to tell himself what article of faith it envisages. Let us admit that we are dealing with the sixth and seventh articles taken together: the remission of sins, the resurrection of the flesh, and eternal life. Although Avicenna admitted part of these truths, notably a certain kind of eternal life with its rewards and its punishments, he certainly did not understand it in the sense it has in Christianity. That is undoubtedly what St. Thomas means, although he does not specify this point. In his passage he argues from the point of view of those who divide the creed into articles according to the number of credibilia themselves. He classifies them, if we may put it this way, by subject matter. That is what he prefers; it also conforms simply to the letter of the creed by considering the existence of God (understood in the sense of Christian faith) as forming an article distinct from the creation of the world, which the creed also mentions as a distinct article, the fifth: "Si [articulus est de Deo] ratione effectus, aut pertinet ad conditionem creaturae, et sic est quintus: creatorem caeli et terrae."[26] In conformity with this conclusion, St. Thomas opposes a different response to the argument drawn from the fact that Avicenna taught the doctrine of creation, although he did not have Christian faith. He did not teach creation in the sense in which Christians understand it, that is to say as having taken place at a beginning of time and so to speak, preceded by the non-being of creatures.[27] In this sense, according to the language of the Nicene Creed, it is even better to say that God is *factor* rather than *creator* of heaven and earth. In his *De Civitate Dei* (book XI, chapter 4), Augustine had already noted that certain philosophers taught the creation of the world all the while holding it to be eternal. This is why the Nicene Creed puts God as *factor*, the word best suggesting a production analogous to that of things that begin to be because they are made by an artisan, so also the operation of God who does not act by necessity of nature but by will.[28]

These remarks do not simplify our interpretation of St. Thomas Aquinas. It is no doubt wise for those who merely desire to form a clear image of his thought to confine themselves to the overall view given by a careful first reading of his doctrine. That is the classical Thomism of the *Summa Theologiae*, the only one with which the teaching of scholastic philosophy and theology concerns itself. Wisdom consists in sticking to it for all useful purposes, because the *Summa*, along with St. Thomas's whole theology, contains everything that his reason can say in order to facilitate the comprehension of faith at all its levels and in whatever measure is possible. Such an endeavor demanded constant recourse to philos-

---

26. *In III Sententiarum*, distinction XXV, question 1, article 2, solution, III:789.

27. Ibid., distinction XXV, question 1, article 2, ad 2, III:788, 790–91. Here are the texts of the objection and of the response: "2. Praeterea, Deum esse unum est probabile per demonstrationem, et similiter Deum esse creatorem rerum; unde etiam quidam philosophi, ut Avicenna, demonstratione moti hoc concedunt. Sed articuli qui essentialiter ad fidem pertinent non possunt per demonstrationem probari, ut ex dictis patet. Ergo inconveniener ponuntur in symbolis pro articulis.—Ad secundum dicendum quod Deum esse simpliciter, non est articulus; sed Deum esse sicut fides supponit, scilicet habentem curam de omnibus, remunerantem et punientem, ut patet per Apostolum, *Ad Hebreos* 11: quia sic determinat, quis est, et quia remunerator est. Similiter Deum esse creatorem non cognoverunt philosophi sicut fides ponit, ut scilicet postquam non fuerunt [scilicet: caelum et terra], in esse producta sint; sed secundum alium modum accipiunt creationem, ut in libro 2, distinctione 1, dictum est." See above 170 n. 22.

28. *In III Sententiarum*, distinction XXV, question 1, article 2, ad 9, III:792.

ophy, particularly first philosophy and natural theology. Everything true that natural theology could say about God and the last end of man ought to be integrated into natural theology by a theologian as St. Thomas conceives him. But there always remains a margin of error to correct in what philosophers have said about God, even when what they said was essentially true. The theologian ought to proceed to fine-tune the philosophical truth in order to be able to integrate it into the doctrine of faith and into sacred science. It is very difficult to say in what measure St. Thomas proceeded to that adaptation in his commentaries on Aristotle. He did it on certain points, not on others. In any case, it is certain that the *Summa Theologiae* only contains the philosophy that the theologian needs and that it is always presented there in a form that makes it capable of being directly assimilated by Christian theology. At that moment the preparatory work has ended. If there is a philosophy peculiar to St. Thomas, it is that and, in effect, when we try to reduce it to the philosophy of any one of his sources, even when he cites them expressly, we come up against inextricable difficulties, because what the historian finds in the source to which he is remitted is not the doctrine of St. Thomas himself, but only the doctrine from which he drew his doctrine by transforming it with a view to his own ends. A rational view of the world, of man, and of their first cause is achieved in this way. It is completely philosophical because it is completely rational, and yet it transcends the order of philosophy pure and simple, as nature in the state of grace transcends nature alone, because the light of reason enjoys the assistance of a higher light here, although one from the same source.

This situation is not at all inconceivable. On the contrary, it is made inevitable by the very nature of scholastic theology, which expressly professes to put philosophy at the service of understanding faith. Starting from this position, it remains possible to put at *sacra doctrina*'s service philosophies that were initially conceived by themselves and without reference to any religious revelation, Christian or otherwise. It is even impossible to do otherwise, because philosophy like science is of this world, but it is impossible to make it serve religious ends, which transcend it, without forcing a reinterpretation upon it, which is carried out in the light of those ends. The example of the great Scholastics lets us see well enough that the endeavor could be crowned with success and to the profit of rational truth itself, and the constructive influence that the great Scholastics had on the development of modern philosophy allows it to be demonstrated, but that is precisely why we are caught up in inextricable difficulties when we try to reduce this philosophy to any one of those from which it drew its material. The longstanding habit of identifying St. Thomas's thought, even his philosophical thought, with Aristotle's has caused innumerable difficulties. No doubt it always will cause them, but only for those who, instead of being satisfied with harmonization made easy by shared technical vocabulary, want to push their work of comparison further. Then the issue is to know whether the meaning of the borrowed doctrines remains the same in the doctrine of the person who borrows them to make them serve his own ends. Naturally the borrowed doctrines retain their essential meaning there but since they serve new ends, their sense is inevitably qualified, modified, and finally transformed. They cannot be correctly understood either without reference to their respective origins or solely in function of their origins. It is necessary to read them in their new doctrinal context to give them their true meaning.

Here the history of philosophy can be of service. Indeed, since its peculiar function is to describe doctrines as they are, let us measure the distance that separates what they were first from what they have become subsequently. Nothing is more delicate than such a task and whoever works at it is often mistaken, but he at least disposes of fairly certain means of forming a fairly well justified overview, so as to reasonably authorize certain conclusions. In this regard, the knowledge of Avicenna can be said to be as necessary as that of Aristotle in order to interpret St. Thomas Aquinas correctly. It is certainly simpler to read the Angelic Doctor as if all the doctrines whose data he combines constitute philosophically homogeneous elements, but insuperable difficulties of interpretation are created in that way. Finally, St. Thomas himself is the victim of this, because his critics reproach him with having mixed different philosophies indiscriminately, which his interpreters indeed do mix, while he himself had arranged them under a higher truth.

In St. Thomas's eyes, Aristotle does not represent the peak of metaphysical progress. Assuredly, he is the Philosopher par excellence, but metaphysics continued to progress after him. Certain of his successors have pushed first philosophy on to being itself, after it had halted at the level of substance in Aristotle's own teaching. In other words, while Aristotle had limited his investigation to substantial being, Avicenna had pushed his onward to the very existence of substantial beings. It is certain that St. Thomas knew that, because he said it. Since he attributed this progress to "certain persons," he had several names in mind, Algazel surely, and probably the author of the *Liber de Causis*, whose doctrine he so curiously interpreted. Whatever the truth is here, it cannot be doubted that the difference between the doctrines of Avicenna and Aristotle on this point was perfectly clear in Aquinas's mind.[29] Moreover, the fact is not in dispute, but it is not taken into account enough.

Indeed, there is an organic link between the manner in which Aristotle conceived being and the way he conceived agent cause. A doctrine where being is substance needs only motor cause to explain the production of generable and corruptible being. Thus, St. Thomas rightly said that Aristotle attributes the production of being to the First Mover, since the being in question is that of physical substance, composed of matter and form, which are born through generation and perish through corruption. By contrast, to explain the production of the total being of the substance, including its matter and consequently its *esse*, the efficacy of the first cause must go beyond that of the simply motor cause. That is what we see in Avicenna's philosophy, and it is why his conception of being contains a new conception of efficient cause. As we have seen, at the same time it contains a new conception of the radical origin of finite being and directs it to the notion of creation.

St. Thomas knew that too. He even saw it so well that what he told us about it exposes us to new misunderstandings. In fact, the Thomist definition of creation is exactly Avicenna's. In his *Metaphysics*, tractate VI, chapter 2, devoted to the nature of agent cause, Avicenna said: "Haec igitur est causa quae dat rei esse per effectum, et haec est intentio quae apud sapientes vocatur creatio, *quod est dare rei esse post non esse absolute*; causatum enim quantum est in se est ut non sit, quantum vero ad causam suam est ei ut sit." St. Thomas in turn repeats that two things suffice to define the notion of creation, that the being of the effect be caused and that it be caused *ex nihilo, quia res creata naturaliter prius habet non esse quam esse*.[30] If there is agreement on these two points, St. Thomas absolves the philosophers for not having taught creation of the world in time, because the thesis then depends on faith and becomes

29. Disputed Questions *De Potentia*, question 3, article 5. *Summa Theologiae*, I, 44, 2.

30. On this point, see the excellent study by Pegis, "St. Thomas and the Origin of Creation," especially 60.

philosophically indemonstrable.[31] The presence of Avicenna is evident here, and he represents a notion of creation that St. Thomas knows to be different from that of Aristotle, even supposing that the Aristotelian production of substantial being could receive this name.

It is necessary to go further, even if things must become more complicated thereby, because that trans-Aristotelian notion of being and of the efficient cause makes its influence felt in the Thomistic proofs of the existence of God. We attempted to make it clear elsewhere that if we hold to the purely philosophical level, it is difficult to regard the "five ways" as homogeneous. The first proof, by the motor cause, stands with the philosophy of Aristotle, etiology and ontology included. The second way, by the efficient cause, presuppose a broadening of the Aristotelian concept of cause that goes beyond Aristotelian scheme. The third way, by the possible and necessary, is directly inspired in Avicenna. The fourth way, by the degrees of perfection, is the one whose Aristotelian character has been so often disputed. The fifth by finality, can certainly invoke Aristotle's name, because the First Mover is also the Last End, but if we attribute to it a providence analogous to that which the Christian God exercises, we profoundly modify its nature.[32] No doubt it will be objected that St. Thomas himself understand each of these proofs in a personal sense that permits him to group them together in his own doctrine, and that is absolutely true, but the difficulties begin again if we attempt to define the conditions of their co-possibility.[33]

To reach the common metaphysical condition upon which the possibility of their coexistence depends, we must in fact push on, if not to the concept of creation, at least to that of perfect divine simplicity, understood in the strictly Thomist sense, that is to say as supreme simplicity of being whose *essentia* is identical with its *esse*. The operation is easily accomplished in writings like the *Summa Contra Gentes* or the *Summa Theologiae* that are theological works. Natural reason moves freely in them and generously deploys its resources, but it always does so with an eye to a super-philosophical end, which belongs to theology, science of the doctrine of salvation. The question is not necessarily posed of knowing where this notion of God comes from, whether from revelation, from reason, or from reason fortified and enlightened in so far as reason

---

31. See above 170 nn. 21–23.

32. See, Gilson, "Trois leçons."

33. Ibid., lesson one, "Le labyrinthe des cinq voies," 4–26.

itself by faith in the word of God. If it is posed, the answer will in no way alter the positions of the theologian who, in any account of the dispute, professes to employ philosophy for his own ends, by rectifying it if necessary, by deepening it always. The theologian might be said to look at philosophy as a transparency against the background of a brighter light than that of natural reason. If this perspective on Thomistic wisdom is admitted, it immediately recovers its perfect coherence and its unity. The perspective would be admitted more frequently, if so many of our contemporaries had not lost the magnificent conception of theology that in the thirteenth century belonged to St. Thomas and the other masters of what today we call medieval scholasticism. We have made it into a doctrine that excludes philosophy instead of leading it to its perfection.

AVICENNA IN THE WEST
DURING THE MIDDLE AGES[1]

INVITED TO PRESENT A paper on "Avicenna in the West during the Middle Ages," I will limit myself to consider four principal questions within this immense subject: 1) Avicenna and Latin scholasticism. 2) Avicenna and Christian theology. 4) Some noteworthy causes of Avicenna's doctrinal influences. 4) Is it true that there was real Latin Avicennism in the Middle Ages?

AVICENNA AND LATIN SCHOLASTICISM

Avicenna only became familiar to scholastic theologians and philosophers through the Latin translations made during the second half of the twelfth century. Consequently, it is from that period that the problems I am to discuss with you began to be posed. We will set aside the *Canon*, which, nevertheless, made Avicenna one of the most respected authorities in medieval medicine and which, furthermore, is rich in philosophical concepts. We will confine ourselves to the Latin version of the *Kitab*

1. The present essay was written for a meeting devoted to the relations between the Latin West and Islamic culture (*East and West in the Middle Ages: Philosophy and Science*), organized by the Academia Nazionale dei Lincei at Rome and Florence, April 9–15, 1969. It is to be published in the *Acts of the Congress* as a report on its specific topic. We thank our distinguished colleague Enrico Cerulli for authorizing its publication in the *Annnales d'histoire doctrinale et littéraire au moyen âge*, as well.

al-Shifâ (*The Book of Healing*), a philosophical encyclopedia where every part of Avicenna's philosophy, from logic to metaphysics,[2] is set forth.

Let us also note that the mode of exposition employed by Avicenna is characteristic and widely imitated. Averroes will adopted the method of literal commentary, following Aristotle's text, dividing it, explaining its different parts word by word, and finally extracting its meaning. As they said in the Middle Ages, he will write *per modum commentarii*. St. Thomas Aquinas's commentaries on Aristotle are inspired by this model. The method is suited to someone like Averroes who proposes to set out someone else's thought (in this particular case, Aristotle's) and to disappear from his presence. By contrast Avicenna thinks of expressing his

2. For the history of twelfth-century Latin translation of Avicenna, see d'Alverny, "L'Introducion d'Avicenne." The translators of Avicenna's encyclopedia, *Kitâb al-Shifâ*, were a Jew named Ibn Daud and one Domingo, archdeacon of Toledo. Ibn Daud (*Avendauth Israelita philosophus*) translated word for word from Arabic to Spanish. Domingo retranslated into Latin. The translation of *De Anima* (titled *Liber Sextus Naturalium* for its place in the encyclopedia) is dedicated to Archbishop Juan, who occupied the see of Toledo from 1151 to 1166. The translation of the *Shifâ* remained incomplete, even though the first (twelfth century) team of translators was replaced by a second "a century later" (d'Alverny, "L'Introducion d'Avicenne," 134). The little treatise *De Caelo et Mundo* included in the collection is spurious. The opusculum *De Intelligentiis* printed with Avicenna's works is likewise spurious, or it is still more spurious if we may put it this way. Mlle. d'Alverny's very prudent conclusions are "that a first body of Avicenna's philosophical works must have been finished about 1180 and was circulated in Europe"; the physicians "who quickly adopted the teachings of the *Qânûn* [Avicenna's *Canon*] [probably] played an important role in spreading his philosophical works, particularly *De Anima* [of which] we still find the greatest number of manuscripts today" (135); that "testimonies of the diffusion of Avicenna's works are infrequent before 1220" (136–37); that the most widely known work after *Liber VI Naturalium* (or *De Anima*) was the *Metaphysics*; finally that "it is particularly after 1260 that Avicenna's major theses of on essence and existence are discussed in the Faculty of Theology and the majority of manuscripts known to us are from that period" (137). Despite their attempted objectivity, these remarks go much further than might be first believed.

The presence of philosophical elements in Avicenna's medical *Canon* did not escape certain theologians, for example Thomas Aquinas, *In Boethium de Trinitate*, question 5, article 1, ad 4: "*Sicut dicit Avicenna in principio suae medicinae . . .*"

On the present state of our knowledge of medieval translation of Avicenna, see note 24 below in this paper on research by d'Alverny. By the same author: "Notes sur les traductions," "Avendauth?," and "Les traductions."

The most impressive picture of the invasion of the Christian West by Arab science and philosophy at the start of the thirteenth century seems to me to be the list of Muslim scholars and philosophers cited by William of Auvergne, which is found in de Vaux, *Notes et textes*: 19–20, "The Scholars"; 20–22, "The Philosophers." Having neither objection nor addition to make about this picture, I simply remit the reader to it.

own thought. Thus he wrote, again as they said in the Middle Ages, *per modum auctoris*: as the principal author of the thoughts he expresses.

From the end of the twelfth century and still more by the middle of the thirteenth, writings of this sort are often found. Albertus Magnus's great philosophical encyclopedia is a free re-working of this genre, which deals with the whole of philosophy like the *Shifā* without being tied in any way to Aristotle's text. Before him William of Auvergne was inspired by Avicenna's example, but Avicenna's first imitator and his first victim, if we can put it that way, was his principal and first translator, Archdeacon Dominicus Gundissalinus (Gundisalvi or son of Gonzalo) of Toledo. His intimate familiarity with Avicenna's writings instills the desire in him to become an author. The treatise entitled *Libre Avicennae in Primis et Secundis Substantiis et de Fluxu Entis*, also called *De Intelligentiis*, printed in Avicenna's *Opera Omnia*, Venice, 1508, folios 64 verso to 67 verso, is a strange mixture of Avicenna, Dionysius Areopagite, and Augustine, with even a touch of Bernard of Clairvaux. Father Roland de Vaux reprinted it in the twentieth century in *Notes et texts sur l'Avicennisme latin*. Another of Gundissalinus's writings is largely a compilation of texts taken from his own translation of Avicenna's treatise on the soul, *De Anima* or *Liber Sextus naturalium*. The complete texts with references to the corresponding passages in Avicenna is found in J. T. Muckle, C.S.B., "The Treatise *De Anima* of Gundissalinus." We will return to a third text by Gundissalinus, packed with Avicenna, which will be taken over unchanged by William of Auvergne. As translator and author, Gundisallinus made Avicenna's Latin style fashionable.

Every reader of Latin Avicenna is struck by the oratorical character of his style and the constant use of the personal manner. He often speaks in the singular: *Videtur etiam mihi . . . Concedo autem quod genus . . . .* But more often he uses the first person plural, which in him is a modest rather than a royal *we*, to avoid the always slightly pretentious *I*: *Dicemus quod verbum . . . Dicemus ergo quod primum . . . Dicemus igitur quod illud . . . Consideremus autem . . . Debemus autem certificare . . .* , etc.

Avicenna addresses his reader personally and readily takes him to one side: *Debes etiam scire . . . Indagator etiam dicet tibi, adapta diffinitionem relativorum cum diffinitione generis et speciei, et fac scire quomodo . . . scitur unum per alterum . . . Non debes autem persistere in dicendo . . .* , etc.

Avicenna strongly emphasizes links and transitions: *Postquam autem jam ostendimus . . . Jam praemisimus in praedictis . . . Nunc autem debemus cognoscere . . . Postquam autem jam locuti sumus de virtutibus apprehendentibus animae sensitivae, oportet loqui de virtute ejus motiva. Dicemus igitur . . . Nunc autem adhuc a capite revolvemus hoc . . .* Avicenna loves digression, but he does not fail to warn the reader when he returns to the thread of his discourse. Returns to the theme and recapitulations are favorite procedures of his, almost trade marks. We have just seen an example. Here are others selected randomly in reading: *Redeamus igitur et dicamus . . . Redeamus ad id in quo eramus . . . Redeo igitur ad caput et dico . . . Redeo autem ad id in quo eram . . . Repetemus autem ea a capite et recolligemus ad declarandum alio modo . . . Redibo igitur et dicam . . . Nos autem adhuc a capite revolvemos hoc . . .* , etc.[3]

An almost complete collection of these and other stylistic procedures of Avicenna is found in *De Intelligentiis*. It is enough simply to read folio 65 recto and verso in the 1508 Venice edition. We are dealing with chapter IV of this apocryphal work. *Redeamos igitur ad id in quo fuimus . . . Sequitur ut aperiemus id in quo pertransivimus . . . Postulamus autem ut tu te non turberis . . . Postquam autem hoc praecessit redibimus ad causam primam . . . Studeas autem scire . . . Et non lateat te . . . Sed si consideres rationem . . . Et scias quod intelligentia est causa rerum . . .* , etc. All of Latin Avicenna's literary mannerisms appear in that astonishing *in the manner of*, by which an overly trusting young Thomas Aquinas let himself be captivated.

The style of *Avicenna Latinus* may also be detected in certain thirteenth-century theologians. The *Magisterium Divinale* by William of Auvergne, Bishop of Paris, could appear without incongruity in Migne's *Patrologia Latina*, but its style often recalls that of the Latin versions of Avicenna. There is the same continuous discourse divided into parts and chapters, with none of Averroes or Thomas Aquinas's literal commentary. William writes "as an author" and speaks in the same personal manner as Avicenna with the same care to bring his reader into the game. Let us open the 1674 Paris edition of *De Universo* randomly at volume I, I^a-I^{ae},

3. Avicenna, *Opera Philosophica*, Venice, 1508. Reproduction, Louvain, 1961 (which rapidly became as difficult to find as the original). These or other similar expressions are found, folio 6 recto, 11 recto, 12 recto; cf. *Liber VI Naturalium*, part II, ch. 6, folio 9 verso, *Metaphysica*, tractate I, ch. 7 folio 75 recto. tractate VI, ch. 2 and 3, folio 92 recto; tractate VIII, ch. 4, folio 99 recto; ch. 6, folio 100 verso. On old editions of Latin Avicenna, see d'Alvernuy below, note 24.

ch. 42 in the single left hand column on page 644: *Propono tibi satisfacere nutu dei . . . Debes etiam reminisci ejus quod praetetigi tibi . . . Dico igitur . . . Addam et aliam manifestationem . . . Dico quod sermo iste erroneus est . . . Post hoc investigabo partes universi corporei . . .* The Avicennist habit of digressing and going back is equally familiar to him. We have Avicennist flashbacks: *Revertar autem ad id, in quo eram et dicam* (Iᵃ-Iᵃᵉ, ch. 44, 648). *Jam autem dixi tibi in praecedentibus* (649). *His autem ita declaratis revertar ad motus planetarum* (651). William gladly recognizes that he often writes off the subject: *multa de his, imo major pars eorum quae hic audivisti, est praeter intentionem propositi . . . Verum ego digressus sum ad illa ut patefacerem tibi* (649). But he ends by coming back to his subject, and he points that out to us: *Revertar autem ut respondeam* (IIᵃ-Iᵃᵉ, ch. 21, 719). Many other examples of this sort of post-Avicennist mannerism could be cited: *Revertar igitur ad id . . .* (IIᵃ-Iᵃᵉ, ch. 24, 729). *Post haec autem revertar . . .* (ch. 30, 735). *Nunc autem revertar ad id unde longe digressus sum, et dicam* (IIᵃ-Iᵃᵉ, ch. 35, 739).

Roger Bacon, whose *Opus Majus* is also written in Avicennist Latin, uses the same direct, personal style, with similar digressions and returns to the thread of discourse: *Dico ergo . . .* (*Opus Majus*, IV, 8, I:145); *Et ideo redeo ad propositum dicens . . .* (IV, 5; I:137); *et nunc ponam unum exemplum . . .* (IV, 6; I:139); *quoniam autem diutius tenui persuasionem . . .* (IV, 8; I:143). *Sed rediens spiritualiter ad propositum pono exempla . . .* (IV, 15; I:214). For Bacon, Avicenna is the principle interpreter and imitator of Aristotle: *praecipuus imitator et expositor Aristotelis* (*Opus Majus*, II, 13, I:55). Bacon tries to write a Latin *Shifâ* himself in the long series of hitherto unpublished works, which Robert Steele has edited for Oxford University Press. For example, it is significant that when Bacon has to explain physics, he begins like Avicenna, by expounding the *Communia naturalium*, and does so in the same discursive almost oratorical style as his model. *Postquam tradidi grammaticam . . . et logicalia cum hiis expedivi . . . Declaravi igitur* (Steele ed., ch. 1, 2 and 5). *Exposui . . .* (ch. 2, 9). *Intendeo facere . . .* (ch. 3, 10). *Cupio tamen . . .* (ch. 3, 13).

Albert the Great's philosophical encyclopedia is written in the same continuous style,[4] *per modum auctoris*, as William of Auvergne's *Summa*.

---

4. Albert the Great used different styles and manners of composition according to the type of work he was writing, but in all his writings, he always retained a freedom of tone and of style that link him to Avicenna. It does not seem that he ever attempted the method of literal exegesis dear to Averroes. His long career (ca. 1193–1280) spans

He employs the personal manner less, but he does not hesitate to use the first person plural: *jam at veram philosophiae sapientiam accedamus . . .* (*Metaphysica*, book I, tractate 1, ch. 1, 1); Albert raises digression to the rank of a method: *Et est digressio declarans quod tres sunt scientiae theoricae . . .* (ch. I, 1). *Et est digressio declarans quid sit hujus scientiae proprium subjectum . . .* (ch. II, 4). *Et est digressio declarans qua unitate et qualiter haec scientia sit una . . .* (ch. III, 7). Everyone who is familiar with the language of the Latin translations of Aristotle will recognize the passage's Avicennist resonance in the phrases like *dicamus igitur, quod sicut diximus . . . , dico autem* (I, 6, 11), which Albert uses spontaneously in many places. Even if the title *digressio* is not from his pen, no other title better suits the numerous chapters where, because he does not follow Averroes's exegetical method, Albert himself has to create the framework into which his teaching is set.

These remarks hold only for Albertus Magnus's great encyclopedia, in which, even more than Roger Bacon would do, he clearly proposes to compose a *Shifâ* written for Latins in the Latin language. This does not apply to Albert's *Summa*s, governed by the technique of the *quaestio*, whose style and manner of composition are different. Even in the encyclopedia where he sets out to completely make over Aristotle in Latin, adding where needed writings missing from Aristotle's own corpus, Albert is only slightly marked by the literary habits that Gundissalinus popularized as translator and author. However, it would be impossible for us to point out his most characteristic borrowing from Avicenna's doctrine without pointing out at the same time examples of the contagion of his Latin imitators by that of their model.

AVICENNISM AND CHRISTIAN THEOLOGY

Avicenna's personal position predestined him to play an important role in the formation and development of medieval philosophies and theologies. Coming from a long line of Muslim theologians (the creators of the *Kalam*) and heir to Alfarabi, a powerful philosophical mind whose writings we hardly know but to whom Avicenna owed much, he was considered an Aristotelian, which could only give him authority (*Avicenna*, Roger Bacon will say, *et caeteri de domo Aristotelis*), but at the

---

almost a century, but in many ways he remained a representative of the pre-Averroist age. This is even true in his language and style.

same time he was a religious thinker, careful to link his philosophy with the essence of Koranic truth and thereby impelled to elaborate a technically Aristotelian philosophy that promoted the teaching of the Koran. If we accept the disputed but handy expression, *Christian philosophy*, to designate the kind of philosophical speculation that Christians incorporated in their Christian theology, perhaps we can speak of Muslim philosophy in Avicenna's regard. Since Islam and Christianity share the Old Testament and the belief in the future life, it was natural that thirteenth-century Christian theologians were tempted to take inspiration from the parts of his works that offer a philosophical justification for their faith.

Averroes, who did more than anyone else to discredit Avicenna and limit his influence, reproached precisely his tendency to seek accommodations between philosophy and religion. Furthermore, this explains why Averroes's influence on Muslim thought has always been slight, almost null, whereas Avicenna's has lasted up to our time. This also explains how we can speak of "Avicenna's religious thought" and study the phases of his thought where "a possible reference to religious values and more precisely to the Muslim faith,"[5] can be perceived.

The reality of this connection with religious belief is confirmed by the bitterness with which Averroes reproaches Avicenna for it. His predecessor's philosophy seems to him to be an impure mixture of reason and belief, of metaphysics and religion. We should always re-

5. Gardet, *La pensée religieuse*. Cf. the essay by Mehren, "Les rapports." He remits to an earlier work: "La philosophie d'Avicenne," 389, 506.

On this point Avicenna himself should be read, *Metaphysica*, tractate X, ch, 1, 2, and 3, folios 108 verso to 109 recto, where we find valuable indications about the Muslim philosopher's theology: the First, Angels, prophecy and the Prophet, inspirations and prayer. Thomas Aquinas knew these texts well, and before the Christian theologians of our days wondered about the matters, he clearly established that, as Avicenna conceived it, prophecy is a *natural* state. Thomas acknowledges and grants Avicenna the reality of this "natural prophecy," which is a kind of foresight, but "the philosophers who have spoken about prophecy, only spoke about natural prophecy, not about the one we consider here, [which is a gift of the Holy Spirit!]," Thomas Aquinas, *Quaestiones Disputate de Veritate*, question XII, article 3 ad 8. Cf. Objection 8: "In the science of nature, philosophers deal only with what can be naturally produced. Now Avicenna deals with prophecy. Thus prophecy is natural." This remits directly to Avicenna, *Metaphysica*, tractate X, ch. 1–3, notably ch. 2, "De stabiliendo Prophetam et qualis est oratio Prophetae ad Deum altissimum et de promssione." A careful examination of Thomas's attitude toward Avicenna in this disputed question would be revealing, because his attitude is very nuanced: the distinction between rational foresight, that is to say, philosophical or scientific, and supernatural, properly religious prophecy (in the Judeo-Christian sense) is the issue here.

member what he wrote in his commentary on the *Physics*, book II, ch. 3, vol. Com. 22: *Via autem qua processit Avicenna in probando Primum Principium est via Loquentium, et sermo ejus semper invenitur quasi medius inter Peripateticos et Loquentes.*[6] Those of our contemporaries who maximize the importance of Averroes's influence on the thirteenth century cannot exaggerate, because it was immense, but it was exercised in the philosophical order, not the theological, where Avicenna principally impacted the philosophy of Christian theologians. We will return to the consideration of this matter in the fourth part of our presentation.

Historical divisions are always frivolous, because at any instant the historical past flows through the present and often even announces the future. Thus, if I may be allowed a simplification for which I myself feel embarrassment as a sign of being simplistic, in one of those moments when historians succumb under the weight of facts and out of pure fatigue allow the detail to sort themselves out into a few general vistas, I would say that I see a first, ascendant period of Avicenna's influence. Roughly, it coincides with the time when books were written in Avicennist style, as we have described. William of Auvergne is its most characteristic representative. A second period, which is prepared and ripens *during* the first, witnesses Averroistic Aristotelianism's invasion of the schools and proceeds to eliminate the form of Aristotelianism represented by Avicenna, not completely but very thoroughly. Thomas Aquinas offers excellent testimony of this evolution, because his admirable *Commentary on the Sentences of Peter Lombard* shows the predominant influence of the Avicennist type of Aristotelianism, whereas all his later works seem to regard as settled that Averroes's Aristotle is the genuine one except for some necessary doctrinal rectifications. At that point the Commentator, he, *che il gran Commento feo*, becomes the great authority in the schools.

However, this movement was always resisted by the persistent influence of Augustine's theology, which by carrying within itself the influence of characteristic themes of Plotinian origin, gives rise to the quarrel of the two great schools, whose boundaries are not precise, but whose identity is felicitously defined by an appropriately famous text of the Franciscan John Peckham. This opposition to the Averroistic version of Aristotle perhaps can be symbolized by the well known condemnation pronounced in 1277 by Étienne Tempier, Bishop of Paris. The

6. Averrores, *Aristotelis Opera cum Averrois commentariis*, vol. IV, folio 57 recto B.

condemnation did not mean the end of Averroes's influence, but it did end the ascendant phase of that influence, in the sense that after that point, it ceases to be taken for granted that the genuine Aristotle is that of Averroes. The letter of John Peckham the Franciscan Archbishop of Canterbury to the Bishop of Lincoln is dated June 1, 1285. It defines with striking precision the principal positions around which the two doctrinal groups were confronted and divided.[7] We are now on the far side of Averroist influence, which, from the point of view of *theology* properly speaking, is that of its decline. It is not completely certain that the claim would be equally true from the point of view of medieval *philosophy*, but its truth seems evident when we refer to properly theological reflection.

This far side, where Averroes's influence is descending, coincides with a renewed increase in that of Avicenna, or if one prefers, of the Avicennist interpretation of Aristotle. All of the elements of Avicennism that foreordained it to form an alliance with Christian theology (with the safeguards of necessary theological rectifications) took on the fullness of their meaning and importance at this point. Aristotle will always remain the Philosopher par excellence but many among the most important will understand him as Avicenna's Aristotle, no longer that of Averroes.

One of the most typical representatives of this second Avicennism (that is to say, after 1277) seems to me to be Henry of Ghent, a metaphysician of the first order, who had no fault except to not leave behind him a religious order that might take charge of perpetuating his influence. Others, including St. Thomas himself, had come to dash off the phrase: *Aristoteles et veritas dicunt.* Henry of Ghent wrote with the same ease

---

7. The text is so familiar that we hesitate to reproduce it one more time, were it not for the fact that what is familiar to historians of medieval philosophy and theology is not necessarily familiar to scholars whose discipline is different: "I do not disapprove at all of philosophical studies, as long as they serve the mysteries of theology, but I disapprove of disrespectful innovations in language introduced during these last twenty years in the foundations of theology to the detriment of philosophy and of the Fathers, whose positions are rejected and openly held in contempt. What doctrine is more solid, the doctrine of the sons of St. Francis, that is to say of Fray Alexander [of Hales] of blessed memory, or of Fray Bonaventure or of others who, like him, are based on the Fathers or on philosophers whose writings are above all reproach, or rather that other very recent and almost completely contrary doctrine, which fills the whole world with verbal quarrels, weakening and depriving Augustine's teaching of all its strength concerning the eternal rules [of truth], the faculties of the soul, the seminal reasons enclosed in matter, and innumerable other questions of this sort. May our elders judge, since wisdom resides in them, may God in heaven judge of this, and may he deign to bring a remedy" (Peckham, *Registrum Epistolarum*, III:901).

and as if it were obvious: *Et ita cum secundum Avicennam et secundum rei veritatem.*[8] Or again: *Ideo in talibus conceptibus propositionum universalium contingit, secundum Avicennam et Augustinum . . .*[9] and even, attesting in a single sentence to the dual literary and doctrinal influence of the Muslim master: *Revertentes igitur ad propositum dicamus secundum Avicennam et veritatem . . .*[10]

8. Henry of Ghent, *Summa Quaestionm Ordinarium*, article 22, question 5, folio 124 verso, letter D.

9. Ibid.

10. Ibid., article 25, question 3, folio 156 recto, letter S. A long study ought to be made focused exclusively on Avicenna's influence on Henry of Ghent. After 1277 this theologian undergoes a real *conversio ad Avicennam*. By way of example, let us take at random his *Quodlibetum* I, question 7: "Utrum creatura potuit esse ab aeterno" (folio IV recto). Avicenna appears there several times and always in the context of key metaphysical notions: "Sic enim dicit Avicenna in sexto *Metaphysicae* suae. Quod aliquid [inquit] sit causa existendi causatum cum prius non fuit, hoc convenit quia non est causa ejus per suam essentiam, sed per aliquam determinatam comparationem quam habet ad illud, cujus comparationis causa est motus." We are already grappling with the choice between Avicennist efficient causality and Averroist motor causality. Henry's decided choice goes to Avicenna. "Et hoc modo habere esse ab alio post non esse vocabat Avicenna creationem, secundum quod dicit in sexto *Metaphysicae* suae. Haec est intentio quae apud sapientes creatio vocatur, quod est dare esse post non esse absolute." *Summa Quaestionum Ordinarium*, folio IV, R. We find the same recourse to Avicenna in Thomas Aquinas in regard to the same central notion of creation. — "Unde Avicenna bene videns quod id quod de sua essentia est non ens, non intellectu solo sed in re esse non recipiat ab alio nisi ex tempore, dicit in fine quinti *Metaphysicae* suae: Postquam autem res ex seipsa habet non esse, sequitur tunc ut esse ejus sit post non esse et fiat postquam non fuerat. Unde et de hoc modo inceptionis dicit in principio sexti: Si autem taxaverit aliquis nomen inceptionis . . ." *Summa Quaestionum Ordinariarum*, folio IV, T: "Manifeste probat Avicenna in fine quinti *Metaphysicae* suae duobis ultimis capitulis . . ." Avicenna's thought is evidently integrated into that of Master Henry of Ghent.

In his excellent *Henri de Gand*, Jean Paulus proposes (6) with one qualification, to add Henry's name to the list of representatives of Avicennist Augustinianism. "*The notions of being, thing, necessary . . .* This essential text of Avicenna—with the chapter of commentaries that the Arab philosopher devotes to it—inspires Henry's whole doctrine of the idea of being, as some years later it will inspire Duns Scotus's well known affirmations regarding the first object of the human intellect." Paulus, *Henri de Gand*, 7.

"The noetic thesis of a priority of the *intentio entis sive rei* imposes upon Avicenna as upon his disciples Henry of Ghent or Duns Scotus the choice of a metaphysics centered on the idea of being." Paulus, *Henri de Gand*, 25. — For the doctrine of *natura communis* in Henry of Ghent, 69–80 cf. 98. Regarding the overall problem, we can repeat what Jean Paulus remarks about one of the numerous questions on which he contrasts Henry and Avicenna: "Thus Henry depends on Avicenna both in vocabulary and doctrine" (224). Of course, this dependence is not servile, because if the influence of Averroes engendered servility, that of Avicenna was rather exercised in a spirit of freedom.

Avicenna's doctrinal influence reaches is zenith in John Duns Scotus's theology. Henry of Ghent had, as it were, prepared the doctrinal material that Duns Scotus needed for the construction of a new system in which Aristotle revised by Avicenna would furnish the principal element. This second *aetas avicenniana* was not to last, because the positivist logicism of William of Ockham would soon bring it to an end, just as it would classical scholastic theology itself, since henceforth faith was going to grapple with a purely logical dialectic, metaphysics having ceased to exist.

However, Avicenna's influenced did not cease to be felt up to modern times. The mere fact that his writings were collected and printed in Venice during the last years of the fifteenth and first years of the sixteenth century testifies to the existence of a center of interest in his thought near Padua, perhaps as an antidote against the effects of Averroism that rampaged through the philosophical schools at the time, notably at Padua.[11] It would be desirable for research to be done in this area.

MAJOR DOCTRINAL THEMES

For a necessarily brief overview, it seems reasonable to select a few doctrinal themes of great importance, which present themselves as connected to the name of Avicenna in the minds of the medieval masters themselves.

1) In the letter I mentioned above, John Peckham places in the first rank of disagreements between the Order of Preachers and the Friars Minor the Augustinian doctrine of the knowledge of the true in eternal rules. This is what is commonly called the Augustinian doctrine of divine illumination. From the time when Aristotle's *De Anima* was known, it was necessary to adjust this Augustinian doctrine to the Aristotelian distinction of the two intellects, agent and possible. Avicenna offered an interesting possibility in this regard, because he attributed a personal possible intellect to each individual (by which he, unlike Averroes, rendered personal immortality and salvation for each individual conceivable), and he identified the agent intellect with a Separated Intelligence,

---

11. In the absence of a modern edition of Latin Avicenna, we must content ourselves with the old editions in Gothic letters, Venice, *Metaphysica*, 1495 (the best edition of this text that I know); *Opera Omnia*, Venice, 1508 (the edition most often used because it contains in one volume all of Avicenna's writings translated into Latin). On this point, see d'Alverny, "Editions anciennes."

the same for all men, whose illumination caused intelligible knowledge and truth in them.

The Christian theologians were soon tempted to identify Avicenna's separated Agent Intellect with Saint Augustine's Illuminating God and thus with the Divine Word, second person of the Trinity. However one designates it, this symbiosis of Augustine's theory of knowledge with Avicenna's is indisputable. The somewhat clumsy and pedantic name *Avicennist Augustinianism* that I once proposed (in the absence of a better one), signifies no more than this very fact.

A remarkable witness to the contagion of Augustinianism by the Avicennist doctrine of the agent intellect is the author of the apocryphal Avicennian book we have already cited, *De Intelligentiis* or *Liber Avicennae in Primis et Secundis Substantiis et de Fluxu Entis*. Today no one would hold that it is a work by Avicenna, if only because its author copies John Scotus Eriugena whom Avicenna never knew. I myself have attributed it, with many reservations, to Dominicus Gundissalinus, but I have never been certain of that, and it is simply for want of being able to find an author for it. After I involved myself with the problem for the first time in 1929, others have taken up the study, but we have not advanced further. In his *Notes et textes sur l'avicennisme latin* of 1934, after noting that "the work's scheme and principal themes are certainly Avicenna's" (65), Fr. Roland de Vaux, O.P., undertakes a closely argued analysis to conclude that "Everything invites us to date the composition of *Liber de Causis Primis et Secundis* [which he holds to be the true title] at the beginning of the last years of the twelfth century or the first quarter of the thirteenth century." To be sure, it is hard to tell exactly whether the reasons justify his conclusion or they depend on it, because the probable date of the Latin translation of *De Causis* plays an important role in the discussion. However that may be, Father de Vaux concludes that "the treatise is posterior to 1180" (69).

That indeed would eliminate the possibility of attributing it to Gundissalinus, if we still hold that his translations of Avicenna were made in the first half of the twelfth century, but if we admit with Mlle. Marie-Thérèse d'Alverny "that a first *Corpus* of Avicenna's philosophical works must have been finished toward 1180," if we, furthermore, take into account the dedication of *De Anima* or *Liber VI Naturalium* to Juan, Archbishop of Toledo from 1151 to 1166, then the dates of Gundissalinus's life, uncertain as we see, are no longer obviously incompatible with the supposition that he is the author of the treatise.

Besides, it does not much matter, because whoever is its father, a book is always someone's son, and whoever composed this little treatise remains in every way a distinguished witness of the substitution of the Augustinian God for Avicenna's Agent Intellect as the cause of our knowledge of the truth. Whether or not it is the origin of this history, it is part of it. Chapter 10 of the text published by Father de Vaux (132–33) refers to the *Soliloquies* of St. Augustine in a development that transforms what comes to us from the Avicennist *intellectus adeptus* into a divine illumination.

The same observation most be held for the *De Anima* traditionally attributed to Gundissalinus himself. Whoever the author is, he is a Christian imbued with Avicenna's philosophy, who follows his guide as long as possible and only abandons him at the last moment to follow Christian guides whose doctrinal authority places his own teaching above suspicion. This hundred or so texts borrowed from Avicenna ends with some ten from inspired texts, from St. James, St. Paul, St. Augustine, Boethius, Alcher of Clairvaux, and even St. Bernard of Clairvaux among other Christian authorities. The notes of Father Roland de Vaux's edition (169–78) give all the useful clarifications in this regard. Here, as in Avicenna, knowing is receiving in the soul forms that come to it from a separated Intelligence, but the true and ultimate source of all wisdom is the Christian God that the author, whoever he is, insistently claims as inspiration in the conclusion of his treatise. The author is full of Avicenna, but he is not an Avicennist. He is a Christian.

It is hardly possible to speak of this contagion of Christian theology by Avicenna as a doctrine properly speaking. The author of *De Anima* rather clearly conveys the predicament of the first Christian theologians in the presence of Muslim philosophers, full of problems new to them and of solutions that they needed to adapt to their own project. They began by taking wholesale, like looters who initially seize things without really knowing what they carry off in their booty. We only encounter real symbiosis between Avicennism and Augustinianism in the first half of the thirteenth century, when the theologians of the first rank began to assimilate what others had initially been content to borrow.

William of Auvergne, Bishop of Paris, is a privileged witness of how this occurred. Father de Vaux devoted a chapter to constructing an inventory of "William of Auvergne's Arab readings of scholars first, then philosophers" (18–20). Averroes only appears twice in this list, and it even seems that William does not quite know of whom he is speaking.

Avicenna is cited about forty times. It can be concluded that not only is the latter "the principal representative of Arab philosophy and thought" (22) in William's eyes, but even that the influence of Avicenna on Christian thought has decisively outstripped what Averroes will soon exercise.

William of Auvergne has no illusions about what separates the Muslim Avicenna from the Christian Augustine. The Muslim, Koranic conception of eternal happiness cannot be reconciled with the Christian understanding. It is true that today some wonder whether "Mohammed's paradise" was no more than an exoteric doctrine for Avicenna, something for the people.[12] But, whatever may have been his true thought on the matter, Christian theologians could only take what literally he had written, and they did not hide their disapproval. William of Auvergne writes that we see "that it is impossible that paradise should be carnal and that it is a ridiculous idea that happiness consists of sensuous pleasures . . ." However, in his *Prima Philosophia* Avicenna explicitly subscribes to these delirious notions," which he understands have to be believed by the faith of Mohammed: "cujus damnatio tanto justior, quanto ista deliramenta tantus philosophus magis videre potuit, et videre neglexit."[13] Thus William suspects almost what today's historians

12. Modern historians wonder whether Avicenna really believed in what is often called "Mohammed's paradise," with its material, even carnal pleasures. Some have gone so far as to doubt that he really believed in the resurrection of the body. Anawati, O.P., "Un cas typique," 68–94. If he did not believe, he contradicts the teaching of both the Koran and the Gospel on this point. Cf. Gardet, *La pensée religieuse*, ch. 3, 2: "The dogma of the resurrection of the body," 86–105. Another dogma on which the scholastics had to take a position in regard to Avicenna is that of the creation of the world in time. We do not discuss it, because its positive influence on Christian philosophy is the point that concerns us in the present study. On this issue it is useful to consult Fackenheim, "Possibility."

13. William of Auvergne, *De Legibus*, ch. 19, I:54. The anti-feminism of the medieval clergy, a simple defense mechanism, is freely expressed there. The discussion of the immortality of the soul in William's *De Universo* (see *De Anima*, part XXII, 147–49) is also presented under the Avicennist form of direct discourse personally addressed to the reader: "Jam autem audivisti . . . Dico igitur . . . Dico etiam insuper . . . Nec te conturbet . . . Jam autem feci te scire . . . , etc." Any reader of Latin Avicenna feels at home. William of Auvergne's treatise *De immortalitate Animae* is printed in the same edition, I:329–36; reprinted in Bülow, "Des Dominicus Gundisalvi," 39–61. This work contains the text of *Gundisalinus de immortalitate animae*, 1–38. Comparing the two texts, we see that William's has been plagiarized from Gundissalinus's. Now Gundissalinus's treatise itself, according to Georg Bülow's personal conclusion, is "a compilation whose greater part plausibly depends on an Arab source. The author and title of the source remains unclear" (107). The style of Gundissalinus's treatise is naturally that of his own Latin translations of Avicenna: "Nosse debes . . . Et jam nosti . . . Nunc autem ex propriis

judge to have been the true, esoteric thought of Avicenna on this point. It is not Christian thought, but his true thought on the matter is not at all ridiculous nor base.

On the contrary, when it is a question of knowing whether the Agent Intellect is a faculty belonging to each individual soul, or a Separate Substance, William does not hesitate to opt for the second position, which was Avicenna's, but in his thought it is closely associated with St. Augustine's Divine Word.

An extraordinary text, in a sense unique, assures us that this doctrinal position was not peculiar to William of Auvergne, but common to a group of thirteenth-century theologians. I think we can do no better than to cite here Roger Bacon's whole testimony on this point. Bacon is one of the traditionalist theologians who maintained the teachings of the Fathers (read: of St. Augustine) on the nature of divine illumination in the knowledge of the true.

Let us recall that the agent intellect is the cause of true knowledge in us: "Intellectus agens dicitur, qui influit in animas nostras illuminans . . . possibilem ad cognitionem veritatis." Roger Bacon continues:

> Et sic intellectus agens, secundum majores philosophos, non est pars animae, sed est substantia intellectiva alia et separata per essentiam ab intellectu possibili. Et quia istud est necessarium ad propositi persuasionem, ut ostandatur quod philosophia sit per influentiam divinae illuminationis, volo illud efficaciter probare, praecipue cum magnus error invaserit vulgus philosophantium in hac parte, necnon multitudinem magnam theologorum, quoniam qualis homo est in philosophia, talis in theologia esse probatur. Dicit igitur Alpharabius in libro De Intellectu et Intellecto, quod intelligentia agens, quam nominavit Aristoteles in tertio tractatu suo De Anima, non est in materia sed est substantia separata. Et Avicenna quinto De Anima et nono Metaphysicae idem docet. Necnon ipse Philosophus dicit quod intellectus agens est separatus a possibili et immixtus . . .
>
> Non enim est dubium experto in philosophia quin haec sit sua [Aristotelis] sententia, et in hoc omnes sapientes antiqui ex-

---

immortalitatem ejus astruere temtabimus . . . Redeamus autem et dicamus . . . Revertamur autem ad id in quo eramus . . . , etc." Perhaps the possible influence of Avicenna has not been considered closely enough in this regard, *Liber VI Naturalium*, V:2: *"De affirmanda existentia animae rationalis non impressa in materia corporali,"* and V:4: *Quod anima non desinit esse neque tranformatur in alia corpora*, folios 22 verso and 24 verso. The Avicennist notion of soul of itself leads those who accept it to maintain the soul's personal immortality. That implies in turn the acknowledgement of a future life.

perti concordant. Nam universitate Parisiensi convocata, bis vidi
venerabilem antistitem dominum Gulielmum Parisiensem epis-
copum felicis memoriae coram omnibus sententiare quod intellectus agens non potest esse pars animae, et dominus Robertus
episcopus Lincolniensis et frater Adam de Marisco et hujusmodi
majores hoc idem firmaverunt.

Et sic nullo modo sequitur quod intellectus agens sit pars animae, ut vulgus fingit. Et haec sententia est tota fidelis, et a sanctis
confirmata; sicut enim omnes theologi quod Augustinus dicit in
Soliloquiis et alibi, quod soli Deo est anima rationalis subjecta in
illuminationibus et influentiis omnibus principalibus.[14]

Thus William of Auvergne, Robert Grosseteste bishop of Lincoln,
Adam Marsh, and *hujusmodi majores* agreed in holding against the
opinion of the Averroist crowd that the agent intellect is a separate substance, which is not part of the soul. Furthermore, their opinion was
confirmed by the joint shared authority of the Muslim philosophers,
Alfarabi and Avicenna, and the Christian theologian Augustine. This
position of capital importance in philosophy and theology attests to the
profound influence exercised by Avicenna on Western thought.

2) It would be easy to discover other traces of Avicenna's presence in
circles dominated by the influence of St. Augustine. All those for whom
the real Aristotle was Avicenna's Platonist Aristotle were predestined,
as it were, to associate him with Augustine's neo-Platonist Christianity.

14. Roger Bacon, *Opus Majus*, Pars II, ch. 5; vol. III: 45, 47, 48. For light on the
historical reality of this movement and its ramifications in different areas, two old essays [of mine] can be consulted, whose conclusions still seem valid to me: *Les sources
gréco-arabes*, and "Roger Marston." See also Ferreira, *Presença do Augustinismo*.

Thomas Aquinas clearly discerned the nature of the problem and that a choice
had to be made between philosophy and religion: "Verum est quod principium illustra-
tionis est unum, scilicet aliqua substantia separata, vel Deus secundum Catholicos, vel
Intelligentia ultima secundum Avicennam" (*De Unitate Intellectus*, par. 54). This article
is very interesting in regard to the nature of the problem and the position that ought to
be attributed to Avicenna in the discussion. Thomas attacks the Averroists who claimed
that all philosophers, except for the Latins, agreed in holding the unicity of the intellect:
"Algazel enim Latinus homo non fuit, sed Arabs [sic]. Avicenna etiam, qui Arabs [sic]
fuit, in suo libro De Anima sic dicit . . ." (*Liber VI Naturalium*, V, 3, folios 24 verso—25
recto). As for Averroes, he is less the commentator of Aristotle than his corrupter: "Unde
merito supra diximus eum philosophiae peripateticae perversorem. Unde mirum est
quomodo aliqui solum commentum Averrois videntes, pronuntiare praesumunt, quod
ipse dixit, hoc sensisse omnes philosophos Graecos et Arabes, praeter Latinos" (*De
Unitate Intellectus*, par. 54). On this essential point, the Latin theologians (Avicennists
or not) and Avicenna are thus in the same camp, against those who appeal to Averroes.

The famous *Theologia Aristotelis* is a bridge between the two doctrinal tendencies. It is all the more remarkable to see a decided partisan of the Averroist interpretation of Aristotle submit to Avicenna's influence on a point as central as the metaphysics of being, which conditions a corresponding metaphysics of God. After the action exercised by Avicenna in epistemology, we are going to experience it in ontology and natural theology in the doctrine of the (philosophically) peripatetic Thomas Aquinas.

It is generally admitted that the overall interpretation of Aristotle to which St. Thomas Aquinas arrived was that of Averroes. And that is true. When dogmatic truth is not in play and it is necessary to choose between Avicenna's Aristotle and Averroes's Aristotle, Thomas follows Averroes. Otherwise, he follows only himself when he deals with the philosophical conclusions with which theological truth is linked, but this very general view does not consider the different periods that mark the short life of Thomas Aquinas, nor the nature of the works where we can try to detect Avicenna's influence. Indeed, this influence was early, deep, and lasting. The honor of having detected and put it in evidence belongs to Aimé Forest in his work *La structure métaphysique du concret selon saint Thomas d'Aquin*. Later, the project was taken up again and completed,[15] but since 1931 the "Table of quotations of Avicenna in the

15. C. Vansteenkiste, "Avicenna-citation." By the same author, "Autori Arabi e Giudei," A table that is still useful and has the merit of being the first, is located at the end of Aimé Forest's always indispensable *La structure métaphysique*, 331–60. This doctoral thesis was so personal and so new that two of members of the tribunal, although highly qualified historians, did not understand it. Both agreed in affirming that everything that the author attributed to St. Thomas "was already in Aristotle." Since too many neo-scholastics only asked to believe that, at least in that far away period, this remarkable work fell victim of its own novelty.

Vansteenkiste's count turns out as follows: Commentaries on Scripture, three references to Avicenna; *In Boethium De Trinitate*, 10; commentaries on Peter Lombard's *Book of Sentences*, 170; commentaries on Aristotle, 25 (which suffices to show that the Commentator par excellence is not Avicenna but Averroes); *Quaestiones Disputatae* and *Quaestiones Quodlibitales*, 132; *Summa Contra Gentiles*, 17; *Summa Theologiae*, 27; authentic opuscula, 21. In all there are 405 references from which we should subtract two or three extracted from Gundissalinus, *De Intelligentiis*, which Thomas initially takes as being Avicenna's, but to which Vansteenkiste adds the references made in doubtful or spurious opuscula; also three in lines eliminated from the *Contra Gentiles* and ten in the *Supplement* to the *Summa Theolgiae* (a huge proportion in relation in relation to the 27 references in the authentic part). The bulk of the references to Avicenna are found in the *Disputed Questions* and in the *Commentary on the Sentences*. It sufficed for a careful historian to point out the texts of Thomas dealing with essence and existence in his early writing to establish without trying that Avicenna's influence was exercised mainly in the ontological order: Sweeney, "Existence/Essence." Incidentally, it is unsurprising

work of St. Thomas" compiled by Aimé Forest made this influence evident as well as the complexity of the problems it poses.

It is evident, firstly, that the considerable proportion of references to Avicenna in the early works diminishes in later ones: 170 references in the Commentary on the *Book of Sentences* of Peter Lombard against merely 17 in the *Summa contra Gentiles* and 27 in the *Summa Theologiae*. It is generally concluded that Avicenna's influence on Thomas Aquinas notably decreased over the years, but to be sure of that numerous, careful studies would be necessary, which have not yet been made. If we may conjecture about the overall result to which such studies would come, I believe they would make us see that Avicenna's influence on the young theologian reached its peak early, but I doubt that it noticeably decreased afterwards. Thomas cites Avicenna less, because the success Averroes enjoyed in the schools as Commentator *par excellence* led Thomas to prefer to define his own positions in function of those of Averroes. But he would have assimilated Avicenna for good. Also, Thomas desires to convince the Averroists above all, and since their interpretation of Aristotle seemed more faithful to the Philosopher's thought than Avicenna's, a theologian anxious to be heard naturally found himself tempted to accept the equation philosophy = Aristotle = Averroes, in whatever measure in which Christian faith was not opposed to it.

Moreover, the question and the answer vary according to the nature of the works in question. As a commentator on Aristotle, Thomas only cites Avicenna infrequently, and he is inspired by Averroes even more often than he cites him. Even in a work as personal as the *Contra Gentiles*, where he wants to get a hearing from philosophy professors who were keen on Averroes, he often abstains from referring to Avicenna in places where he could do so, because in the university circles of his time it was understood that the true philosopher was Aristotle in the purely rationalist interpretation given him by Averroes. Averroes's fundamental objection against Avicenna—that the latter taught a mixture of philosophy and revealed theology—recommended him to the attention of theologians, but disqualified him in the eyes of pure philosophers, those "Averroists" who, however much they differed from each others,

---

that neither of these historians gives precise references to the passages of Avicenna cited by Thomas Aquinas, because what Thomas attributes to Avicenna is always there, but Thomas cites ideas and doctrines rather than passages. We would say the reason is that Latin Avicenna's language is so rough, and to be frank, so un-Latin, that it is difficult to quote without glossing.

had a common wish to philosophize by the light of natural reason alone, without any reference to revelation—Jewish, Christian, or Muslim. Even a pure theologian like Thomas Aquinas could not hope to make philosophers listen to him or simply make himself read by them, if he put forward Avicenna's doubtful Aristotle rather than Averroes as the guarantee of his own philosophy. In his oldest theological writings, where he addresses only Christian readers and theologians like himself, Thomas Aquinas lets Avicenna speak freely. If, as Fr. Ignatius T. Eschmann thinks,[16] Thomas's work on the *Sentences* was composed around 1256, it

16. Eschmann, "A Catalogue." If I am not mistaken, this is the most recent study of its sort. In regard to the *Summa contra Gentiles* (ca. 1261–1264), its late author recalls that "the defense of orthodoxy against a kind of Averroism before the fact, which had invaded the teaching of Parisian professors was (according to Gorce) St. Thomas's target in this work." In agreement with Salman, Eschmann rejects this interpretation, but leaving aside the term "Averroism," subject to dispute like all *isms*, it is certain that Thomas had Averroes's commentary at hand on his writing table. He uses it more than he quotes it, and the work is certainly intended for those who practically did not distinguish the authority of Averroes from that of the Philosopher. If the questions *De Potentia* date from around 1265 (ibid., 391), they bear witness that at the moment when he was finishing *Contra Gentiles* Thomas still found the occasion to cite Avicenna thirty times. The more the subject is metaphysical, the more frequently Avicenna is quoted. Questions relating to prophecy and the last ends of man also invite Thomas to take a position on the final chapters of Avicenna's *Metaphysica*. For example, *De Veritate*, question XII, article 3, objections and replies 8 and 9 about the question of knowing whether prophecy is natural or supernatural. Here, Thomas seems to remit to Avicenna, *De Anima* (*Liber VI Naturalium*), IV, 4, ed. 1608, folio 20 verso. But it is in the metaphysics of being and consequently of God, or natural theology, that Avicenna's influence is most visible and deepest. Studying what he terms "the genus argument" in favor of the distinction between essence and existence, Fr. Leo Sweeney ("Existence/Essence," 109) finds four passages (without having sought them out) which explicitly refer to Avicenna: 1) "Secundum Avicennam, II parte Logicae, cap. 2 ubicumque est genus et species, oportet esse quidditatem differentem a suo esse, ut prius dictum est . . ." (*In I Sententiarum*, distinction 19, question 4, article 2, solution, I:483). 2) "Non oportet illud quod est in praedicamento substantiae habere quidditatem compositam, sed oportet quod habeat compositionem quidditatis et esse; omne enim quod est in genere suae quidditatis non est suum esse, ut Avicenna, *Metaphysica*, tract. VII. cap. 4 etc, dicit" (*In II Sententiarum*, distinction 3, q. 1, article 1, ad 1, II:88). [Translator: In references to Aquinas's *Commentary* on Lombard's *Sentences*, I have indicated the volume and page of the 1929 Mandonnet edition against which I have checked the quotations.] 3) "Secundum Avicennam ubi supra (*Metaphysica*, tract. V, cap. 5, 6, 7) omne id quod habet esse aliud a sua quidditate, oportet quod sit in genere; et ita oportet quod omnes angeli ponantur in praedicamento substantiae, prout est praedicamentum, cum secundum Avicennam, loc. cit., substantia sit res quidditatem habens cui debetur esse per se, non in alio, scilicet quod sit alio a quiddate ipsa." *In II Sententiarum*, distinction 3, question 1, article 5 solution, II:99–100. 4) "Ut Avicenna dicit in sua *Metaphysica*, tract. II, c. 1, et tract. VI, c. 5, ad hoc quod aliquid sit proprie in genere substantiae requiritur

is not surprising to find Avicenna everywhere. His presence is as visible as it will still be in *De Ente et Essentia*, composed in 1256 at the latest in the same Avicennist fervor

Thus the study of Avicenna's influence on Thomas Aquinas remains to be done. Moreover, it is not certain that the nature of the question will ever permit a final, simple response to the question. Someone who has lived with the question for long years becomes more and more modest in his expectations.

Roughly, we must distinguish three situations: the very rare instances in which Thomas refers nominally to Avicenna and quotes him literally or almost so; the frequent instances where Thomas names Avicenna and attributes to him, often insistently, formulas that are not literally found in his text. These cases are particularly troublesome, because in the absence of a concordance of Latin Avicenna and without reading his *Opera Omnia* each time we look for this sort of passage, we are never sure that we have not failed to notice the text in question. We do not know whether it does not exist or whether we have missed it. What incites us to think that a text does not exist is that in such cases the formula attributed by Thomas to Avicenna is a concision, a precision, in short, a completely Thomist verbal perfection. It is Avicenna's as Avicenna could have thought it in Arabic and as an Avicenna whose language was Latin would have written it. The certainly very understandable clumsiness of the Latin translation invited Thomas to reformulate Avicenna's thought in quoting it. But this makes the work difficult of those who read in St. Thomas *ut dicit Avicenna* and expect a literal quote, but do not manage to find it. The third case is where Thomas writes with the text of Avicenna at hand or present in is memory but paraphrases it and freely

---

quod sit res quidditatem habens cui debeatur esse absolutum, ut per se esse dicatur vel subsistens . . ." *In II Sententiarum*, distinction 3, question 1, article 6 solution, II:102–3. I would recall that all references to Avicenna should be taken with caution, without blaming the person who makes them. Thus, the notions of being, substance, God, angel, in short of any created substance, depend on the principle posited by Avicenna and adopted by Aquinas (*In I Sententiarum*, distinction 8, question 1, article 1, solution, I:195) "in qualibet re creata essentia sua differt a suo esse." However, I have never managed to find in Avicenna's own text the literal formula that Thomas certainly seemed to attribute to him (See Sweeney, 109): "ens per se non est diffinitio substantiae, ut Avicenna dicit . . ." The references that editors transmit have not yet led me to any passage of Avicenna that says these simple words. Those who live long enough to read the Leonine edition of the disputed questions *De Potentia* will doubtless be happier than us. But I am not certain of that. Thomas Aquinas did not suffer from literalist scruples in quoting. See however, 108–9.

uses Avicennist themes to express his own thought. This is a question of exegesis that is infinitely detailed and that we cannot confront here. It is not even certain that such exegesis could be other than oral, spoken rather than written.

Examples of almost literal quotations—Avicenna: "Dicemus igitur quod ens et res et necesse talia sunt quae statim imprimuntur in anima prima impressione" (*Metaphysica*, tractate I, ch. 6, folio 72 recto A). Often quoted by Thomas Aquinas in an abbreviated form: "Ens est illud quod primo cadit in conceptione human, ut Avicenna dicit . . ." (*In I Sententiarum*, question 1, article 3, 3. [Trans: sic]). "Primum cadens in apprehensione intellectus est ens, ut Avicenna dicit . . ." (*In I Sententiarum*, distinction 38, question 1, article 4, 4, I:905). "Primo in intellectu cadit ens, ut Avicenna dicit" (*In Metaphysicam*, book I, 2). "Illud autem quod primo intellectus concipit quasi notissimum et in quo omnes conceptiones resolvit, est ens, ut Avicenna dicit in principio *Metaphysicae* suae" (*Quaestiones Disputatae de Veritate*, question 1, article 1, respondeo) "Cum autem ens sit id quod primum cadit in conceptione mentis, ut dicit Avicenna" (*Quaestiones Disputatae de Veritate*, question 21, article 1, respondeo) "Ens autem et essentia sunt quae primo intellectu concipiuntur, ut dicit Avicenna in principio *Metaphysicae* suae" (*De Ente et Essentia*, I, 1). Furthermore, we observe that Thomas seems to avoid *necesse*, which would give rise to endless, but not useless glosses.

Distinction between *being* and *thing*: "Nomen entis imponitur ab esse et nomen rei a quidditate, ut dicit Avicenna" (*In I Sententiarum*, distinction 25, question 1, article 4, objection 2, I:611) Or again: "Secundum Avicennam, ut supra dictum est, hoc nomen ens et res differunt secundum quod est duo considerare in re, scilicet quidditatem et rationem ejus, et esse ipsius" (*In I Sententiarum*, distinction 25, question I, article 4, solution, I:611). This distinction is the root of the renowned Thomist doctrine of the composition of essence and existence in the finite. Thomas refers to Avicenna to establish their distinction (from which their composition follows): "Tertia ratio subtilior est Avicennae: . . . omne quod est in genere habet quidditate differentem ab esse" (*In I Sententiarum*, distinction 8, question 4, article 2, I:222). We read in effect in Avicenna that every thing has its own quiddity, which is other than its being: "Unaquaeque res habet certitudinem propriam quae est ejus quidditas, et notum est quod certitudo cujusque rei quae est propria rei, est praeter esse, quod multivocum est cum aliquid" (*Metaphysica*, I, ch. 6 folio 72 verso). We are going to see that this is even why God has no genus, because he has not quiddity or essence: "Primus etiam non habet genus; primus enim non habet quidditatem; sed quod non habet quidditatem non habet genus . . ." (*Metaphysica*, tractate VIII, ch 4, folio 99 recto A).

In contrast to finite substances, God is pure being without essence: "Quidam enim ducunt, ut Avicenna et Rabbi Moyses [*who follows Avicenna*] quod res illa quae Deus est, est quoddam esse subsistens, nec aliud nisi esse in Deo est. Unde dicunt quod [Deus] est sine essentia" (*In I Sententiarum*, distinction 2, question 1, article 3, body of article, I:67). And in *De Ente et Essentia*, ch. V: "Aliquid enim est, sicut Deus, cujus essentia est suum esse; et ideo inveniuntur aliqui philosophi dicentes quod Deus non habet quidditatem, quia essentia sua non est aliud quam esse suum." This is Avicenna's thought purified and clarified: "Dico enim quod necesse esse non potest habere quidditatem quam comitetur necessitas essendi" (*Metaphysica*, tractate VIII, ch. 4, folio 99 recto A), and again, *ibidem*: "Igitur necesse esse non habet quidditatem nisi quod est necesse esse . . ."

Avicenna is led by this to ask himself whether, since God has no essence and is not in a genus, he is substance? His answer involves a modification of the notion of substance: "Contra quod dico quod hoc non est intentio substantiae quod posuimus genus; imo intentio ejus est quod est res habens quidditatem stabilem, cujus esse est esse quod non est in subjecto . . ." (*Metaphysica*, tractate VIII, ch. 4, folio 99 recto C). Here is what these and other analogous texts become once filtered through Thomas Aquinas: "Ens per se non est definitio substantiae ut Avicenna dicit, ens enim non potest esse alicujus genus, sed substantia est res cujus quidditati debetur non esse in aliquo. Et sic non convenit definitio substantiae Deo, quo non habet quidditatem suam praeter suum esse. Unde Deus non est in genere substantiae, sed est supra omnem substantiam" (*Quaestiones Disputatae De Potentia*, question VIII, article 3 ad 4).

The consequences of these doctrinal positions affect all of St. Thomas's metaphysics and consequently his theology: "Respondet Avicenna in sua Metaphysica. Dicit enim omnes res a Deo creatas esse, et quod creatio est ex nihilo, vel ejus quod habet esse post nihil" (*In II Sententiarum*, distinction 1, question 1, article 5 ad 2, II:38). Conceived thus, creation is a mode of causality peculiar to God: "Secundum Avicennam duplex est agens: quoddam naturale quod est agens per motum, sicut naturale, et quoddam quod est sine motu, dando esse" (*In II*

Sententiarum, distinction 1, article 2, ad 1, II:46). The distinction of the motor and efficient causes brings a remarkable deepening of the understanding of the latter. With a remarkable grasp of the significance of this deepening, Émile Meyerson called efficient causality "theological causality," and indeed it is because this is so that Averroes rejected any demonstration of the existence of God by efficient causality. He knew that the motor cause is the true Aristotelian cause, and that it is a physical, not metaphysical, cause.

Since even quasi-literal quotations are hardly literal and resemble paraphrases or glosses, we cannot here engage in a discussion of any case where Thomas Aquinas visibly took from Avicenna the doctrinal themes or notions to be used for his own ends. I believe that a detailed comparison of Thomas Aquinas, *Summa Theologiae*, I, 3, *De Simplicitate Dei*, with Avicenna, *Metaphysica*, VIII, 4 and 5, at some points would permit us to see Thomas at work gathering, interpreting, adapting, and sorting out as necessary several of the Muslim philosopher's doctrinal positions. It is striking that St. Thomas has confided more in Averroes in everything that concerns the order of finite things and so in physics, and more in Avicenna for everything that concerns the metaphysical order, that of being and God. The cause of this is perhaps that there is some Plotinus in Avicenna, therefore some metaphysics. But let us keep from dreaming.

3) However, it is not in Thomas Aquinas but in Duns Scotus that Avicenna's influence asserts itself most strikingly. Deciding whether the Thomistic proofs of the existence of God are physical or metaphysical is a frequently debated historical problem, or, to put it more exactly, whether their true place is in physics or in metaphysics. Averroes judges that the existence of God is proved in physics. Thomas Aquinas refrains from insisting on this difficulty and offers proofs whose point of departure is sense experience of physical reality but whose conclusion is metaphysically demonstrated. Duns Scotus plainly opts for Avicenna, according to whom proving the existence of God belongs to metaphysics: "Sed non potest concedi quod Deus sit in hac scientia ut subjectum, imo quaesitum est in ea."[17] In the controversy that sets Scotists and Thomists at

17. Avicenna, *Metaphysica*, tractate I, ch. 1, folio 70 recto C. This initial decision accepted by Duns Scotus controls the whole structure of his own doctrine. It would be challenged by Averroes and St. Thomas Aquinas. See Scotus, *Quaestiones in Metaphysica Aristotelis*, question 1, and *Reportata Parisiensia*, Prologus, question 3, article 1. The title

odds during the course of the fourteenth century, the Scotists merely take the side of Avicenna against Averroes and proclaim it openly.

The point where Avicenna's metaphysics most deeply left its imprint on the doctrine of Duns Scotus is his notion of the *natura* or nature of beings. Thomas had noticed what was peculiar to Avicenna's position on this point: "Secundum Avicennam in sua *Metaphysica*, triplex est alicujus naturae consideratio."[18] Indeed, according to Avicenna a thing's nature can be considered either in its physical, concrete reality, that is as particular, or in thought, that is as universal, or finally, and here is the noteworthy point of his doctrine, in itself, that is to say as neither universal nor particular, but indifferent to generality and particularity. This is what is called the doctrine of *natura communis*, whose Avicennist

---

of the first question on the *Metaphysics* exactly defines the elements of the problem. "Is the subject of metaphysics being in so far as being, as Avicenna maintained, or God and the Intelligences as the Commentator Averroes held?" We can easily grasp the immediate result of this initial choice. All of Averroes's natural theology, which St. Thomas attributes to metaphysics, for Duns Scotus becomes physics. The so called "physical" proofs of the existence of God proposed by Averroes and apparently accepted unchanged by Thomas Aquinas, will be replaced in Duns Scotus by properly metaphysical proofs. The two theologians establish themselves on two different planes whose opposition faithfully reflects that of Averroes and Avicenna. Duns Scotus said so in his own words: "Item Commentator [*Averroes*] *I Physicorum*, commento ultimo, dicit quod Avicenna multum peccavit ponendo metaphysicam probare primam causam esse, cum genus substantiarum separatarum sit ibi subjectum et nulla scientia probat suum subjectum esse; sed ratio illa Averrois non valeret, nisi intelligeret quod Deus esset primum subjectum ibi; ergo, etc.—Ad Commentatorem *I Physicorum* dico quod Avicenna bene dixit, et Commentator male." *Opus Oxoniense*, Prologus I, q 3, article 1, number 3. In *Reportata Parisiensia*, Prologus, q 3, number 1. For an overview of the question, see Gilson, *Jean Duns Scot*, 77–80. It is apparent there that the Christian theologies of the Middle Ages were not just influenced by Avicenna or Averroes, nor even by both, but also by their own historical relationships. The doctrinal quarrel between Averroes and Duns Scotus is reflected in the quarrel that divides Duns Scotus from Thomas Aquinas. The well-known antagonism between the Thomist and Scotist schools that will last beyond the sixteenth century and up to our days is rooted in that of Averroes against Avicenna.

18. Thomas Aquinas, *Quaestiones Quodlibetales*, q. VIII, article 1, respondeo. This passage sums up clearly the position that had been Avicenna's before becoming that of Duns Scotus: "Respondeo dicendum quod, secundum Avicennam in sua *Metaphysica*, triplex est alicujus naturae consideratio. Una, prout consideratur secundum esse quod habet in singularibus, sicut natura lapidis in hoc lapide et in illo lapide. Alia vero est consideratio alicujus naturae secundum esse suum intelligibile, sicut natura lapidis consideratur prout est in intellectu. Tertia vero est consideratio naturae absolute, prout abstrahit ab utroque esse; secundum quam considerationem consideratur natura lapidis, vel cujuscumque alterius, quantum ad ea tantum quae per se competunt tali naturae."

origin is undeniable[19] and which occupies an important place in John Duns Scotus's theology.[20] It can be said, in this sense, that the Avicennist notion of common nature or of the triple way of looking at nature, constituted a point of departure for the reflection of Duns Scotus.[21]

Hardly any part of his doctrine lacks this mark. The notion of equivocal being, which, as is well known, impacts the Scotist conception of the proofs of the existence of God in such a way that we conceive divine being (analogous in Thomas, univocal in Scotus) by the relation Scotus asserts and by the distinction he introduces between the universal and the singular, by his personal conception of individuation, and so forth. To say which first notion controls all these consequences in Duns Scotus, we would have to agree first on what is the key notion in Avicenna. At least it is certain that what is still taken today as the trademark of Scotism, the univocity of being, merely translates the direct consequence of the

---

19. "Essentiae vero rerum aut sunt in ipsis rebus, aut sunt in intellectu; unde habent tres respectus: unus respectus essentiae est secundum quod ipsa est non relata ad aliquod tertium esse, nec ad id quod sequitur eam secundum quod ipsa est sic. Alius respectus est secundum quod est in his singularibus. Et alius secundum quod est in intellectu." Avicenna, *Logica*, ch. 1, folio 2 recto. "Ergo universale ex hoc quod est universale est quoddam, et ex hoc quod est aliquid cui accidit universalitas est quoddam aliud. Ergo de universali ex hoc quod est universale constitutum signatur unus praedictorum terminorum; quia cum ipsum fuerit homo vel equus erit haec intentio alia praeter intentionem universalitatis, quae est humanitas vel equinitas. Diffinitio enim equinitatis est praeter diffinitionem universalitis, nec universalitas continetur in diffinitione equinitatis. Equinitas enim habet diffinitionem quae non eget universalitate, sed est cui accidit universalitas, unde equinitas non est nisi equinitas tantum. Ipsa enim ex se nec est multa nec unum, nec est existens in his sensibilibus nec in anima, nec est aliquid horum potentia vel effectu ita quod contineatur intra essentiam equinitatis. Sed ex hoc quod est equinitas tantum, unitas autem est proprietas quae, cum adjungitur equinitati, fit equinitas propter ipsam proprietatem unum" (Avicenna, *Metaphysica*, tractate V, ch. 1, folio 86 verso).

20. See my study "Avicenne et le point." The distinguished commentator on Scotus, Mauritius Hibernicus O.F.M., gave Avicenna as Duns Scotus's source on this point: Scotus, *Opera Omnia* Vivès, I:103.

21. Avicenna left an easily detectable clue for future researchers on his influence. The example he chose to illustrate his notion of *natura communis* (neither universal, nor singular), as we have seen above in note 19, is the nature of horse, equinity. *Equinitas* reappears frequently in those influenced by him, and first of all in Duns Scotus himself, who readily remits to the text of Avicenna's *Metaphysica*: *ubi vult quod equinitas sit tantum equinitas*. On this Scotist teaching, see my *Jean Duns Scot*, 447–51. It is unnecessary to stress that this agreement about the nature of the universal situates a doctrine within medieval philosophy as a whole. In this matter, it is impossible to recommend highly enough the important study by Johann Kraus, "Die Universalienlehre."

Avicennist teaching on *natura communis*, when it is applied to being. Just as equinity stays the same, whether we consider a horse or the horse, in the same way being is entity itself and its sense is the same for any being of which it is predicate: *In ista quaestione videtur opinio Avicennae, quod ens dicitur per unam rationem de omnibus de quibus dicitur.* This is also the being that constitutes metaphysic's peculiar subject; Avicenna's influence determines the area occupied by a whole great natural theology, one of the three or four great scholastic theologies. The importance of this influence cannot be exaggerated.

But it would not be impossible to be mistaken about its nature. By their essence, scholastic theologies appeal to philosophies, including those of Averroes and of Avicenna, in order to acquire the *intellectum fidei* that St. Augustine (who had asked it of Plotinus) held to be the specific goal of theological speculation. But theology is not faith. To ask a philosophy for intelligence of the faith is to become involved, not in a particular faith, but in a particular theology. We should understand the classical adage of medieval schools in this sense, *qualis in philosophia, talis in theologia.*

All these Christian theologians have the same faith, and although they interpret it differently according to the different philosophies by which they are inspired, none of them can ever be held to be a disciple of that philosopher whose doctrine the theologian uses for his own ends. Augustine is not a Plotinian, because his God is not that of Plotinus. Thomas Aquinas is not an Aristotelian, still less an Averroist, because his God is neither that of Aristotle nor that of Averroes. For the same reason, no theologian could be said to be an Avicennist pure and simple, because no theologian could become one without becoming a Muslim and betraying his Christian faith. Absolutely speaking, one could be Christian and Averroist at the same time, precisely because the philosophy of Averroes was not a Muslim philosophy in any sense, and claimed to be completely free of all ties with any religion. It acknowledged the existence of the Prophet and even his preeminence, but the transcendent manner in which the Prophet possessed the total and absolute truth, according to Averroes, exercised no influence on the purely rational manner in which the philosopher can know it. Accordingly, the influence of Averroes on medieval Christian speculation may be considerable, but it differed in nature from that of Avicenna, which was what Averroes might have agreed to call (disdainfully) a scholastic theology, rather than a philosophy truly worthy of the name. We should never forget, pondering these questions, the implacable condemnation of Avicenna by Averroes: *sermo Avicennae semper invenitur quasi medius inter Peripateticos et Loquentes.* Since this mixture of philosophy and theology was a deadly confusion for philosophical truth,[22] he could say nothing worse against his predecessor.

However, it is just this that explains that Avicenna's philosophy should have furnished materials, intelligible materials, if we can use the expression, to many Christian theologians. Even when they ultimately would have to separate from him or submit his teaching to radical reinterpretations, they found in him material to borrow to be used positively with a view to specifically religious goals.

That is what the examples we have supplied attempt to make clear. No theologian conceded to Avicenna that our agent intellect was a Separate Intelligence, but many conceived God as playing the role of that substance, and in that sense of being our true agent intellect. The distinction is important, because it is what dissuades us from speaking of a real "Christian Avicennism."[23] Indeed, and we will come back to the point, none of these "Avicennizers" was an "Avicennist" in the sense in which the followers of Averroes were "Averroists." They followed Avicenna in his doctrine of separate Agent Intellect, specifying that this intellect was not the lowest of the Intelligences, a kind of Intelligence of earth, but indeed the Christian Word.

To study the nature of Avicenna's influence on Thomas Aquinas is a task that each of us can take up himself, if he has the desire, but he cannot hope to attain the end of such reflections and still less involve others than himself in them. The thirteenth century was not only the golden age of scholastic theology. It was also, and at the same time, one of the great periods of metaphysics. In large measure this was thanks to the example of Avicenna, who, I always have thought, must not be separated from his master Alfarabi. Each of them gave a fertile example of

22. In the abundant literature on this topic, I still know nothing better than Léon Gauthier's work, which is old but strikes the right tone, translating Averroes, moreover: "Accord de la religion." From the same author, *Ibn Rochd (Averroes).* Cf. Gardet, *Bulletin Thomiste* 8 (1931) 248–52. For want of something better, Gilson, *Reason and Revelation,* 37–66.

23. However, in favor of this notion that we have intentionally rejected as unjustified by the facts, see de Vaux, *Notes et textes.* The question is secondary and de Vaux's work is important in any case, but we do not think we should modify the observations we made in *Mediaeval Studies* 2 (1940) 25–27. See further, 116–20; *sed contra* de Contenson, "Avicennisme latin."

metaphysical thought nourished by Plotinus's and anxious to go beyond Plotinus's in the direction of biblical revelation. They attempted to conceive Plotinus's One as being and creator of being, the God of the Old Testament, whose heirs they were by the Prophet. By committing themselves to the same endeavor after their example, Christian theologians between about 1250 and 1350 were led to enlarge and deepen Greek metaphysics of being. While Augustine, who cared chiefly about the noetic in these matters, had applied his genus mainly to the doctrine of the true, accepting Plotinus's being nearly as he had received it (here we mean in philosophy), Avicenna and those Christian theologians whom he inspired took up again Plotinus's teaching to deepen in it in the direction of ontology rather than of noetic and epistemology. Thomas did not cease to repeat: *ens est primum quod cadit in intellectu, ut Avicenna dicit*. In both accounts God is the pure act of being without any essence added to it, and being is the first principle of reality as of knowledge. Can we see more striking convergence and broader consequences? Yet at the heart of this very convergence we feel a profound difference, whose consequences are infinite. Avicenna's God is *necesse esse* par excellence, a first necessity source of all other necessities, something not without relation to the spirit of the Koran and its prophet. Because pure act of *esse* transcends every essence, Thomas Aquinas's I AM is first of all free creative fecundity. He is a Christian God. There is no doubt in this regard, but in reading Thomas Aquinas we feel the presence of Avicenna's First, deepened and transformed. Without Avicenna we would doubtless have had a Thomas Aquinas, but we would not have had him as he is.

What should be said about Duns Scotus? More than three centuries ago his illustrious Franciscan interpreter, Maritius a Portu, said everything essential in this regard: *Favet namque Avicennae inter philosophos ubique nisi sit contra fidem*. Could one say more? Scotus, says Maurice a Portu, is always for Avicenna among the philosophers, "for Augustine among the Catholic doctors, for Paul among the apostles, for John among the evangelists, and there is nothing surprising about that since, as Boethius says, we desire everything that resembles us." Wonderful Maurice a Portu, who says it all in so few words! However, we cannot be content with Avicenna's God in ontology if we adhere to St. John's God in theology. Beyond the *Necesse Esse* is the Gospel's *Deus caritas est*. That is why, even in metaphysics, Duns Scotus's God contradicts the God of the philosopher from whom he borrows his technique. Instead of being a Necessity that causes necessities, as he is in Avicenna, the God of Duns Scotus is a freedom that causes freedoms. Universe of necessity in Avicenna, universe of contingency in Duns Scotus, the two creations differ like their respective sources, that of Duns Scotus everywhere carries the mark of its initial contingence, to which it owes its being. Without Avicenna we would perhaps have a Scotism. We would have one in the measure in which Scotism is a theological expression of Christian faith, but we can say about him, as we were saying an instant ago about Thomas Aquinas, that without Avicenna the doctrinal synthesis Scotus left us would be different from what it is. Avicenna permitted our greatest scholastic theologians to create in a realm where innovation is so rare, that of ontology and of natural theology that crowns ontology, by going beyond Avicenna although by his example and with his help.

4) In drawing a conclusion on this point, I wish to formulate two requests. First, that inquisitive minds who care about historical objectivity might undertake to construct lexicons of the different medieval Latins that came out of translations made from Arabic. It is easy to distinguish those who learned their philosophical Latin in the translation of Avicenna's *Shifâ* or in Averroes's *Great Commentary*. No doubt there are sub-species. The task is not only dry but difficult, because these different Latins are contaminated by each other. However, I would be surprised if this sort of research did not produce results.

This research presupposes another line of research that happily has begun,[24] on the text of Latin translations of Avicenna, with a view to

24. "One of the most urgent tasks would be the re-edition of the medieval Latin translations of Arab philosophers in general and Avicenna in particular. This task . . . is beyond the capacity of a single individual as far as the great works of Avicenna and Averroes go. It would be highly valuable for an international organization of medievalists to be established and assume the direction of an undertaking upon whose success the future of our common studies seems to be directly involved." Gilson, "L'étude des philosophies arabes," 596. My appeal was heard as regards Averroes, for whom, however, we already had relatively numerous editions usable for practical purposes. Needless to say, the modern re-edition of the Commentator's writings is welcome. It renders great services. But it does not compensate us for the lack of a similar re-edition of Avicenna, whose work occupies a specifically different and more important place than that of Averroes in the history of Muslim and Christian thought. All the more acknowledgement is due the author of the first preparatory works required for this great undertaking: d'Alverny, "Avicenna latinus," numbers 28, 29, 30, 31, 32, 33, and 34.

[Trans. Note: Brill (Leiden and Boston) has published the following works of Avicenna between 1968 and 1999, edited by Simone van Riet with doctrinal introduction

their eventual re-edition.[25] Forty-two years ago at the Sixth International Congress of Philosophy held at Harvard University, I publicly expressed the desire for an edition of the *Shifâ* with fewer gaps and imperfections than the one we have. We are still dependent on the *Metaphysica Avicennae sive ejus Prima Philosophia, optime castigata et emendata per canonicos regulares sancti Augustini in monasterio divi Joannis de Viridario commorantes.* It would be most ungrateful to criticize these religious men without whom the medieval Latin Avicenna would be still more difficult to know than he is thanks to their work. However, these Canons of St. John in Verdara flattered themselves, and it would be easy to improve on them simply producing a less defective edition, if not a critical edition, at least revised in the light of selected manuscripts. Those who see the first volume of such a future edition will be able to say with the Canons of St. John *Ad laudem Dei.* For us who only see this promised land from the distance, *Insh'allah* is all we can say, but we say it with all our hearts.

WAS THERE A LATIN AVICENNISM?

It is customary to speak of medieval Latin Averroists and Latin Averroism. Seeing the influence Avicenna had on certain scholastic theologians, it is tempting to speak of Latin Avicennism corresponding to Latin Averroism, but the notion of Latin Avicennism is a painted

by Gerard Verbeke. *Liber de Anima seu Sextus de Naturalibus* appeard in two volumes. *De Philosophia Prima sive Scientia Divina* appeared in three volumes. A volume is devoted to *Liber Primus Naturalium.* Finally, a volume collects Marie-Thérèse d'Alverny's studies of the codices of Avicenna updated by Sione van Riet and Pierre Jodogne. The project seems to have been stopped at this point.]

At present the following can already be beneficially consulted in *Archives d'histoire doctrinale et littéraire du moyen âge* 28 (1961) 282–94: 1. description of the Arabic text of *Kitab al-Shifâ*; 2. the Latin translation; 3. old editions; 4 *descriptio operis.*

25. There are already excellent partial studies of the history of certain Greek technical terms and their various translations into Hebrew, Arabic, and Latin. For example, Wolfson, "The Internal Senses," by the same author, "The Amphibolous Term," again by Wolfson, "The Terms *tasawwur* and *tasdiq*". Gundissalinus, translator of the *Metaphysics*, seems to have started from Boethius's Latin for the basis of his vocabulary, but since Boethius was insufficient, he had to invent. See Marie-Thérèse d'Alverny, "Anniyyaanitas."

The stylistic studies of which I am thinking would be completely different. They would deal with vocabulary and style of authors who did not know Greek and Arabic, who used the Latin of the translations just as they received it. From there, works derive written like those of Boethius, Latin Avicenna, or Latin Averroes, or even mixing the three (not to mention several others like Maimonides, Ghazzali, etc.)

window invented by the need of a non-existing symmetry. As paradoxical as it seems, it is easier for a Christian to be an Averroist than to be an Avicennist, precisely because the philosophy of Averroes was free of any religious influence, even Muslim influence, which is not true of Avicenna's philosophy.

Averroes's teaching is a rationalism, a philosophism alien to any theology except natural theology, which is the coronation of metaphysics. The so-called doctrine of "double truth," which the condemnation of 1277 attributed to the Latin disciples of Averroes, expressed precisely their desire to keep the two orders separate. The work of Averroes was the condemnation, not of all religion or religious preaching, but certainly of the speculative theology carried out by the masters of the Kalam, and later by the masters of Christian scholasticism. In so far as that theology desired to understand faith, in Averroes's eyes it became a hybrid, neither philosophy—because religious faith was mixed up in it—nor religion—because it purported to demonstrate the indemonstrable and thus put faith in danger without thereby clarifying reason.

Thus it was possible to be Muslim and Averroist, or Christian and Averroist, at the same time, as long as one kept the two orders separate. Any difficulty arose from the mixture of the two orders, which, however, was the very substance of speculative theology, whether Muslim or Christian.

This lets us understand how a Latin Averroism existed. Someone who was a Latin, and thereby a Christian, could think what he wanted in philosophy, provided only that he continue to believe the teaching of his religion or even that he made the appearance of believing it. In fact, this was seen in the case of many masters who claimed to be Christians in religion, all the while following the opinions of Averroes in philosophy. Siger of Brabant, Boethius of Dacia, John of Jandun were genuine Latin Averroists and taught a real Latin Averroism because, in philosophy, these Latin Christians accepted and taught essentially Averroes's philosophy. They judged that the creation of the world *ex nihilo* in time is indemonstrable. They taught that the possible intellect and the agent intellect are Separate Substances that do not belong to individuals as such. That consequently there is no personnel immortality of the soul, nor eternal rewards or punishments in another life. A Christian could think all this freely in philosophy, if he was an Averroist. It was enough for him to think or to say that he held such conclusions to be "necessary" in philosophy, but that the authority of God justified his holding the contrary to be "true" from the point of view of faith. Thus there could be and in fact there were Christians who professed that the philosophical conclusions necessary for reason were those of Averroes. They were the genuine "Latin Averroists." They cannot be regarded as "Christian Averroists," because, since Averroism excludes any alliance with religion, the notion of Christian or Muslim Averroism would be contradictory, but Latin Averroism remained possible.

The position of Avicenna was completely different. Although he was not essentially a theologian but, in his intention, a pure philosopher as Averroes must have been, he never thought of teaching philosophical conclusions openly contradicting the teaching of the Koran. On the contrary, without setting out to justify the literal truth of religious revelation, he always tried to teach philosophical conclusions that could be regarded as rational justifications of revealed truth. Unlike Averroes, Avicenna sincerely desired to take Mohammed's prophetic preaching into account and teach nothing contrary to it. So Christian theologians could use for their own purposes a philosophy anxious by nature to be in harmony with Old Testament revelation, shared by the two religious confessions. Avicenna taught the existence of One God, pure act of being, creator *ex nihilo* of a universe governed by providence where men, all submitted to one Agent Intellect but each endowed with a personal possible intellect, could hope for eternal happiness or fear endless punishment. Obviously, the philosopher did not think about these things as naively as a member of the faithful believes them. It can even be feared that Avicenna naturalizes belief as he turns in into philosophy, but he does not want either to combat it or separate himself from it.

The intrinsic impossibility of Latin Avicennism properly speaking comes from its belonging not to the religion of the Gospel but of the Koran. Because the Old Testament offered some common ground, that whole part of Avicennism that taught there is one God, being and creator of beings, with the consequences that follow for the ontological status of participated being, assisted the Christian masters in the elaboration of their own theology *De Deo Uno*. Also it is understandable thereby that epistemologically the Avicennist doctrine of separated Intellects should have furnished Christian theologians with a sort of model to formulate philosophically their own doctrine of the human possible intellect by the light of the divine Word. St. Augustine's Platonism, springing from

Plotinus and Marius Victorinus, effortlessly joined that of Avicenna. Thus an alliance of Christian theology and Avicenna's philosophy was natural, but it had no less natural limits, because in the very measure in which it took the teaching of Islam into consideration, a Muslim's philosophy is spontaneously oriented in directions where that of a Christian cannot follow. The Muslim God is above all the First Necessary, cause of all created necessities. That of Christians is rather the liberty of pure being, creator of other liberties. The second person of the Christian Trinity, the Word, directly illuminates human intellects, whereas Avicenna's strict monotheism only authorizes illumination by interposed intelligences. Even if he is a Christian, a Latin Averroist can let himself teach an illumination of the human intellect by the lowest of the separated Intelligences, because, as a Christian, he can simultaneously believe that the Word illuminates every man coming into this world. A disciple of Avicenna must choose to either renounce the illumination by the Word or else identify it with the separate Agent Intellect of Muslim philosophy. The second solution prevailed. The Christians did not make the separated Agent Intellect the Word. They did the opposite, and they were constrained to do so, because they could not allow themselves to separate their philosophy from their religion, their reason from their faith. Thus there was no Avicennist doctrine of double truth. For that very reason, there was no Latin Avicennism properly speaking. Of all the Latin theologians I have managed to read, not a single one identified philosophical truth with the philosophy of Avicenna as others at that very moment identified it with that of Averroes. The Latin Averroists deserve the label because they made Averroes their master by following him. Those who used Avicenna could only do so by transforming him.

Reading the chapter that Fr. Roland de Vaux devoted to William of Auvergne as "witness to Latin Avicennism" confirms this. De Vaux first establishes an impressive list of the principle points where William distances himself from Avicenna:

> The world did not begin in time.—The first cause acts out of necessity in the manner of a natural cause.—The first cause could only produce one creature immediately, namely the first Intelligence.—The world has been created by degrees, each Intelligence creating the following Intelligence, and there are only ten Intelligences.—The heavenly substances govern the perpetual cycle of generations, and human affairs do not escape

their influence.—The agent intellect is a separate substance, namely the motor intelligence of the last sphere.—The agent intellect is the efficient cause of human souls.—The happiness of human souls consists in their union with the separated intellect.— Since the principle of individuation is matter, there are no two separated intelligence that belong to the same species.—Human souls are individuated by their bodies. It must be concluded that the separated souls lose their individuality.—Intelligence as such does not grasp singulars. Souls share in this state. It follows from that that they cannot grasp God.[26]

To this first observation, Father de Vaux adds a second, whose implications seem very important to me, namely: "We have only to read this list to also notice that almost all the errors could as well be called Averroist as Avicennist, and that they are encountered again in the condemnation of 1277."

It is enough to place these two observations together to see how the problem is posed. We can speak of Latin Averroism, because, from the thirteenth century on, there were Latins who maintained on Averroes's authority that those propositions were true *in philosophy* if not in theology. We cannot speak unequivocally of Latin Avicennism because, in the actual state of our knowledge, there were never Latins who maintained them all as true on Avicenna's authority. Furthermore, let us recall that it would have been impossible to do so appealing to Avicenna, whose case was entirely different in this regard from that of Averroes: Avicenna never taught as philosophically true any doctrine he considered to be opposed to that of the Koran on the same point. Avicenna can be adapted and utilized by modifying him to accommodate the demands of religious truth, but it would have been contradictory to the spirit of his own philosophy to receive it unchanged into a theology with which it was in disagreement on important points. Thus it was possible to Avicennize in Christian theology (as it was to Aristotelize), but not to be a true Avicennist or Aristotelian properly speaking. Since the theoretically absurd is never historically impossible, it is necessary to make a reservation dictated by prudence: in the present state of our knowledge, we know of no Christian who accepted the principal theses of Avicenna's philosophy, while continuing to call himself a Christian theologian. Logic consisted thus in remitting to Averroes rather than to Avicenna, as did, moreover, those whom we know.

26. de Vaux, *Notes et textes*, 37–38.

Therefore, it is also understandable that, as Ernest Renan observed in his book *Averroès et l'Averroïsme*,[27] the fable of a personally anti-religious Averroes finds a pretext in the separation he indeed maintained between philosophy and theology. Renan observes that Averroes's tendency to always contradict Avicenna, "had been noticed by Roger Bacon" (*Opus Majus*, 13, Jebb ed). He adds "Benvenuto da Imola confirmed the same tradition (*ad Infernum* Canto IV, v. 141, ms. Bibliothèque Impériale, number 4146, suppl. Fr. folio 25). He claims that Averroes devised his teaching of contempt for established religions through opposition to Avicenna, who sustained that we should "respect the religion into which we were born."[28]

---

27. The first edition dates from 1852. Michael Lévy's edition (1861) that I have before me, contains a very interesting observation. Notably, we read: "In my view we have there the most curious lesson that comes out of this whole history. Arab philosophy offers an almost unique example of a very high culture almost instantaneously suppressed without leaving traces, and virtually forgotten by the people who created it" (111). The observation perhaps holds for Averroes but not for Avicenna who naturally only has a shadowy place in Renan's book. For my part I would say rather: "In my view we have there the most curious lesson that comes out of this whole history. Arab philosophy offers an almost unique example of a very high culture, to which Muslim theology opposed an impenetrable barrier, but which was accepted with favor, even gratitude, in spite of necessary reservations, by Christian theology. It is not possible to conceive a history of Christian theologies in the Middle Ages that does not take Avicenna into account and even Averroes. It is in Christian theology, much more than in Muslim theology, that medieval Arab philosophy found a climate favorable to its development."

28. Renan, *Averroès*, 111. Dante places Avicenna between two illustrious physicians (Hyppocrates, Avicenna, and Galen), *Divine Comedy, Inferno* IV:143. Thus it is the author of the *Qânûn* that Dante intends to honor. In the *Convivio* Avicenna is mentioned with Algazel and Plato, in the context of the giver of the forms (II:14); with Aristotle and Ptolomy in relation to astronomy (II:15); in connection with the distinction between *raggio* and *splendore* (III:14); finally about the origin of the difference of nobility among souls (IV:21). In his commentary on the *Inferno*, IV:14, Benvenuto da Imola evidently thinks that Dante's intention was to honor Avicenna as physician: "iste [*Avicenna*] fuit per multa saecula post Galienum, tamen praefertur sibi merito. Fuit enim Avicenna universaliter excellens in omni parte medicinae et colegit artificialiter omnia dicta Galieni, et redigit ad ordinem et brevitatem. Fuit enim Galienus diffusissimus, et multa volumina fecit, in quibus multa superflua dixit. Unde ipse Avicenna dicit quod Galienus multa scivit de ramis medicinae, pauca vero de radicibus . . . Avicenna fuit filius regis Hispaniae, vir magnae virtutis et scientiae, aemulus Averrois. Averrois. Hunc ultimo autor post philosophos et medicos nominat singulariter . . . iste enim dicitur fuisse alter Aristoteles. Fuit tamen superbissimus omnium philosophorum, conatus semper damnare dicta Avicennae . . . Damnavit etiam omnem sectam fidei, cujus contrarium fecit Avicenna, qui dicit quod unusquisque debet colere fidem suam." Imola, *Commentum*, I:181.

There is some inaccuracy in these remarks. Averroes never taught scorn for established religions, but he certainly taught that the respective domains of philosophy and religion ought to be kept scrupulously separate. That is exactly why his philosophy could help Christians as long as they dealt with sciences of nature but not when they dealt with metaphysics and natural theology. Avicenna could serve in both cases. This symbiosis with Christian theologians is where Avicennism manifested its speculative fecundity to the Middle Ages. It is in a similar symbiosis with Islam that it finds the promise of new fecundity again today.

BIBLIOGRAPHY

Adloch, Dom B. "Glossen zur neuesten Wertung des Anselmischen Gotteseweises." *Philosophische Jahrbuch* 16 (1903).

Alanus de Insulis. *Liber de Planctu Naturae. Patrologia Latina* 209. [See Migne.]

Albert the Great [Albertus Magnus]. *Opera Omnia.* 38 vols. Edited by Auguste Bourgnet. Paris: Vivès, 1890–1899.

———. *In Libros Metaphysicorum. Opera Omnia* 6.

Algazel. *Metaphysica.* In *Algazel's Metaphysics: A Medieval Translation*, edited by J. T. Muckle. Toronto: Pontifical Institute of Medieval Studies, 1933.

Allen, Percy Stafford, and Helen Mary Allen. *Opus Epistolarum Desiderii Erasmi Rottero-dami.* 12 vols. Oxford: Clarendon, 1906–1958.

Alverny, Marie-Thérèse d'. "Anniyyaanitas." In *Mélanges offerts à Étienne Gilson*, 59–91. Paris: Vrin, 1959.

———. "Avendauth?" *Homenaje a Millás Vallicrosa* 1 (1954) 19–43. [See *Homenaje*.]

———. "Avicenna latinus." *Archives d'histoire doctrinale et littéraire du moyen âge* 28 (1961) 281–316; 29 (1962) 217–33; 30 (1963) 221–72; 31 (1964) 271–86; 32 (1965) 257–302; 33 (1966) 305–27; 34 (1967) 315–43.

———. "Editions anciennes." *Archives d'histoire doctrinale et littéraire du moyen âge* 28 (1961).

———. "L'Introduction d'Avicenne en Occident." *La Revue du Caire* (June 1951) 130–39.

———. "Notes sur les traductions médiévales des oeuvres philosophiques d'Avicenne." *Archives d'histoire doctrinale et littéraire du moyen âge* 19 (1952) 337–58.

———. "Les traductions d'Avicenne (Moyen Âge et Renaissance)." In *Avicenna nella storia della cultura medioevale.* Quaderno 40. Rome: Accademia dei Lincei, 1957.

Anselm, St. *Ad Lanfrancum, Epistula. Patrologia Latina* 158. [See Migne.]

———. *De Fide Trinitatis. Patrologia Latina* 158. [See Migne.]

———. *De Veritate. Patrologia Latina* 158. [See Migne.]

———. *Liber Apologeticus contra Gaunilonem. Patrologia Latina* 158. [See Migne.]

———. *Monologium. Patrologia Latina* 158. [See Migne.]

———. *Proslogion. Patrologia Latina* 158. [See Migne.]

Anselme de Cantorbery. *Fides Quaerens Intellectum.* Translated by Alexandre Koyré. Paris: Vrin, 1930.

Aquinas, St. Thomas. *De Ente et Essentia.* Edited by Marie-Dominique Roland-Gosselin. LeSaulchoir, Kain, Belgium: Revue des sciences philosophiques et théologiques, 1926.

———. *De Unitate Intellectus*. [No edition cited by Gilson. It is found in Aquinas, *Opuscula Omnia necnon Opera Minora*. Vol. 1. Edited by Joannes Perrier. Paris: Lethielleux, 1949. See also Pierre Mandonnet, *Opuscula Omnia*, Paris: Lethielleux, 1927. A critical edition, *Tractatus de Unitate Intellectus contra Averroistas*. Edited by Leo W. Keeler. Rome: Gregorian University Press, 1936, 1957 was also available.]

———. *In Boethium de Trinitate*. [No edition cited by Gilson. It was available in Aquinas, *Opuscula Theologica*. Edited by M. Calcaterra. Turin: Marietti, 1954. See also Pierre Mandonnet. *Opuscula Omnia*. Paris: Lethielleux, 1927.]

———. *In Dionysius, De Divinis Nominibus*. Vol. 2. Edited by Pierre Mandonnet. In *Opuscula Omnia*.

———. *Opuscula philosophica et theologica*. Edited Pierre Mandonnet. In *Opuscula Omnia*.

———. *Quaestiones Disputatae de Potentia*. [No edition cited by Gilson. Likely choices are Aquinas, *Quaestiones Disputatae*. Edited by Raimundo Spaizzi. Turin: Marietti, 1949, 1965. *Quaestiones Disputatae*. Edited by Pierre Mandonnet. Vol. II, Paris: Lethielleux, 1925. An older French edition is *Quaestiones Disputatae*. *Accredit Liber de Ente et Essentia*. Vol. 1, Paris: Blood et Barrel, 1883.]

———. *Quaestiones Disputatae de Veritate*. [No edition cited by Gilson. It is found in Pierre Mandonnet, editor. *Quaestiones Disputatae*. Vol. I. Paris: Lethielleux, 1925, *Quaestiones Disputatae*. Vol. I, Turin: Marietti, 1964. An older French edition is *Quaestiones Disputatae*. *Accedit Liber de Ente et Essentia*. Vols. 3 and 4. Paris: Bloud et Barral, 1883.]

———. *Quaestiones Quodlibetales*. [No edition cited by Gilson. It is found in Raimundo Spiazzi, editor. Turin: Marietti, 1956.]

———. *Scriptum super libros sententiarum magistri Petri Lombardi Episcopi parisiensis*. [Cited as *In I Sententias*. Edited by Pierre Mandonnet. Paris: Lethielleux, 1929.]

———. *Summa Contra Gentes*. Leonine *editio manualis*. Turin-Rome: Marietti, 1934.

———. *Summa Theologiae*. [No edition cited by Gilson. In other works, Gilson declares that the Leonine edition of Aquinas's *Opera Omnia* is the best and mentions the Turin-Rome: Marietti, 1948 separate edition of the *Summa Theologiae*.]

Auerbach, Erich. *Dante als Dichter der irdischen Welt*. Berlin: de Gruyter, 1929.

———. "Dante und Virgil." *Das humanistiche Gymnasium* 4–5 (1921) 126–44.

Augustine, St. *Contra Julianum Pelagianum*. Patrologia Latina 44. [See Migne.]

———. *De Civitate Dei*. Patrologia Latina 41. [See Migne.]

———. *De Gratia et Libero Arbitrio*. Patrologia Latina, v. 44. [See Migne.]

———. *De Libero Arbitrio*. Patrologia Latina 32. [See Migne.]

———. *De Moribus Manichaeorum*. Patrologia Latina 32. [See Migne.]

———. *De Spiritu et Littera*. Patrologia Latina 44. [See Migne.]

———. *De Trinitate*. Patrologia Latina 42. [See Migne.]

Averroes. *Aristotelis Opera cum Averrois commentariis*. 12 vols. 1562. Reprint, Frankfurt: Minerva, 1962.

———. *Tahafut Al-Tahafut* (*The Incoherence of the Incoherence*). See Bergh, *Averroes' Tahafut Al-Tahafut*.

Avicenna. *De Intelligentiis* [spurious]. In *Opera Philosophica*.

———. *Liber VI Naturalium*. In *Opera Philosophica*.

———. *Logica*. In *Opera Philosophica*.

———. *Metaphysica*. Venice: Bernardinus de Vitalibus, 1495 also in *Opera Philosophica*. Venice, 1508. [There is now a critical edition: *Liber de Prima Philosophia sive Scientia Divina*. Leiden: Brill, 1977–1983.]

———. *Opera Philosophica*. Venice: Apud Junctas, 1508 [French and Latin selections Louvain: Editions de la bibliothèque S.J., 1961.]

———. *Sufficientia*. In *Opera Philosophica*.

Bacon, Roger. *Opus Majus*. Edited and introduction by John Henry Bridges. Oxford: Clarendon, 1897–1900.

Barth, Karl. *Fides quaerens intellectum: Anselm's Proof of the Existence of God in the Context of His Theological Scheme*. Translated by Ian W. Robertson. 1960. Reprint, Eugene, OR: Pickwick, 1985.

———. *Fides quaerens intellectum: Anselms beweis der Existenz Gottes*. München: C. Kaiser, 1931 (Zurich: Theologischer Verlag, 1981).

Barth, Karl, and Heinrich Barth. *Zur lehre vom Heiligen Geist*. Munich: Kaiser, 1930.

Baruzi, Jean. "Le commentaire de Luther à l'Épitre aux Hébreux." *Revue d'histoire et de philosophie religieuse* XI (1931).

Baumgartner, Matthias. *Die Erkenntnislehre des Wilhelm von Auvergne*. Münster: Aschendorff, 1893.

Becker, Josef. "Der Satz des hl. Anselm: *Credo ut Intelligam*." *Philosophisches Jahrbuch*. 19 (1906).

Bédier, Joseph, and Paul Hazard, editors. *Histoire de la littérature française illustrée*. 2 vols. Paris: Larousse, 1923–1924.

Bergh, Simon Van Den, translator. *Averroes' Tahafut Al-Tahafut (The Incoherence of the Incoherence)*. 2 vols. Oxford: Oxford University Press, 1954.

Bernard of Clairvaux, St. *Tractatus et Opuscula*. Vol. 3 of *Opera*. Edited by Jean LeClercq and Henri Rochais. Roma: Cistercienses, 1963.

Boethius. *In Categorias Aristotelis. Patrologia Latina* 64. [See Migne.]

———. *De Hebdomadibus. Patrologia Latina* 64. [See Migne.]

———. *In Librum De Intepretatione editio prima. Patrologia Latina* 64. [See Migne.]

Bonaventure, St. "Christus Unus Omnium Magister." Sermon IV in *Opera Omnia* 5.

———. *In III Sententiarum*. In *Opera Omnia* 3.

———. *Itinerarium mentis in Deum*. Quaracchi: Ex Typographia Collegii S. Bonaventura, 1938.

———. *Opera Omnia, Ad Claras Aquas*. 10 vols. Quaracchi: Ex Typographia Collegii S. Bonaventurae, 1892–1902.

Bouchitté, Louis Firmin Hervé. *Le rationalisme chrétien à la fin du XIe siècle, ou Monologiun et Proslogiun de Saint Anselme, sur l'essence divine*. Paris: Amyot, 1842.

Bülow, Georg, editor. *Des Dominicus Gundisalvi Schrift von der Untsterblichkeit der Seele. Beiträge zur Geschichte der Philosophie des Mittelalters* II.3. Münster: Aschendorffschen buchhandlung, 1897.

Cajetan. *In De Ente et Essentia*. Edited by M.-H. Laurent. Turin: Marietti, 1934.

Carame, Nematallah. *Avicennae Metaphysices Compendium*. Rome: Pontifical Institute of Oriental Studies, 1926.

Carra de Vaux, Bernard. *Saint Anselme*. Paris: Alcan, 1901.

Chenu, Marie-Dominique. "Javelli." In *Dictionnaire de théologie catholique*, 8:535–36.

———. "Note pour l'historie de la philosophie chrétienne." *Revue de sciences philosophiques et théologiques* 14 (1932) 231–35.

Cicero. *De Inventione Rhetorica*. [Edition not cited by Gilson. A possibility would be *Rhetoricae Libri Duo, qui sunt De Inventione Rhetorica*. Leipzig: Teubner. 1884.]

Cohen, Gustave. *Mystéres et moralités du manuscrit 617 de Chantilly*. Paris: Champion, 1920.

———. *Ronsard, sa vie et son oeuvre*. Paris: Boivin, 1924.

Contenson, P.-M. de, O.P. "Avicennisme latin et vision de Dieu au début du XIIIe siècle." *Archives d'histoire doctrinale et littéraire du moyen âge* 26 (1959) 29–97.

Denzinger, Heinrich. *Enchiridion Symbolorum*. Freiburg: Herder, 1928.

Duhem, Pierre. *Le système du monde: Histoire des doctrines cosmologiques de Platon et Copernic*. 5 vols. Paris: Hermann, 1917.

Dunphy, William P. *The Doctrine of Causality in the* Quaestiones in Metaphysicam *of Peter of Auvergne*. PhD diss., University of Toronto, 1952.

Edie, Callistus James. "The Writings of Étienne Gilson Chronologically Arranged." In *Mélanges offerts à Étienne Gilson*, 15–59. Toronto: Pontifical Institute of Medieval Studies, 1959.

Ehrle, Cardinal Franz, "Die päpstliche Encyklika von 4. August 1879 und die Restauration der christlichen Philosophie." In *Stimmen aus Maria Laach*, 1880.

Erasmus. *Colloquia, Convivium Religiosum*: XXVI in *Colloquia Familiaria*.

———. *De Contemptu Mundi*, in *Opera Omnia*, vol. 5.

———. *Enchiridion Militis Christiani*, in *Opera Omnia*, vol. 5.

———. *Epistola Apologetica ad Martinum Dorpium Theologum*, in *Opera Omnia*, vol. 9.

———. *Hyeraspistae Diatribes* in *Opera Omnia*, vol. 10.

———. Letter to Henry VIII, number 1390. In Percy Stafford Allen and Helen Mary Allen, editors. *Opus Epistolarum Desiderii Erasmi Rotterodami*. Vol. 5.

———. Letter to Johann Vlatten, number 1390. In Percy Stafford Allen and Helen Mary Allen, editors. *Opus Epistolarum Desiderii Erasmi Rotterodami*. Vol. 5.

———. *Opera Omnia*. Leyden: Cura & Impensis Petri Vader Aa, 1703–1706.

———. *Paraclesis id est Adhortatio ad Christianae Philosophiae Studium*, in *Opera Omnia*, vol. 5.

———. *Ratio sive Methodus* in *Opera Omnia*, vol. 5.

———. "Responsio ad Albertum Pium, art. 'Scholastica Theologia,'" in *Opera Omnia*, vol. 9.

Eschmann, Ignatius T. "A Catalogue of St. Thomas's Works." In *The Christian Philosophy of St. Thomas Aquinas*, by Étienne Gilson, 381–439. 1956. Reprinted, Notre Dame, IN: University of Notre Dame Press, 2002.

Fackenheim, Emil L. "The Possibility of the Universe in Al-Farabi, Ibn Sina, and Maimonides." In *American Academy for Jewish Research*, New York, 1947.

Faral, Edmund. "Le Roman de la Rose et la pensée française au XIIIe siècle." In *Revue des Deux Mondes* (September 15, 1916) 430–57.

Ferreira, J., O. F. *Presença do Augustinismo avicennizante na teoria dos intellectos de Petro Hispano*. Braga: Editorial Franciscana, 1959.

Filliatre, Charles. *La philosophie de saint Anselme*. Paris: Alcan, 1920.

Finance, Joseph de. *Être et agir dans la doctrine de saint Thomas*. Paris: Beauchesne, n.d., [1943].

Fonck, A. "Mystique." In *Dictionaire de théologie catholique*, vol. 10, column 2600.

Forest, Aimé. *La structure métaphysique du concret selon saint Thomas d'Aquin*. Paris: Vrin, 1956.

Gardet, Louis. *La pensée religieuse d'Avicenne (Ibn Sina)*. Paris: Vrin, 1951.

Gauthier, Léon, translator. "Accord de la religion et de la philosophie d'Ibn Rochd (Averroès). Traité d'Ibn Rochd (Averroes) traduit et annoté." Algiers, 1905.

———. *Ibn Rochd (Averroes)*. Paris: Presses Universitaires de France, 1948.

———. *La théorie d'Ibn Rochd sur les rapports de la religion et de la philosophie*. Paris: Leroux, 1909.

Gilson, Étienne. "Avicenne et la notion de cause efficiente." In *Atti del XII Congresso Internazionale di filosofia*, 121–30. Florence: Sansoni, 1961.

———. "Avicenne et le point de départ de Duns Scot." *Archives d'histoire doctrinale et littéraire du moyen âge* 2 (1927) 89–149.

———. *The Christian Philosophy of St. Thomas Aquinas*. New York: Random House, 1956.

———. "La cosmogonie de Bernardus Silvestris." *Archives d'histoire doctrinal et littéraire du moyen âge* 3 (1928).

———. *L'ésprit de la philosophie médiévale*. 2nd ed. Paris: Vrin, 1944.

———. "L'étude des philosophies arabes et son rôle dans l'interpretation de la scholastique." In *Proceedings of the Sixth International Congress of Philosophy*, Harvard, September 13–17, 1926. Edited by E. S. Brightman. New York: Longmans, Green, 1927.

———. *Études de philosophie médiévale*. Strasbourg: Faculté des lettres de l'Université de Strasbourg, 1921,

———. *Études sur le rôle de la pensée médiévale dans la formation du système cartésien*. Paris: Vrin, 1930,

———. *Introduction à l'étude de saint Augustin*. 2nd ed. Paris: Vrin, 1943.

———. *Jean Duns Scot, Introduction à ses positions doctrinales*. Paris: Vrin, 1952.

———. *Philosophie au moyen âge*. Vol. 1. Paris: Payot, 1922.

———. *La philosophie de Saint Bonaventure*. Paris: Vrin, 1924.

———. "Pourquoi saint Thomas a critiqué saint Augustin." *Archives d'histoire doctrinale et littéraire du moyen âge* 1 (1926).

———. *Reason and Revelation in the Middle Ages*. New York: Scribners, 1938.

———. "Roger Marston, Un cas d'augustinisme avicennissant." *Archives d'histoire doctrinal et littéraire du moyen âge* 8 (1933) 37–42.

———. *Les sources gréco-arabes de l'augustinisme avennissant* in *Archives d'histoire doctrinale et littéraire du moyen âge* 4 (1929) 5–149. [English translation, James G. Colbert. *Greco-Arabic Souces of Avicennist Augustinism*. New York: Global Scholarly, 2003.]

———. *Le thomisme, Introduction à la philosophie de saint Thomas d'Aquin*. 5th ed. Paris, J. Vrin, 1942.

———. "Trois leçons sur le problème de l'existence de Dieu." *Divinitas* 1 (1961) 23–87.

Goichon, Amélie-Marie. *La distinction de l'essence et de l'existence d'après Ibn Sina (Avicenne)*. Paris: Desclée de Brouwer, 1937.

Gouhier, Henri, "La pensée médiévale dans la philosophie d'Auguste Comte." In Edie, *Mélanges,* 299–313.

Grabmann, Martin *Die Geschichte der scholastischen Méthode*. 2 vols. Feiburg: Herder, 1909.

———. "Die Opuscula *de summo bono sive de vita philosophi*, und *De Sompniis* des Boetius von Dacien," in *Archive d'histoire doctrinale et littéraire du moyen âge*. Vol. 6 (1931).

Gundisaliunus. *Gundisalinus de Immortalitate animae*. In Georg Bülow, "Des Dominicus Gundisalvi Schrift," 1–38.

Henry of Ghent. *Summa Quaestionum Ordinarium*. 1520. Reprint, St. Bonaventure, NY: Franciscan Institute, 1953.

Hilary, St., *De Trinitate. Patrologia Latina* 10. [See Migne.]

Histoire littéraire de la France: ouvrage commencé par des religieux bénédictins de la congrégation de Saint Maur, et continué par des membres de l'institut (Academie des inscriptions et belles-lettres). Paris: Imprimerie Nationale, 1733–2002.

Hocedez, Edgar. "La vie et les oeuvres de Pierre d'Auvergne." *Gregorianum* 14 (1933) 3–36.

Homenaje a Millás Vallicrosa. 2 vols. Barcelona: Consejo Superior de Investigaciones Científicas, 1954–1956.

Hommage à Monsieur le professeur Maurice de Wulf. Louvain: Institut supérieur de philosophie, 1934.

Humbert, Auguste. *Les origines de la théologie moderne.* Paris: Lecofre, 1911.

Imola, Benvenuto da. *Commentum super Dantis Comoediam.* Edited by Warren Vernon. Florence: Barbera, 1887.

Isidore, St. *Etymologiae. Patrologia Latina* 82. [See Migne.]

Koyré, Alexandre. *L'idée de Dieu dans la philosophie de saint Anselme.* Paris: Leroux, 1923.

Kraus, Johann. "Die Universalienlehre des Oxforder Kanzlers Heinrich von Harclay." *Divus Thomas* 10 (1932) 36–38, 475–508, and 11 (1933) 288–314.

Lefranc, Abel. "Diverses définitions de la Renaissance." *Revue des cours et conferences* 16:28 (1910) 494.

Leo XIII. *Aeterni Patris: De Philosophia Christiana in Scholis Catholicis Instauranda.* Papal Encyclical, August 4, 1879.

Levasti, Arrigo. *Sant'Anselmo, vita e pensiero.* Bari: Laterza, 1929.

Lombard Peter. *Petri Lombardi: Libri IV Sententiarum,* studio et cura PP. Collegii S. Bonaventurae, Ad Claras Aquas: Ex Typographia Collegii S. Bonaventurae, 2nd ed. 1916.

Lorris, Guillaume de and Jean de Meun. *The Romance of the Rose.* Translated by Harry Robbins. New York: Dutton, 1962.

Luther, Martin. *Commentary on the Epistle to the Galatians* in *Werke,* vol. 2.

———. *De Servo Arbitrio,* in *Werke,* vol. 18.

———. *Disputatio contra Scholasticam Theologiam,* in *Werke,* vol. 1.

———. Letter to Georg Spenlein, April 8, 1516. *Briefwechsel, Werke,* vol. 1.

———. Letters to Johann Lang, March 1, 1512 and February 8, 1517. *Briefwechsel,* ed. Weimar, vol. 1, 88–89.

———. Letters to Spalatin, October 19, 1516 and September 2, 1518, Weimar edition, *Briefwechsel, Werke,* vol. 1.

———. *Werke.* 127 vols. Weimar: Böhlaus, 1883–1929.

Madkour, Ibrahim. *La place d'al Fârabi dans l'école philosophique musulmane.* Paris: Maisonneuve, 1934.

Maimonides, Moses. *Guide des égarés.* Translated by S. Munk. Paris, 1856.

Mâle, Émile. *L'art religieux du XIIIe siècle en France.* Paris: Colin, 1919.

Malebranche, Nicholas. *Entretiens sur la métaphysique.* 2 vols. Edited by Paul Fontana. Paris: Colin, 1922.

———. *Méditations chrétiennes et métaphysiques.* Edited by Henri Gouhier. Paris: Aubier 1927.

———. *Recherche de la vérité.* Edited by Francisque Bouillier. Paris: Garnier frères, 1880.

Martin, Jules. *St. Augustin.* Paris: Alcan, 1901.

Masnovo, Amato, *Da Guglielmo d'Auvergne a san Tommasso d'Aquino,* I, *Guglielmo d'Auvernge e l'ascesa verso Dio,* Milan, Società editrice Vita e Pensiero, 1930.

Maurer, Armand. "Boetius of Dacia and the Double Truth." *Mediaeval Studies* 17 (1955) 233–39.

———. "Henry of Harclay's Questions on the Divine Ideas." *Mediaeval Studies* 23 (1961) 163–93.

McGrath, Margaret. *Étienne Gilson: A Bibliography. Étienne Gilson: Une Bibliographie.* Toronto: Pontifical Institute of Mediaeval Studies, 1982.

Mehren, A. F. "La philosophie d'Avicenne (Ibn Sina) exposée d'après des documents inédits." *Muséon* 3 (1882).

———. *Les rapports de la philosophie de Avicenne avec l'Islam.* Louvain: Peeters, 1883.

Mélanges offerts à Étienne Gilson. Toronto: Pontifical Institute of Medieval Studies and Paris: Vrin, 1959.

Migne, Jacques-Paul, editor. *Patrologia Cursus Completus*, series Latina. Paris: Garnière fratres, 1844–1864.

Millénaire d'Avicenne. Congrès de Bagdad. Cairo: Matba'at Misr, 1952.

Müller, Alphons Viktor. *Luthers theologische Quellen. Eine Verteidigung gegen Denifle und Grisar.* Giessen: Topelmann, 1912.

Ottaviano, Carmelo. *Anselmo d'Aosta, opere filosofiche.* 3 vols. Lanciano: Carabba, 1928.

Paulus, Jean. *Henri de Gand. Essai sur les tendance de sa métaphysique.* Paris: Vrin, 1938.

Peckham, John. *Registrum Epistolarum.* Edited by C. T. Martin. London: Longman, 1885.

Pegis, Anton. "St. Thomas and the Origin of Creation, in Philosophy and the Modern Mind." Edward Cardinal Mooney Lecture Series, 1960–1961. Detroit: Sacred Heart Seminary, 48–65.

Petit de Julleville, Louis. "Esprit de la littérature française a la fin du xve siècle." *Revue des cours et conférences*, 1895–1896.

Pineau, J.-B. *Érasme, sa pensé religieuse.* Paris: Presses Universitaires de France, 1923.

Randall, John Hermann Jr. *The Making of the Modern Mind.* Boston: Houghton Mifflin, 1926.

Renan, Ernest.*Averroès et l'Averroisme.* 2nd ed. Paris: Michael Lévy Frères, 1861.

Renaudet, Augustin. *Érasme, sa pensée religieuse et son action d'après sa correspondance (1518–1521).* Paris: Alcan, 1926.

Ritter, Heinrich. *Histoire de la philosophie chrétienne.* Paris: Librarie Philosophique de Ladrange, 1843.

Roland-Gosselin, Marie-Dominique. *Le De Ente et Essentia de S. Thomas d'Aquin.* Paris: Vrin, 1926.

Sajó, Géza. *Un traité récemment découvert de Boèce de Dacie De mundi aeternitate. Texte inédit avec une introduction critique.* With an appendix containing an unpublished text of Siger de Brabant, *Super VI Metaphysicae.* Budapest: Akademiai Kiado, 1954.

Saliba, Djémil. *Étude sur la métaphysique d'Avicenne.* Paris: Presses Universitaires de France, n.d.

Sanseverino. *Philosophia christiana cum antiqua et nova comparata in compendium ad usum scholarum clericalium.* 2 vols. Naples: Manfredi, 1866.

Scheel, Otto. *Dokumente zur Luthers Entwicklung.* Tübingen: Mohr/Siebeck, 1911.

Schindele, Stephan. *Beiträge zur Metaphysik des Wilhelm von Auvergne.* Munich: Kastner, 1900.

Scotus, Duns. *Duns Scoti, Opera Omnia.* 26 vols. Paris: Vivès, 1891. [The Vivès edition is a reprint of Luke Wadding's edition, Lyon: L. Durand, 1639, which, however, has only 12 volumes. Vivès was reproduced by Westmead, Franborough and Hants: Greg International, 1969. Wadding was reproduced by Hildesheim: Georg Olm, 1968. Since Gilson wrote, critical editions of Scotus's *Opera Omnia* have begun to appear, which are not yet complete.]

———. *Opus Oxoniense.* In Vivès, vols. 8–21; Wadding, vols. 5–10.

———. *Quaestiones Subtillisimae in Metaphysica Aristotelis.* In Vivès, vol. 7; Wadding, vol. 4.

————. *Reportata Parisiensia.* In Vivès, vols. 23–24; Wadding, vol. 11.

Sertillanges, Antonin-Dalmatius. *Le Christanisme et les Philosophies.* Paris: Aubier, n.d.

Signoriello, Nunzio. *Lexicon Peripateticum Philosophico-Theologicum.* 3rd ed. Naples: 1881.

Stoltz, Anselm. "Zur Theologie Anselms im *Proslogion.*" *Catholica* 2 (1933) 1–24.

Strohl, Henri. *L'épanouissement de la pensée religieuse de Luther de* 1515–1520. Strasbourg: Librairie Istra, 1924.

Sweeney, Leo. "Existence/Essence in Thomas Aquinas Early Writings." In *Proceedings of the American Catholic Philosophical Association,* 97–131. Washington, DC: 1963.

Vansteenkiste, C. "Avicenna-citation bij S. Thomas." *Tijdschrift voor Philosophie* 15 (1953) 437–507.

————. "Autori Arabi e Giudei nell opera di San Tommasso." *Angelicum* 37 (1960) 336–401.

Vaux, Roland de. *Notes et textes sur l'avicennisme latin aux confins des XIIe et XIIIe siècles.* Paris: Vrin, 1934.

William of Auvergne, *Guillermi Alverni episcopi parisiensis, mathematici perfectissimi, eximii philosophi, ac theologi praestantisssimi, Opera Omnia,* 2 vols., in folio. Edited by Blaise Le Féron. 1674. Reprint, Frankfurt: Minerva, 1963.

————. *De Immortalitate Animae,* in *Opera Omnia.*

————. *De Fide et de Legibus,* in *Opera Omnia.*

————. *De Trinitate,* in *Opera Omnia.*

————. *De Universo,* in *Opera Omnia.*

Wilmart, Dom A. "Les Homélies attribuées à saint Anselme." *Archives d'histoire doctrinale et littéraire du moyen âge* II (1927).

Wolfson, Harry Austryn. "The Amphibolous Terms in Aristotle, Arabic Philosophy, and Maimonides." *Harvard Theological Review* 31 (1938) 151–73.

————. "The Internal Senses in Latin, Arabic, and Hebrew Philosophical Texts." *Harvard Theological Review* 28 (1935) 69–133.

————. "The Terms *tasawwur* and *tasdiq* in Arabic Philosophy and their Greek, Latin, and Hebrew Equivalents." *The Moslem World* (April 1943) 1–15.

Wulf, Maurice de. *Histoire de la philosophie médiévale.* Fifth edition. Louvain: Institut supérieur de philosophie, 1924–1925.